WHAT
SIDE
ARE
YOU
ON?

Critical Indigeneities

J. Kēhaulani Kauanui (Kanaka Maoli) and
Jean M. O'Brien (White Earth Ojibwe), editors

Series Advisory Board
Chris Andersen
Emil' Keme
Kim TallBear
Irene Watson

Critical Indigeneities publishes pathbreaking scholarly books that
center Indigeneity as a category of critical analysis, understand
Indigenous sovereignty as ongoing and historically grounded,
and attend to diverse forms of Indigenous cultural and political
agency and expression. The series builds on the conceptual rigor,
methodological innovation, and deep relevance that characterize
the best work in the growing field of critical Indigenous studies.

A complete list of books published in Critical Indigeneities is
available at https://uncpress.org/series/critical-indigeneities.

WHAT SIDE ARE YOU ON?

A Tohono O'odham Life across Borders

Michael Steven Wilson and **José Antonio Lucero**

The University of North Carolina Press
Chapel Hill

This book was published with the assistance of the University of Washington.

Designed by Lindsay Starr
Set in Arno, Helvetica Now, Lato, and Cassino
by codeMantra
Manufactured in the United States of America

Cover art: Portrait of Mike Wilson, Tohono O'odham Nation, 2008.
Courtesy of Michael Hyatt, michael-hyatt.com.

Library of Congress Cataloging-in-Publication Data
Names: Wilson, Michael Steven, author. | Lucero, Jose Antonio, 1972– author.
Title: What side are you on? : a Tohono O'odham life across borders / Michael Steven Wilson
and José Antonio Lucero.
Other titles: Tohono O'odham life across borders | Critical indigeneities.
Description: Chapel Hill : The University of North Carolina Press, [2024] |
Series: Critical indigeneities | Includes bibliographical references and index.
Identifiers: LCCN 2024005598 | ISBN 9781469675572 (cloth ; alk. paper) |
ISBN 9781469675589 (pbk. ; alk. paper) | ISBN 9781469675596 (epub) |
ISBN 9798890887603 (pdf)
Subjects: LCSH: Wilson, Michael Steven. | Tohono O'odham Indians—United States—
Biography. | Social reformers—United States—Biography. | Illegal immigration—Tohono
O'odham Nation of Arizona. | Transborder ethnic groups—Sonoran Desert. |
United States—Emigration and immigration—Government policy. | BISAC: SOCIAL
SCIENCE / Ethnic Studies / American / Native American Studies | BIOGRAPHY &
AUTOBIOGRAPHY / Social Activists | LCGFT: Autobiographies.
Classification: LCC E99.P25 W54 2024 | DDC 973.0497/45520092 [B]—dc23/eng/20240304
LC record available at https://lccn.loc.gov/2024005598

For the thousands of
undocumented migrants
who have died, are dying,
and will die on the lands
of the Tohono O'odham
Nation for lack of a cup
of water.

Contents

Illustrations

Acknowledgments

I thank Tony Lucero for his suggestion that we collaborate on this book, a partnership that began in 2010 following the signing of SB 1070 (Show Me Your Papers) by the governor of Arizona. After a decade of recorded lectures in Tony's classroom and one-on-one interviews with him, we agreed that we had enough material to proceed. I also thank my wife, Susan Ruff, for her tireless and patient editing of the manuscript. We met in 2003 when she was one of the first volunteers who, as a witness, helped me put water in the Baboquivari Valley of the Tohono O'odham Nation. A decade later we hosted almost 200 asylum migrants in our home. With the help of Tony and Susan, this storyteller can, with the permission of his O'odham ancestors, finally tell his story.

MIKE WILSON

I am grateful to Mike Wilson for sharing this life story with me, to my family, to my students, and now to the person holding this book. Susan Ruff was an invaluable editor and interlocutor. Research assistance was provided by Hannah Dolph, Marcus Johnson, Meghan Jones, and Manisha Jha. Manisha did double (and probably triple) duty, copyediting the entire manuscript. Molly Hatay provided a crucial bibliographic assist late in the game. Tsianina Lomawaima and Shannon Speed were the ideal reviewers for this book and provided invaluable feedback. Jason De León read the manuscript with care and generosity. Jeani O'Brien and J. Kēhaulani Kauanui were dream editors, and the University of North Carolina Press's Critical Indigeneities series is the perfect home for this project. We are also thankful to Mark Simpson-Vos and his incredible team at UNC Press. Thanks also go to Julie Bush for the care with which she copyedited this work and to Fred Brown for his indexing skill.

The incomparable early-morning Garage Band writing group helped keep this project on track. Lydia Heberling and David Kamper were more helpful than most humans should be expected to be at 7 a.m. I am also thankful to Chad Allen, Vince Diaz, Hokulani Aikau, and many amazing cohorts of the Summer Institute on Global Indigeneities for years of support on this project. The H. Stewart Parker Endowment and the UW College of Arts and Sciences provided valuable support in the book's final stages. Colleagues and friends in the Jackson School of International Studies, the Comparative History of Ideas department, the Latin American and Caribbean Studies program, and the Center for American Indian and Indigenous Studies, all at the University of Washington, provided support for this collaboration. And last, but always first, María Elena García read every page, more than once, and this book is all the better for her sharp eyes and unwavering support. Our son, Toño Lucero-García, grew up as this book was written and completed. I hope one day he sees how Uncle Mike's story is connected to his.

TONY LUCERO

WHAT SIDE ARE YOU ON?

Introduction

Crossings and Collaborations

JOSÉ ANTONIO LUCERO

On a hot summer day in 2004, Mike Wilson drove his truck down a road outside of Tucson, on the lands of the Tohono O'odham Nation. Wilson was waved down by a hobbling Mexican man, one of thousands of migrants who have attempted to cross the Sonoran Desert in hopes of finding work in the United States. This man had been walking for days and could barely stand. His paid guide, or coyote, and fellow travelers had left him behind when his blistered feet made him too slow. Carrying a jug of brackish brown water that he had drawn from a cattle pond, the man was exhausted. Wilson was on his way to refill the water stations that he had maintained since 2002, when he was a Presbyterian lay pastor on the reservation.

Wilson gave the man a bottle of fresh water and asked him to sit on the ground so that he could treat the man's wounded feet. As he applied iodine to the migrant's blisters, he explained in Spanish, "I am a member of this tribe

FIGURE 1. Mike Wilson aiding a migrant in the desert, as shown in the documentary *Walking the Line* (directed by Jeremy Levine and Landon Van Soest, 2005). Transient Pictures, LLC.

and I have permission, even if the tribe does not like it, to put out water. They say if I put out water, more migrants will come."[1]

This striking scene, from the 2005 documentary *Walking the Line*, is almost biblical as Wilson, a tall Tohono O'odham man with long hair, wearing a white short-sleeved shirt and a cross around his neck, washes the stranger's feet in the desert. Some fifteen years earlier, Wilson would have cut a very different figure, as one might have seen him in his battle dress uniform as a US military advisor to the repressive right-wing government of El Salvador during the late 1980s. By Wilson's own admission, he was a very different person then. "I felt as though we were to the right of Attila the Hun; I mean we were the reactionary right. We were the tip of the spear against creeping communism in Central America. And so, to come out of that experience and now ask the Central American migrant, 'Mi hermano, ¿quieres comida, quieres agua? My brother, want some food, some water?' How do you move from that to this?"[2] This book uses that question and Mike Wilson's life history to illuminate the histories and tensions of Indigenous sovereignty, US empire, and immigration politics in the Americas.

An O'odham Life across Borders

Mike Wilson's life story is a journey through multiple horrors: poverty and seg-regation, imperialism and colonialism, and a humanitarian tragedy caused in large part by US foreign and immigration policies. It is also a journey through communities that try their best to stand up to those horrors. Although there have been many excellent academic treatments of these themes, this work ap-proaches them through both the intimacy of a first-person narrative account and a historical analysis of the forces that make these man-made disasters sadly familiar features of global politics.

Wilson spent a year (2001–2) working as a Presbyterian lay pastor in Sells, Arizona, on the lands of the Tohono O'odham Nation. His work coincided with a sharp increase in border crossings, largely by Central American and Mexican migrants fleeing violence, poverty, and political in-stability. The surging rates of migration through the Sonoran Desert in the first years of the twenty-first century can be explained largely as the result of a new Border Patrol policy called "prevention through deterrence." This policy was an extension and amplification of the actions of previous oper-ations to blockade traditional urban points of crossing like El Paso/Juárez and San Diego/Tijuana, leaving migrants no choice other than to cross through the "hostile terrain" of the Chihuahuan and Sonoran Deserts. Sadly, migrants did just that. These policies produced a dramatic spike in migrant deaths.[3] Between October 1999 and July 2021, the remains of 3,937 migrants were found in the Sonoran Desert.[4] The majority of these deaths happened on the officially demarcated lands of the Tohono O'odham Na-tion.[5] One could find bodies, or what was left of them, across the reserva-tion. Wilson saw it as his moral duty to do something about it. For twelve years, he created and sustained, almost single-handedly, as many as ten water stations on the lands of the Nation.

The water stations were controversial because in the eyes of some tribal members they were seen as encouraging more crossing, environmental dam-age, and criminality. Such concerns make more sense when one considers that it was not unusual for 1,500 desperate migrants to cross tribal lands in a *sin-gle* day.[6] Hungry, thirsty, desperate, and lost, migrants sometimes broke into houses or damaged property. Making matters worse, cartels became involved in smuggling operations that were moving people and drugs across Native lands. The tribal government did not have the financial or human resources to manage the security and humanitarian disaster that came with these flows, so it reached out to the US federal government for assistance. This has meant an increased presence of US Border Patrol officers, detention facilities, drones, and other forms of surveillance on the reservation. Needless to say, there are mixed opinions about what Wilson calls "an occupying army."[7] He was among the tribal members who disagreed with the increased Border Patrol presence and also with what he viewed as a lack of concern for the lives of migrants, spurring him to create and maintain several water stations on reservation lands.

While Wilson, as an enrolled tribal member, felt that he had the moral and legal authority to put water out on tribal lands, he did not have the approval of his government or local church. Eventually, he chose to resign his position at the church and move off the reservation to Tucson. With the help of another tribal member, whom we will call Daniel,[8] Wilson continued his work on the water stations for the next eleven years and gained attention from several film-makers and various news outlets.[9]

However, those films and media coverage say little about Wilson's journey through life, a journey that took him from the segregated mining town of Ajo, Arizona, to the ranks of the US Army Special Forces in Central America. It was a crisis of conscience during his service in El Salvador that changed the direction of Mike Wilson's life, one that would take him to theological seminary, to humanitarian work in the desert, and into conflict with his tribe and church. This book offers an autobiographical and analytical exploration of the large lessons that Wilson's life holds for understanding the histories of indigeneity, empire, religion, and immigration debates in the Americas.

The focus on a single life history may raise some questions among some social scientists. What can a single person reveal about the world? Ethnographically and culturally attuned scholars, of course, have long understood, with Antonio Gramsci, that historical processes always leave an "infinity of traces" upon each of us, and thus, "the starting point for critical elaboration" is making "an inventory" of those traces.[10] Oral history, biography, ethnography, and testimonial literature can all be excellent ways to begin making such inventories. Scholars of social movements like Javier Auyero have shown the utility of focusing on a small number of "contentious lives" to understand how movements and activism operate at the "gray zones" of state and society. As his work illustrates, the sites where biography, sociology, politics, and culture meet offer vantage points to see not only the arc of one life but also the sociocultural workings of the world.[11]

Our Method: Toward a "Hyperlinked" Testimonio

As a collaborative oral history and Indigenous studies project, this work offers a hybrid form of "testimonio," a literary form familiar to students of Latin America in which individuals, often activists or leaders, tell their stories, usually in collaboration with an outside interlocutor.[12] We recognize that the testimonio genre has a complicated history and sometimes gets portrayed as the work of parachuting social scientists who seek to make academic careers on Native stories.[13] We want to be clear that this is not the case here. Our project is based on over a decade of sustained conversation and collaboration.

Moreover, our version of a testimonio collaboration differs from previous efforts. In our digital age, we are tempted to borrow a metaphor from the Internet and see our work as a "hyperlinked" testimonio. Across chapters and interludes, specific sites and experiences "link" to broad histories: Ajo links to racial capitalism, military service links to boarding schools, El Salvador links to US foreign policy and Archbishop Óscar Romero, a San Francisco seminary links to Manifest Destiny, and so on. And like hyperlinks, they can be bidirectional or multidirectional and can open new windows (and as we will see in chapter 4, they can even take some windows down). The metaphor of the hyperlink also serves to underline the nonlinear and interactive way that this collaboration came together across various encounters, screens, and locations.

Wilson and I (José Antonio Lucero) first met at the 2010 conference of the Native American and Indigenous Studies Association, held in Tucson, Arizona. Before that meeting, I had come across Wilson's work in the documentary *Walking the Line*, which explores the complex landscape of anti-immigrant vigilantism and also social justice, pro-immigrant advocacy in southern Arizona. Soon after the conference, I invited Wilson to speak at the University of Washington in 2011, which led to a first round of taped conversations about Wilson's life history, conducted in Seattle. A second round of interviews was conducted in Tucson in 2012. It is important to note that none of these conversations were held on the lands of the Tohono O'odham Nation. We conducted a third round of interviews in Seattle in 2016. With the help of research assistants at the UW, I carefully transcribed all those interviews[14] and then formatted them into a first-person prose account of specific periods of Wilson's life. Wilson then used those first-person drafts as the foundations for the five chapters and revised them with a close eye on clarity, accuracy, and style, while keeping the storytelling and genuine emotion of the original conversations. He wrote the testimonial chapters, and I took the first pass at researching and crafting the brief analytical interludes that accompany them.

The final step of the writing process involved Wilson and me coming together—like the rest of the world in the time of the pandemic, by phone or videoconferencing—to review the chapters and interlude drafts. We revised the entire manuscript word by word and idea by idea. The process was itself a journey through the modes of oral and textual knowledge production: our words went from spoken conversations, to transcribed interviews, to written and edited chapters, to a manuscript literally read aloud, and now, finally, to a book that you hold in your hands or read on your screen. In this long process of speaking, writing, and revising, additional memories (like one about Wilson's grandfather at the US government's Carlisle Indian Industrial School circa 1917) and new headlines (like those in 2021 on the mass graves found at the sites of First Nations residential boarding schools in Canada) revealed the new relevance of old stories.

The shape of this book, a conversation between the living archive of Wilson's memories and library-informed discussion of global themes, is not only a product of our intentions but is also informed by respect for Native intellectual sovereignty. We submitted our project, in good faith, for review to the Tohono O'odham Nation's Institutional Review Board (IRB), a body established by tribal legislation.[15] The tribal IRB reviewed our proposal and granted us "permission with modification." The modification communicated to us was that the IRB granted permission for Mike Wilson to explore his "life experiences" but did not grant permission for me to provide a secondary analysis, since such analysis would, in the IRB's view, "not offer comprehensive historical research of the Tohono O'odham Nation."[16] In our reply to the IRB, we made clear that Wilson's life experience would be the core of the book and that my interludes would not offer research or secondary analysis on the Nation but rather would provide accessible, academic reflections on broad themes.

This work represents a dialogue of different forms of knowledge. The core of this book is generated by a rich, textured oral history. That oral history led to engagement with various kinds of academic study, often by Native scholars. These forms of knowledge are produced in relation to each other. Together, they shed light on a remarkable set of questions that are examined in the following chapters of this book. What features of "boomtown" racial capitalism are illuminated by Mike Wilson's hometown, Ajo, Arizona, as it went from an open-pit copper mine to the site of a multimillion-dollar US Border Patrol housing complex (chapter 1)? How did Wilson's decision to join the military connect to other histories of American Indian service in the US military, which is higher (per capita) than that of any other demographic group (chapter 2)? How did his evolving views of US involvement in Central America resonate with debates over US foreign policy (chapter 3)? What questions do his entrance and exit from the church raise about the ambivalent place of Christianity in Indian Country (chapter 4)? Finally, how do conflicts over immigration between Wilson, his tribal government, and human rights activists fit within a broad historical landscape shaped by Native sovereignty, social movements, imperialism, and border politics (chapter 5)? We suggest that these chapters make some specific contributions to broader scholarly and political debates.

Contributions

First, this exploration deepens our understanding of Tohono O'odham and other Indigenous border crossers (and borders that cross Indigenous peoples), troubling the familiar and problematic narrative of the United States as a "nation of immigrants." Scholars working in Native studies, American studies, and (increasingly) borderlands studies have noted that the immigrant-centered construction of the US nation, even if well-intentioned (for example, "this land is your land, this land is my land," and the like), reinforces narratives of Native extinction in the creation of settler republics.[17] Native peoples are, of course, very much alive and constitute over 500 federally recognized sovereign tribes in the United States alone. Indigeneity, as many scholars have noted, is not a racial or ethnic category but a political one. Borders exist, therefore, not only between the United States and Mexico but also between federally recognized tribes and the United States. Those multiple border spaces make questions of politics and sovereignty complex. Moreover, many of the border crossers coming from Mexico and Central America are themselves Native peoples from across Abiayala (the Guna term for "the Americas"), representing Mayan, Zapotec, Mixtec, Aymara, Garifuna, Quechua, and many other Indigenous peoples. Immigration is thus an Indigenous issue.

Second, as the work tacks between "experience-near" and "experience-distant" forms of analysis, we find new ways to appreciate how imperialism is lived.[18] As Mike Wilson tells the story of a life that goes from Ajo to El Salvador, one can appreciate how everyday people across the hemisphere must negotiate the shifting lines of US empire and settler colonialism. In that respect, the presence of the US Border Patrol on Native lands is not just a recent development but a continuation of the oldest story in the Americas, one in which boundary lines between "civilization" and "merciless savagery" (to use the Jeffersonian rhetoric of the Declaration of Independence) must be drawn and maintained.[19]

Similarly, the tragedy produced by "prevention through deterrence" is an updating of the old colonial policies of dislocation and removal that forced (and continued to force) Native peoples from one part of the continent to another. It is also part of a longer history of the surveillance, incarceration, and deportation of racialized "Others." Harsha Walia eloquently describes the imperial and racist genealogies of US border policies, built upon the layered histories of Indian Wars, Chinese exclusion, anti-immigrant violence, and Japanese American incarceration: "The links between empire, race making, and the border are perhaps best symbolized in the construction of the border wall itself: wire mesh recycled from a Japanese American internment camp, repurposed Air Force landing strips and ground sensors from the Vietnam War, and Elbit Systems' 'virtual wall' surveillance technology field-proven on Israel's apartheid wall."[20]

Third, border politics are also another way of understanding the "colonial entanglements" that are part of American Indian political life.[21] The Tohono O'odham Nation, Wilson observes, invited the US Border Patrol onto its lands. To what extent can that decision be seen simultaneously as an example of Native sovereignty and a continuation of colonial dynamics? How much choice did the tribe have in looking to the US federal government to help mitigate the tragic consequences of US border policy? Similarly, why are institutions like the US military and the church part of (ongoing) colonial violence against Native peoples and also spaces in which Native peoples find support and even empowerment against those same forces?

Finally, this work interrogates the crucial role of religion in both the genocidal violence against Native peoples and the emancipatory work of social movements. Missionary violence casts a long and deadly shadow across Indian Country.[22] And yet, religion also represents a crucial terrain of action that involves many actors, including churches, pastors, and social movement organizations. Religion additionally provides an analytical vocabulary for understanding some of the motivations and tensions in prophetic and progressive efforts, like the sanctuary movements of the 1980s and the early years of the 2000s, to reveal the evils of state violence. This project also complements other work that looks at the intersections of social movements, border politics, and religion.[23]

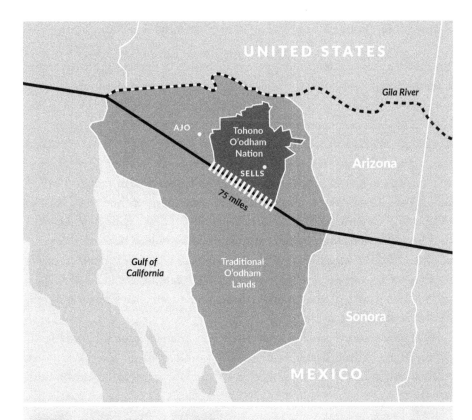

 The US federal government recognizes the Tohono O'odham Nation. Sells is the capital of the Nation. Although approximately 2,000 tribal members live in Mexico and can cross the international boundary as tribal citizens, Mexico does not provide federal recognition of tribal nations in the way that the US federal government does.

 The ancestral lands of the O'odham span from the Gulf of California to the Gila River, based on George S. Barnett's "Report Regarding the Tohono and Hia-Ced O'odham of Mexico Indigenous Peoples' Loss of Their Land."

The Gila River served as the boundary between the United States and Mexico from 1848 to 1854.

This boundary was created by the Gadsen Purchase in 1854. The O'odham were not consulted.

MAP 1. Tohono O'odham lands. Based on a map of O'odham lands created by Catherine D'Ignazio and Forest Purnell, using information provided in George S. Barnett, "Report Regarding the Tohono and Hia-Ced O'odham of Mexico Indigenous Peoples' Loss of Their Land, Violations of Convention 107 of the ILO, Violations of Treaty Rights, and the Lack of Protection for Cultural and Religious Rights of the O'odham of Mexico and the United States," unpublished report, Tucson, Arizona, October 9, 1989.

A Multigenerational Story (and an Intergenerational Collaboration)

Mike Wilson's story is a multigenerational one. Reflecting the storytelling tradition that he inherited from his father, Wilson reveals important insights into his parents' and grandparents' generations. These stories include a discussion of Wilson's maternal (non-Native) grandfather, Alfred Meeden, who worked for the Bureau of Indian Affairs in the 1930s training O'odham carpenters and builders on the reservation. His paternal grandfather, Juan Vavages, was among the first O'odham children to be taken to the (in)famous Carlisle Indian Industrial School. Vavages survived that experience and came back to O'odham lands with the name "Harry Wilson," part of the government's effort to erase Indigenous identity, something that Mike Wilson notes was not successful. Off the reservation, O'odham elders like Ella Rumley helped create community centers and safe spaces for young urban Indians like Mike. Thus, this multigenerational story is about struggle and resilience even as it chronicles adversity and hardship.

Our collaboration itself also represents an intergenerational borderlands conversation. Wilson describes himself as a product of the Cold War 1950s, while I am a child of the 1980s, when the Cold War was winding down. Both of us were born and raised in the desert borderlands, where churches, schools, military bases, and international boundaries serve to keep Native, Mexican, Anglo, Black, and other peoples apart (and sometimes together) in unexpected ways. As this project has spanned many years, it has provided ample time and opportunity for multiple trips to Arizona, Washington, and California, along with countless phone and Zoom conversations. These years of work have happily also provided the conditions for the establishment of the trust, knowledge, and friendship required to translate a life's worth of experience into the pages of a book. That is no small thing, and it comes with great responsibility. Beyond the charge to get the story right and do justice to the nuances and complexities of a remarkable life, there is an obligation to contribute to a better understanding of the challenges faced by the Tohono O'odham people and the migrants who find themselves crossing O'odham lands. We hope that the following pages offer some steps in the right direction.

Chapter 1

Ajo, Arizona

An Idyllic, Progressive Community, Which Included the Racism

MIKE WILSON

I am a very nontraditional Tohono O'odham.

I am what we call an "urban Indian." I don't speak O'odham, because our father never taught us. I speak Spanish because I developed an ear for it growing up in Mexican Town in Ajo and then later in South Tucson. I grew up in Ajo, Arizona, a booming mining town at the time, until my family moved to Tucson during the summer of 1960. Ajo is, as the crow flies, about twelve miles from the western edge of the Tohono O'odham Reservation. There are not many Native folk who live in Ajo anymore, not since the mine shut down in the mid-eighties.

Ajo was still segregated when I lived there in the 1950s. Mexican Town and Indian Village were separate housing areas of town. The original site plan of Ajo, circa 1917, included a "Mexican Townsite," an "Indian Townsite," and an "American Townsite" for Anglos. Jim Crow's ugly reach extended to my hometown.

FIGURE 2. Historic Ajo townsite sector.
Photograph by Phillip Capper.

Indian Village was a cluster of Phelps Dodge company-owned houses where predominantly Tohono O'odham families lived. It was high up on the hill and overlooked the open-pit copper mine. At its center was St. Catherine's Mission Church, where many children, me included, attended catechism. I was an altar boy there for a short period when the priest was Father Justin. Across the road from the church was a community center with a "feast house" and an outdoor basketball court with a cement floor. Traditional "waila" dances were held there. Our house was just a stone's throw away from the church. Its cement slab is still there; it's about twelve by twenty feet. Twelve by twenty feet for a family of seven! Our toilet was an outhouse.

Mexican Town sat on company-owned land where predominantly Mexican American families built their homes. When the mine closed, Phelps Dodge told the homeowners they had to leave, because they didn't own the land. Many of the families lost money, a *lot* of money. What choice did these poor miners have? If you worked for Phelps Dodge, you were beholden to the company, but you had a good job. You had security. You had food on the table. You had a roof over your head. You know, compared to your cousins in Sonora, Mexico, who didn't have economic stability, didn't have a guaranteed income, medical care, free education for the children. You weren't going to complain.

I was born in the San Xavier District of the Tohono O'odham Nation. I was born there in 1949 in the only Indian hospital in the area. The previous Indian Health Service hospital burned down in Sells, the capital of the Nation, in 1947. Another hospital wasn't built there until probably the early sixties. So, post–World War II, the only hospital serving Native Americans was the one in the San Xavier District, which was originally built as a tuberculosis sanatorium.

The Tohono O'odham Reservation is the second-largest reservation in the United States, about the size of Connecticut. The Tohono O'odham Nation has nine districts on the main reservation. Then there is the Gila Bend District, which is forty-four miles north of Ajo, and the San Xavier District, which is south of Tucson. Geographically, these two small districts are separated from the Tohono O'odham Reservation.

I had six siblings. I was the third oldest. My oldest brother, Stanley, whose nickname was Tykie, died in the summer of 1957. He was actually my half brother, but at the time I didn't know that. He was güero, güero, güero (Spanish: light-skinned). I never knew who his father was. Still don't. My mother never talked about it.

Family History: Navigating Race, Poverty, and the Bureau of Indian Affairs

My mother, Bertha, was born in 1929 in Hayden, Arizona, a mining town north of Tucson. She was part Spanish and also Native American, Quechan, one of the Colorado River tribes near Yuma. Her father, Alfred Meeden Sr., we think, was German American from Pennsylvania. He was a master carpenter by trade. He moved from town to town—Hayden, Sacaton, Tucson, Sells, Ajo—because that was where he could find carpentry work. During the Depression of the 1930s, he worked for the Bureau of Indian Affairs in Sells, the capital of the Tohono O'odham Nation. This is when the BIA established an Indian agency in Sells, which contained a BIA compound, housing for government employees, and other buildings. During that time, he also worked for the Civilian Conservation Corps in its Indian Division as a carpentry instructor. President Roosevelt began these work programs to put unemployed Americans back to work, including on reservations.[1]

The first time I climbed Baboquivari Mountain was in the summer of 1965. I remembered my grandfather telling me that they, the CCC, built the trail up Baboquivari Mountain. When they got to the cliff face below the summit, they

FIGURE 3. An artistic rendering of a Civilian
Conservation Corps–Indian Division patch at
the Uintah and Ouray Agency, c. February 1939.
National Archives Record Group 75, Records of
the Bureau of Indian Affairs, National Archives
and Records Administration, reproduced in
White, "The CCC Indian Division."

built a wooden staircase to reach the top. They had to use mules to haul the lumber. On my hike, when I reached the cliff face there were still remnants of the wooden staircase. When I made it to the summit, I found that a fire-watch shed, that they also built, was still standing, although it was disintegrating due to weather and age. I looked down and I saw rusted nails on the ground. I put some of them in my pocket because I wanted a physical and spiritual connection to my grandfather. I was never close to my grandfather, although he lived with us for a while after we moved to Tucson in 1960. He died probably the next year. My maternal grandmother, María Refugia Gonzales Meeden, died in Ajo in 1955.

My parents met in Sells where my mother was working at a grocery store. According to my aunt Flora, my father walked into the store in his army uniform, and it was love at first sight. After World War II, my father returned to the reservation where there were few jobs. There were no industries on the reservation. Well, I take that back. The only industries were cattle ranching and governments. There was probably a small tribal government and an even smaller BIA agency with oversight responsibilities of the tribal government. You worked for one bureaucracy or the other. And those who didn't were ranchers. But if you were a rancher with a family—with, say, four or five kids—only one of your sons could continue in the family business. What about the other kids, when they became of age, where were they going to find work? Well, the daughters could marry another ranching son, but what about the other sons? They couldn't stay in ranching. This is why many O'odham, including returning veterans, were forced to leave the reservation in search of jobs in mining towns like Ajo.

My dad worked in Ajo for a while. Remember, if you worked for the Phelps Dodge company, you got company housing. Because of that, we lived in Indian Village. As far as I recall, my father never worked *in* the mine, but he worked *for* Phelps Dodge. My earliest memory of him working was him doing maintenance at the Curley Elementary School repairing my first-grade classroom's swamp cooler. And then he probably lost his job. Well, he *did* lose his job because we had to move out of Indian Village. We moved to Mexican Town, two blocks from where my Meeden grandparents lived.

My dad grew up in Pozo Verde, a place traditionally called Ce:dagi Wahia, in the Mexican state of Sonora. There were no schools on the Mexican side for Mexican kids, let alone for O'odham kids. But his mother wanted him to get an education, so he was born on the US side in Topawa, where she had relatives. By 1920, the year he was born, there was already a Presbyterian day school on the reservation in the village of San Miguel. He attended the school through the fifth grade.

My father was an alcoholic. He was a good person when he was sober and working. And then come Friday night, he'd come home drunk. I don't know where he found the money to get drunk because he wasn't working much, and he certainly wasn't contributing money to the family. For all practical purposes, my mother was a single working mom who kept a family with six hungry kids together.

While we were still living in Ajo, he moved to Tucson to look for work. He found a job doing yard work for a church. I guess if he had wanted steady work, he could have stayed there because the pastor also had several other properties. But I don't remember him ever keeping a steady job.

My parents eventually split. You know, I don't think they ever married, and we never questioned it. In Arizona, there were—what are they called?—miscegenation laws. And they weren't repealed until 1954 or later.[2] For all social and legal purposes, my mother passed for white. She was güera, very light-skinned. My father was a dark-skinned Tohono O'odham. I suspect if they had ever tried to apply for a marriage license, the racist miscegenation laws would have prevented their marriage.

Ajo: A Progressive, Racially Segregated Town

We have a tendency to demonize corporations, but in my brief study of the histories of the Ajo community and of the mine, I learned the township was built following a progressive model. This was the Progressive Era, the 1910s, 1920s, and it included a national movement called "City Beautiful." Its philosophy was that if American corporations built good, healthy, beautiful cities *for* their employees, the employees would be happy *and* more productive.

By the time I was growing up in Ajo, there was a beautiful central park surrounded by the business district. There was also a public swimming pool. And a public library. And a public cinema. And a public school. And a *hospital*. Those are things that we take for granted today. Back in the 1910s and 1920s, that didn't exist, certainly not for the majority of American laborers. Ajo is emblematic of that era, of township *and* social planning, the idea that if you take care of your employees, then they will take care of the corporation.

Now, with that comes the racism of the era. Yes, Ajo was planned as an idyllic, progressive community, which also included the racism. Housing development was based on the division of the races: Indian Village, Mexican Town, and then American Townsite for everybody else outside those two communities. Except for the force of racism, my hometown was progressive in many ways.

Thinking about my childhood in Ajo, those years were some of the best years of my life. I remember everything was an adventure; everything was exciting. I loved the thrill of climbing to the top of a tamarisk tree and swaying in the wind. I remember my best friend Max Kisto and I would collect soda and beer bottles, and we'd redeem them for two and five cents each. For a quarter, we could watch a movie in the air-conditioned Oasis Theater and have money left over for a candy bar and soda! Or we'd spend the entire afternoon at the swimming pool, where admission was fifteen cents, and a candy bar and a record on the jukebox were a nickel each. One family in Mexican Town had a black-and-white TV, and they would let the neighborhood kids come over to watch it. We would sit like packed sardines on their living room floor and watch TV for hours after school. *American Bandstand* was my favorite, with *The Mickey Mouse Club* a close second. My other big thrill was putting on my metal roller skates and skating from NiNi's candy store in Mexican Town to the "downtown" plaza. I remember a sense of joyfulness in being alive. That sense of wonder is my life's companion.

I didn't know we were poor. I didn't know we were *desperately* poor. I had a sense that our family was struggling. I could see the strain on my mother's face and hear the desperation in her voice. But the wonder and joy I found in my daily life kept me hopeful and became the key to my survival. At least once a year, there's something in the wind that calls me back to Ajo, that calls me back specifically to Saint Catherine's Indian Mission Church.

There's something lovely and divinely feminine about Saint Catherine's. And, over sixty years later, she still speaks to me. When I speak of Saint Catherine's I mean both the church and the shrine on the hill behind the church. It's where I go to contemplate. She is my Vatican in the Desert, my personal Mount Sinai. I go there and it's as if the burning bush calls me.

I remember the nuns, who were our catechism teachers, but I don't see their faces or remember their names. But I remember their collective spirits, so much so that I felt the presence of the sacred. And I remember their love. I've said this before, and I'll say it till my last breath: They loved me first and taught me second. There was one young nun who loved me and inspired me the most. She planted and watered the seeds of an intellectual curiosity that has served me for the rest of my life. And I was in *preschool*. At the time, we were Catholic, but who wasn't? The vast majority of residents in Mexican Town and Indian Village were Roman Catholic.

I attended the Curley Elementary School, first through fourth grades. I remember it being fun and exciting. But I also remember I failed the third grade. I was traumatized by a very mean teacher. I remember her as being hateful. And because I feared her so much, I shut down and performed poorly academically. In 2003, I was part of an Ajo oral history project. Some of the other participants shared similar stories about the same teacher.

From Ajo to South Tucson

I didn't recognize the official de facto racial segregation in Ajo until I moved to South Tucson. In 1964, maybe 1965, I was subpoenaed to testify at a United States Civil Rights Commission hearing in Phoenix.[3] It was a hearing concerning alleged civil rights violations by the Phelps Dodge company in Ajo. I don't know where the complaints came from, and I certainly don't know how the commission got my name. They had enlarged black-and-white photographs of Indian Village and Mexican Town. I told them about growing up in both communities. I hadn't been conscious of the racial separation until that hearing. Looking at those photos I realized there *was* segregation by housing. For me that was eye-opening. But that didn't happen until I moved to Tucson. Looking at the photographs and saying, "Wow, these are really poor communities"—it didn't make me angry. It made me confused.

Growing up in Ajo I knew I was O'odham, but I didn't know what that meant. My dad, the church, and Indian Village formed my O'odham identity. It wasn't until I started the first grade that I knew I was "different" from other kids, but I wasn't self-conscious. After we moved to Tucson and I met more O'odham, that was when my sense of O'odham identity really came to the fore.

We left Ajo when I was young. My first conscious memory is of a sacred space, although I certainly didn't know it was that at the time. In fact, for many years I thought this memory was just a recurring childhood dream. It wasn't until we moved to Tucson that I realized what I had been dreaming about was an actual place. Have I ever told you about the Garden of Gethsemane? It's still there.

The Garden of Gethsemane is an art project by a Mexican American man who survived World War I. His last name was Lucero. During the war, he made a promise to God, that if God allowed him to survive, he would build religious monuments in thanks to him. One of the projects is on the west bank of the Santa Cruz River near Congress Street, west of downtown, in one of the barrio communities.[4] Lucero built a tableau of the Last Supper out of cement and plaster. You know, the same Last Supper picture that you see on the wall in every Mexican American home? That's what's there, but nearly life-size and in three dimensions. Jesus and his apostles overlook the Santa Cruz River. He also built a sculpture of the Crucifixion (again nearly life-size) and a small Roman temple.

The earliest memory I have is being there, at the Garden of Gethsemane. We were probably still living in South Tucson at one of the motor inns, Ingram Court. We were living there when I was born because that's the address on my birth certificate. My mother went to San Xavier Hospital and had me there, and then we moved back to Ingram Court.

I suspect my family took a day trip, maybe a picnic, to the garden. I remember being frightened looking at the tableau. I didn't know who they were or even if they were alive. I was maybe two, three years old. I also remember looking out and seeing a bridge over the river to the other side and horses beyond a wooden fence. This had to have been in the early fifties. I used to think that this was a dream. Until I moved to Tucson in 1960.

My O'odham friend Danny Lopez and I would often hang around downtown. We'd often bike there, him pedaling and me sitting on the handlebars. We'd check out the 45s in the record section at McClellan's and Woolworth's department stores. Or we'd go to the movies at the Fox, Paramount, or Lyric Theaters. When hungry, we'd get hot dogs and hamburgers at Art's or Kippy's, or our favorite, chili dogs at Pat's. Danny knew Tucson better than I did. We were probably about eleven or twelve years old, just hanging around, having a great time downtown.

One day we ended up at the Garden of Gethsemane. I just stood there. I looked and looked, stunned by what I was seeing. I said, "Wait a minute. I've been here before. This place is not a dream. This is as I remember it: the Last Supper sculpture, the river bed, the bridge." The fence and horses were gone, but all the rest were confirmation of my earliest memory. This is now one of my three sacred sites that I make a pilgrimage to when I need spiritual guidance. I also go to the hillside grotto next to San Xavier del Bac Mission and to Saint Catherine's in Ajo.

The Challenge of Growing Up in Poverty

Poverty was always present. Growing up on welfare was a month-to-month reminder of how poor we were. By the time I was in high school, my father had left. He went back to Pozo Verde, Sonora, where he lived in his childhood adobe shack. He took with him his monthly VA disability check that he was receiving because his right calf had been shredded by an enemy bullet in the Second World War. That was money that the family depended upon to survive. So, when he left, his check went with him.

At the first of each month, he would ride on horseback from Pozo Verde through a mountain pass and into Sasabe, Arizona. There, he would pick up his VA check at the post office and go next door to Alice's Market, where he cashed it and paid his grocery bill. Alice told me she used to warn him about stopping at the cantina in Sasabe, Sonora, on his way back home. "They're waiting for you, Joe," referring to the drinking vultures who would be waiting for him. They'd drink until all his money was gone. None of that money ever made it back to us.

We relied on welfare from Pima County and on food from the US Department of Agriculture. My mother was a domestic worker; she cleaned houses. My older brother and I would help out as much as possible doing yard work over the weekends and chopping cotton during the summer. One summer we picked cantaloupes in Dome Valley, east of Yuma, Arizona. You know, we got by.

Poverty can do two things: it can weaken you, or it can make you strong. I survived. I paid the price, though. I'm sure. I remember my mom, out of desperation, told us that she might have to put all of us children in the Arizona Children's Home. I was in the sixth grade. It was then that I developed a severe stutter. I'm sure it was brought on by the fear of us ending up in the Children's Home and the breakup of our family. I was that traumatized! I even negotiated with God, saying, "God, if you untie my tongue, I will serve you." Over time I managed to overcome it, although I still struggle with certain words. In fact, I consider myself a recovering stutterer. As a public speaker, I recognize that my every spoken word is a miracle.

I want to tell you about my brother Tykie, who died in 1957. "Nephritis," my mother said, "kidney failure." Here's what I think happened to him. Ajo had a public swimming pool, but we also liked to go swimming in the watering holes. In the processing of copper extraction, the mine used a lot of water.

They would release the untreated water into an arroyo, which became our alternative swimming holes. What we didn't know was what was *in* the water.

I think a lot of heavy metals and chemicals that they used in the mining industry were released in these waters, including acids and who knows what else. These became the ponds in which we would go swimming and diving. For us in the desert this was a big deal. I mean, there was a swimming pool across the road. But this was more fun. It was free, and it was a wooded area. There was so much water; it was an oasis in the desert, literally an oasis in the desert. I'm thinking that's probably where Tykie got some kind of chemical contamination, which probably destroyed his kidneys. He was eleven years old.[5]

Now, do I have proof? No. But this was pre–Environmental Protection Agency regulations. Also, clouds of smoke discharged out of the smelter almost daily and would fall right onto Mexican Town. And there was no EPA in place to protect residents from chemical contamination. Decades later I was driving through El Paso, Texas. The smelter there was discharging clouds of smoke, and I remember thinking, *Wow, this feels like Ajo.* That's why the University of Texas at El Paso has los mineros, the miners, as its mascot.[6]

INTERLUDE 1

Boomtown Lessons

Capitalism, Race, and Environment

As I listened to Mike's story and especially his mention of my hometown of El Paso, Texas, I was struck by how much he reminded me of people in my family. My paternal grandfather, like Mike's father, was also employed by a mining company in neighboring New Mexico. His death was a result of the slow but steady damage that the mines did to his lungs. Like Mike's O'odham family, my Mexican, Chicano, and Mexican American family straddles the US-Mexico boundary line.[1] My brothers, cousins, and I crossed the US-Mexico line to go to school and work and to spend time with family. The houses where I grew up in Ciudad Juárez, Chihuahua, and later El Paso, Texas, are only a few hours' drive from Mike's Tucson home.

Mike mentioned ASARCO (American Smelting and Refining Company) and UTEP to me as we sat in my office at the University of Washington. I joked that those ASARCO smokestacks were El Paso's answer to the

Seattle Space Needle. Constructed in 1966, just a few years after the Space Needle (1961), El Paso's 828-foot smokestack was the tallest in the world.[2] When I made that joke, I did not realize that the Pacific Northwest had had its own answer to El Paso's "Smeltertown": an ASARCO copper smelting plant with its own towering smokestack located in Tacoma, Washington, on the lands of the Puyallup Tribe, a forty-minute drive from where my family lives now in Seattle. A Tacoma postcard from 1909 gives pride of place to plumes of smoke that bellow out of the smelter, seamlessly joining the clouds above, conveying the image of boomtown modernity that, we now know, had a dirty underside. In 1917, a new smokestack was built in Tacoma. At 571 feet tall, it was the largest in the world at the time. As a result of this industrial activity, arsenic, lead, and other heavy metals are still in the soil of more than 1,000 square miles of the Puget Sound basin.[3]

Many of these monuments of boomtown modernity have come down. The Tacoma smelter was demolished in 1993. The smokestacks in El Paso were demolished two decades later, in 2013. While I have been back to El Paso many times since 2013, I somehow never noticed that the ASARCO smokestacks were gone. Like a sort of visual illusion, my brain inserts them into the landscape as I drive along I-10.

FIGURE 4. American Smelting and Refining Company's Smeltertown in El Paso, Texas, 2009. Courtesy of Wikimedia Commons.

ASARCO and its toxic remains connect the Indigenous borderlands of the desert Southwest with those of the Pacific Northwest. The locations of ASARCO smelters (in El Paso, Tacoma, and eighteen other communities in the United States) are part of what we might broadly call the "Superfund" geography of the borderlands, locations where legal action was often required to begin the work of cleaning up toxic substances related to extractive industries often located on or near Native, Black, or Latinx communities.[4] As if this history of environmental racism were not enough, El Paso, Tacoma, and other cities on this list of environmental cleanup sites are also connected as points in the growing network of immigrant detention centers and Border Patrol stations across the United States. Indeed, on the very location of the Tacoma Superfund site, private contractors built the Northwest Detention Center, one of the largest immigrant detention centers in the country.[5] El Paso was also the place where the Border Patrol strategy later known as "prevention through deterrence" was first developed in the 1990s, a plan that funneled thousands of migrants through the Sonoran Desert, the land of the Tohono O'odham Nation, which has become what anthropologist Jason De León calls "the land of open graves."[6] On the lands of Native peoples in the northwest and southwest borderlands, one does not have to scratch the surface very hard to find the traces of extractive capitalism and environmental injustice produced by boomtowns. Below, I briefly put Mike's hometown of Ajo in a broader historical frame, one that lets us see the workings of race, capital, and progressive urban planning.

Boomtowns and Racial Capitalism

> The development, organization, and expansion of capitalist society pursued essentially racial directions, so too did social ideology. . . . Racialism would inevitably permeate the social structures emergent from capitalism.
>
> —Cedric Robinson, *Black Marxism*

The concept of "racial capitalism," as developed by the political theorist Cedric Robinson, brings into relief some of the forces that Mike and his family encountered in Ajo. To be clear, Robinson uses this phrase not to suggest that there is a particular form of capitalism that is "racial" but rather to say that *all* capitalism is racial capitalism. In other words, the accumulation of capital works through the construction of inequality and difference; the fabrication of cultural categories facilitates the economic work of exploitation, dispossession, and removal. "Racism," in Jodi Melamed's succinct formulation, "enshrines the inequalities that capitalism requires."[7] Arizona, like much of what is now the US Southwest, was a racialized landscape in which dispossession and removal were tools of development. "Arizona was a land of vast mineral and land resources for Anglo pioneers," Nicole Guidotti-Hernandez points out. "Meanwhile, Mexicans were trying to retain what they had gained through Spanish colonization of the New World. Arizona was the homelands of the Apache and Papago [now known as Tohono O'odham]. . . . Capitalism fueled competition for control of territory."[8]

Even a capsule history of Ajo's development reveals the workings of racial capitalism in this part of the desert. The name "Ajo," according to various sources, likely comes from a corrupted version of the O'odham word for paint, "au-auho," which was produced from red copper oxide in this area. This copper-rich land drew Spanish and European settlers. Their initial efforts to extract mineral wealth were limited, but in the early twentieth century, connections made possible by improvements in railroad, drilling, and leaching technology created infrastructure and capacity for greater extraction. New investments by Calumet and Arizona Copper Company in 1911, from nearby Bisbee, allowed for the development of a new leaching plant in Ajo, which would by 1916 make the New Cornelia mine the first open-pit copper mine in Arizona. The entry of the United States in World War I increased the demand for copper production and greatly expanded the mine's profitability and the need for labor. The East Coast founders of the mine addressed the need for workers with a new sense of urban planning, a vision that could rightly be called progressive by the standard of the day.[9] As Mike notes, while "company towns" have acquired a negative and even exploitative reputation, they were often presented as enlightened efforts to create public spaces as well as educational and health opportunities for workers.

This coupling of extraction and urban planning highlights one of the paradoxical characteristics of racial capitalism: it can include the colonizing violence of extractive industry and also progressive social planning that together serve to "value and devalue forms of humanity differentially to fit the need of reigning state-capital orders."[10] Mike captures this contradictory nature of capitalism well when he describes an almost oasis-like quality to the economic opportunities that brought O'odham and Mexican laborers to the mines and related activities in Ajo. Architectural histories of the town confirm Mike's account. Planned in 1914 by Minnesota architects William M. Kenyon and Maurice F. Maine, under the direction of John C. Greenway, Ajo is "an example of comprehensive town planning based on the principles of the City Beautiful movement."[11] Amenities like public schools, libraries, swimming pools, and city plazas were part of this desert urbanism that one finds both in the archival documents of the last century and also in the promotional tourism of the twenty-first. In both historical and contemporary sources, one finds a version of what Renato Rosaldo called "imperialist nostalgia,"[12] not only for the expanding frontier of the United States that sites like Ajo represented but also for the victorious generation of imperial progressivism embodied by figures like Teddy Roosevelt.[13]

The founder of the town of Ajo, John C. Greenway, was one of Roosevelt's "Rough Riders" and a veteran of the Spanish-American War of 1898, a key moment in the expansion of US empire that would push the boundaries of the country beyond the familiar shape of the "lower forty-eight" map to formally include territories in the Caribbean (Puerto Rico and Cuba) and the Pacific (the Philippines, Guam, and Hawai'i).[14] Greenway was a Yale University graduate and, like many East Coast elites, saw opportunities in the West. The New Cornelia Mine and Greenway's plans for the town of Ajo illustrate the influence of the "frontier thesis" that Frederick Jackson Turner articulated in 1893 in a work that placed territorial expansion at the heart of the political project of the United States. Turner performed the intellectual and ideological work of reconciling an expanding US empire with the self-understanding of enlightened democratic rule.[15] Greenway's venture, like other settler-colonial projects, combined heavy-handed coercion with progressive public works.

Greenway's business record was, as one journalist put it, "checkered."[16] While he gets credit for the economic success of the mines he managed and the town he built, a dark spot on his record involved "his role in the notorious 1917 Bisbee Deportation," during which Greenway authorized and helped organize the "illegal round up of Industrial Workers of the World union members—often called 'Wobblies'—and sympathizers," most of whom were immigrants or ethnic Mexicans, during a period of worker unrest. Local media helped provide justification for the deportations by referring to the national security threats that came with the US entry into World War I. One newspaper ran a story with the headline "Strikers Help the Kaiser." Others pointed to the turbulence of the Mexican Revolution just across the border.[17] In a pattern that would become familiar over time, anxiety over race, gender, and violence converged to justify coercive measures to protect homeland and property. The sheriff of Bisbee worried that "Mexicans in Bisbee and along the border would take advantage of the disturbed conditions of the strike and start an uprising, destroying the mines and murdering American women and children."[18]

At the same time, Greenway's work in creating Ajo is celebrated for its progressively minded design. With the aid of Minnesota architects Kenyon and Maine, Greenway made public schools, swimming pools, and a hospital part of the landscape of Ajo. There was also the creation of what we now would call civil society as companies "encouraged fraternal and social organizations, sponsoring such groups as Boy Scouts."[19] The City Beautiful movement imagined and cultivated a new form of public sphere and thus may seem to have been a corrective to the exploitative and differentiating work of capitalism. In Ajo, however, not all forms of humanity enjoyed the amenities equally. This was most obvious in the common practice of residential segregation, designed in Ajo by Kenyon and Maine, who separated the town into discrete sections including "the mine and socially stratified 'American Townsite,' 'Mexican Townsite,' and 'Indian Townsite.'" This was common "in the copper towns of Arizona and New Mexico," in which "a significant portion of the unskilled [sic] labor population was Mexican and Native American. Anglos filled more skilled jobs. As Mexican nationals (mineros) and Native Americans were paid less than Anglo workers, this laid the seeds for many strike attempts. Segregation was evident in all aspects of community life, even regarding the assignment of swimming pool use."[20]

Given the segregation of "public amenities" like the swimming pool, it is perhaps not surprising that Mike and his siblings took to swimming in the "alternative swimming pools," the arroyos, filled by the excess and contaminated water used by the mine. The death of Mike's brother Stanley of kidney failure was a clear indication to Mike of the environmental racism that was literally in the water of his childhood hometown. Mike notes that this happened long before there existed the language of "environmental protection," yet that does not make the practice of environmental racism less real. To return to where this interlude began, this kind of structural and environmental violence can be found in communities as disparate as Tacoma, Washington, and Ajo, Arizona.

Geographer Megan Ybarra notes in her insightful study of Tacoma's Northwest Detention Center that the very location of this immigrant detention center on a Superfund site is part of a long history in which the best land is reserved for whiteness. "If White privilege maps onto whiteness as property, then White supremacy maps onto the interlocking systems of settler colonialism and racial capitalism that dispossess people of colour of land and dehumanises their bodies into devalued pollution sinks, where the less-than-citizen is forced to live on Tar Pits that they cannot even call 'home.'"[21]

In Mike's narrative, one learns that his family moved from Indian Village to Mexican Town, with "village" and "town" replacing the original moniker of "townsite." From his description and the archival materials, one suspects that the move from "village" to "town" was evidence not of social mobility but of shared precarity. Reading the history of his town, it is striking to learn that in the years after Mike's family moved out of Ajo, the residential zones for Mexicans and Indians "were demolished for expansion of the pit."[22] It is hard to think of a more apt image for the logic of racial capitalism than that of a large and growing mining pit literally consuming Mexican Town and Indian Village.

That elimination of these two residential zones also brings us back to the geographies of injustice with which this interlude began. Like the Superfund site turned detention center in Tacoma, the story of Ajo is also a story of the intentional and steady prioritization of whiteness and the erosion of Native spaces and bodies. It is not an exaggeration to say, with geographer Megan Ybarra, that this represents an example of what she calls the "spatialization of White supremacy." In this way, Tykie's death, likely a result of the contaminated waters in which he and other Native and Mexican children swam, represents one more casualty in a broad system of structural violence, one that connects the open pit of Ajo with the Tar Pits of Tacoma.[23]

As a final coda to this story of Mike's early years and a prelude to his future work with organizations like Humane Borders, it is helpful to fast-forward to twenty-first-century Ajo. After the closing of the mine in the 1980s due to labor strikes and decline in profits, the town has been repurposed into a new kind of boomtown. The "company" now is no longer Phelps Dodge but the Department of Homeland Security.[24]

The New Boomtown

In a project on "American Futures," *Atlantic* writers Deborah Fallows and James Fallows profile several cities and towns across the United States.[25] These places, "in the heart of America," represent hopeful signs of a less fractious country, proof that people can "heal the divide" that has become all too visible in a polarized United States. Ajo, according to Deborah Fallows, is such a place. Hearing the echoes of the progressive aspirations of the town's founders, she describes Ajo as "the story of a better America": "Take a walk through the oasis of green grass and palm trees in the central plaza of the tiny Sonoran Desert town of Ajo in southwest Arizona. You're likely to run into a Native American from the Tohono O'odham tribe, a Hispanic from the United States or nearby Mexico, or a white person, whom the whole town refers to as Anglo. These three cultures comprise most of the population of Ajo—and always have."[26]

Ajo's "comeback" story is a multicultural one, including innovative Native, Mexican, and Anglo art collaborations coordinated by the nonprofit International Sonoran Desert Alliance and an idyllic downtown listed in the National Historic Register. I have no reason to doubt the importance of the arts in Ajo or the efforts of its residents to create a more welcoming town that acknowledges its Native, Mexican, and Anglo histories.[27] However, as in the first founding, there are limits to such a progressive vision. A front-page story in the *Arizona Republic* puts the economic comeback in a different light: "Border Agents Add New Life to Arizona Town."[28]

The story of the Border Patrol presence in Ajo is a relatively recent one, but then again, so is the story of the border's intensive militarization. Interviews with a former US Border Patrol agent reveal that, in the 1970s, "there were no crossings."[29] For the decade of the 1980s, the Border Patrol presence was light; about ten agents staffed the local station, rising to twenty-one in 1989. Then in the 1990s, shifting US border policies made crossing through urban ports of entry more difficult and funneled migrants through the Sonoran Desert. The Border Patrol presence grew dramatically. "By 2010 Ajo Border Patrol staffing levels had increased to about 300 agents," writes geographer Scott Warren, "and by 2012 a new Border Patrol station was built, and staffing levels increased to about 500 agents."[30] A government document described the need for a new federally supported housing project and noted that Ajo should get ready: "The local development and real estate community has been encouraged to meet the longer-term projected housing demand."[31] Warren describes the contours of the new boomtown as part of an emerging border-industrial complex: "National Guard personnel, deployed to support Border Patrol from 2006–2008 in Operation Jumpstart Arizona, rotated in and out of Ajo, occupying hotels, RV parks, and restaurants. Ajo experienced a modest real-estate boom as construction contractors came to build border fences, forward operating bases, a new Border Patrol station, and other physical infrastructure. The construction of remote surveillance towers in the desert south of Ajo, for instance, brought five different contractors to town including Boeing, Granite Construction, and the private security firm EODT."[32] The election of Donald Trump as president in 2016 and his subsequent efforts to build a border wall through O'odham lands added to this boom with an influx of construction workers and contractors.

The rise in migrant crossings also fueled a boom on the other side of the border as local economies responded to the increasing needs for specialized water bottles, clothes, and other gear that border crossers would need as they walked through what the Border Patrol called with cruel accuracy "hostile terrain."[33] Border Patrol and smuggling economic booms are mirror images of the monetization of migration. The management of human bodies has replaced the extraction of copper ore as the activity that fuels borderland economies. As in the Phelps Dodge years, this new company has also sought to cultivate support in local civil society. In a striking echo of the early twentieth-century company encouragement of the formation of Boy Scout troops, the Border Patrol began the twenty-first-century "Border Patrol Explorers," a program for young people from fourteen to twenty years old. One Mexican American youth described how "we would sometimes act as the agents, or we would be the illegals. . . . [The agents] would tell us who we were going to be, give us a little background on our life, and then we would act it out."[34] The playacting, of course, was a pale reflection of increasingly aggressive actions by Border Patrol.

Scott Warren understood the increased Border Patrol footprint in Ajo all too well, not only from his vantage point as a scholar but also as part of a growing community of immigrant-rights activists in Ajo who volunteered with the humanitarian organization known as "No More Deaths." The organization has faced increased attention from Border Patrol agents, who, in several videos, can be seen destroying water stations set up by No More Deaths volunteers in the desert. In fact, shortly after No More Deaths released one of those videos, Border Patrol arrested one of the group's volunteers.[35] In January 2018, Warren was arrested for giving "food, water, clean clothes, and beds" to two young migrants, Kristian Perez Villanueva of El Salvador and José Sacaría Goday of Honduras. Warren was indicted on two counts of "harboring and conspiring to transport undocumented immigrants."[36] Warren insisted he was only giving humanitarian aid, in accordance with his religious beliefs. In the first trial, jurors were unable to reach a decision. In the second trial, it took two hours for jurors to acquit Warren.

Warren's case attracted great media attention as it highlighted not only the humanitarian crisis of death on the southern US border but also growing federal attempts to criminalize the activities of humanitarian organizations like No More Deaths. A reporter for the *Washington Post* notes that on the very same day that Warren was acquitted, another high-profile case also came to a close: "In the same courthouse, just two floors down, former Border Patrol agent Matthew Bowen was sentenced to three years of probation and supervised release. In a plea deal, Bowen admitted he had intentionally run over a Guatemalan migrant with his truck—and then lied about it."[37] These cases reveal just how much has been missed in most media accounts of the "border crisis."

The borderlands have arguably always been sites of violence and compassion, progressive inclusion and racial violence, and sources of beauty and tremendous suffering. Mike Wilson considers Ajo one of his sacred places, and I can understand why.

Chapter 2

Shake the Hand That Shook the World

The Path to the US Military

MIKE WILSON

Being Good Neighbors

As a teenager, I was always on the move. I was either involved in school or in the community at the Indian Center or working on the weekends doing yard work. There was always something going on in my community or in my life. I think that kept me occupied; I was always too busy to get in trouble.

Most of my friends in South Tucson were O'odham. We used to run in a group and called ourselves "the gang"—not that we were in any criminal gang but just a gang of kids. We'd say, "Is the gang coming over?" "Where is the gang going after the dance tonight?" There was a sense of belonging. And really, all we did was socialize. We would go to a dance Friday or Saturday night at the Indian Center, and afterwards, we'd go over to somebody's house and put the records on and hang out. I had never done that before, so it was a lot of fun. And because many of our parents knew each other from the reservation, they trusted the family whose house we were going to. There was a sense of tribal trust, of "Oh, I know them. It's okay for you guys to hang out late there. Just stick together." It was a good feeling. There was a sense of belonging to an extended family, and I think kids need that.

I *lived* for the weekend dances. By the mid-sixties, there were a couple of Tohono O'odham rock and roll bands, the Fagens and the Revelations. We had our own Tucson Indian Center in the predominantly Chicano city of South Tucson. We had an open-door policy at our Saturday night dances, and anybody could come in. I felt proud that Latino and Black people came in. I felt like we were being good neighbors. I was very proud of the fact that we had our own Indian Center with a predominantly Native board of directors. There was this core of urban tribal leadership that created and maintained the center for us. Some of the parents must have realized there wasn't any place for the kids to hang out, so they probably said to themselves, "You know what, we better have our own Indian Center for the kids to be able to do something; otherwise they're gonna get in trouble."

I remember one of the founding members, Ella Rumley,[1] told me that one time she was driving by an Indian bar on the south side, and she saw a bunch of O'odham kids outside the bar door listening to music, and it dawned on her: "Well, they're listening to music there because that's the only place they can listen to live music. They can't go in now, but in a couple of years, they will. What do we have for them in the meantime?" She was one of the tribal elders who had a vision for an Indian Center for the community.

Coincidentally, Ella Rumley had gone to the San Miguel day school on the reservation with my dad, back in the 1920s. She remembered him because he had a crush on one of her friends. This was before there were Bureau of Indian Affairs schools out there. There were very few, if any, schools on the reservation, so the Presbyterians opened a school that taught first through the fifth grade. Later, the Roman Catholic Church opened a day school in the village of Topawa. I believe that by the late 1930s and 1940s, public elementary schools were being built throughout the reservation. When I lived in Ajo in the 1950s, I recall students from the reservation attending Ajo High School.

The dances at the Indian Center were always a lot of fun, mainly because there was live music. The first band was called the Fagens. Ella Rumley's son, Darrell, was the drummer. I once asked him, "How did you guys come up with the name 'the Fagens'?" He said, "When I was in a high school English class, we were reading a book by [Charles] Dickens and one of the characters was called Fagin and the name just stuck."[2]

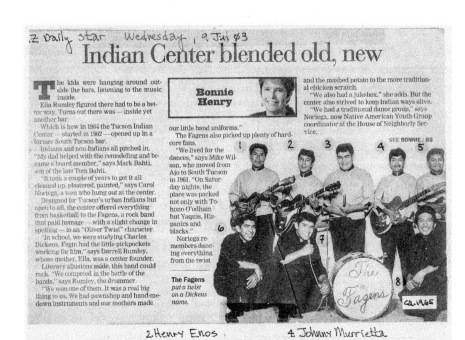

Indian Center blended old, new

Bonnie Henry

The kids were hanging around outside the bars, listening to the music inside.

Ella Rumley figured there had to be a better way. Turns out there was — inside yet another bar.

Which is how in 1964 the Tucson Indian Center — started in 1962 — opened up in a former South Tucson bar.

Indians and non-Indians all pitched in. "My dad helped with the remodeling and became a board member," says Mark Bahti, son of the late Tom Bahti.

"It took a couple of years to get it all cleaned up, plastered, painted," says Carol Noriega, a teen who hung out at the center.

Designed for Tucson's urban Indians but open to all, the center offered everything from basketball to the Fagens, a rock band that paid homage — with a slight change in spelling — to an "Oliver Twist" character.

"In school, we were studying Charles Dickens. Fagin had the little pickpockets working for him," says Darrell Rumley, whose mother, Ella, was a center founder.

Literary allusions aside, this band could rock. "We competed in the battle of the bands," says Rumley, the drummer.

"We won one of them. It was a real big thing to us. We had pawnshop and hand-me-down instruments and our mothers made

our little band uniforms."

The Fagens also picked up plenty of hardcore fans.

"We lived for the dances," says Mike Wilson, who moved from Ajo to South Tucson in 1961. "On Saturday nights, the place was packed not only with Tohono O'odham but Yaquis, Hispanics and blacks."

Noriega remembers dancing everything from the twist

The Fagens put a twist on a Dickens name.

and the mashed potato to the more traditional chicken scratch.

"We also had a jukebox," she adds. But the center also strived to keep Indian ways alive.

"We had a traditional dance group," says Noriega, now Native American Youth Group coordinator at the House of Neighborly Service.

SEE BONNIE / 8S

ca. 1965

1. Ralph Kisto
2. Henry Enos
3. Darrell Rumley
4. Johnny Murrietta
5. Richard Murrietta
6. Tony Parvello
7. Joe Wilson, Jr.
8. Danny Lopez

FIGURE 5. A newspaper clipping, annotated by Mike Wilson. Mike saved a newspaper column from the *Arizona Daily Star* on the Indian Center and the Fagens, July 9, 2003. Mike's brother is in the front row, second from the left. Photograph by Mike Wilson.

I used to live for those Saturday nights. There were so many of us teenagers, and all of us loved to dance. And it was a safe place. There were always parents there, as chaperones, as cooks in the kitchen selling hamburgers and Cokes, keeping an eye on all of us, inside and out.

At Pueblo High School I wasn't a very good student. I certainly never took any college prep courses, because I didn't know that there was a college prep track. If you were brown-skinned or Black, you were not encouraged by the guidance counselors to take college prep classes. For myself, my goal was to get a high school diploma, get a job, and get out of poverty. Or join the military.

I was class president during my freshman and sophomore years, then took a break as a junior. I was student body president my senior year. Somewhere during those first two years, a couple of my teachers saw something in me. The summer after my sophomore year, I and a few other students from Pueblo High School and Ajo High School were selected to attend a six-week program at Yale University.

What the Other World Looks Like: A Summer at Yale

The program was funded by the National Science Foundation and was for male minority students from across the country. There were three of us from Tucson and two O'odham from Ajo. There were many northern inner-city kids and rural southern Black people.

I remember that program very fondly. In fact, I remember when I got back to Tucson, I was offered a scholarship to a prep school, but I would have to repeat my sophomore year. I remember someone saying it was in New England, possibly Exeter Academy. My mother said no. My parents didn't understand the value of higher education. My dad completed the fifth grade and my mother possibly completed ninth. College had never been part of their lives.

I was very disappointed. At summer school I told myself, *Wow, so this is what the other world looks like. This is no ordinary school.* Our teachers took us on weekend field trips to Harvard, the Guggenheim Museum in New York City, and the Newport Jazz Festival, where I saw Nina Simone. I even attended a Supremes concert at the Yale Bowl! For a kid from South Tucson? Ha! By the end of the summer, I realized that an elite prep school was a stepping stone out of poverty. When my mother said no, I remember her saying, "No, you have to stay here and work." Meaning, "You have to help put food on the table for the family." She didn't say it, but I also understood her to mean, "You know that we can't depend economically on your dad."

She was working five, sometimes six days a week cleaning houses across town. Taking long, hot bus rides twice a day, working for The Man. When you've got bills to pay and six children to feed and to shelter, that was her, and our, brutal reality. I had been putting food on the table since I was twelve years old, chopping cotton during the summers and doing yard work on the weekends. That was my world. My world was growing up poor.

College had never been part of my vocabulary before Yale Summer School. The previous summer I picked cantaloupes in the Dome Valley near Welton, Arizona. It was toward the end of the Bracero Program.[3] It was the summer of 1964. I remember that there was a school bus that picked my older brother, Joe Jr., and me up at the Indian Center, then drove to Sells, then Ajo, and finally to Gila Bend, picking up field laborers along the way. The bus continued on Interstate 8 to Welton, where we were discharged at a labor camp. Many braceros were already there. We worked ten-hour days doing stoop labor, picking cantaloupes in the endless fields. I remember the row boss walking behind us yelling, "All I want to see is elbows and asses!" Imagine, then, my transition from Welton, Arizona, to New Haven, Connecticut, from cantaloupes to Dostoevsky!

Parenthood and the Politics of the 1960s

Shortly after I graduated from high school, I became a father. That was a shock; I was certainly not prepared for fatherhood, let alone for being a husband. I married my high school sweetheart, Laura C. Cruz, during our senior year in 1968. Our son, Joseph Anthony Wilson, was born in July 1968. I continued to be the student body president, but the office soon faded into the background. That spring Dr. Martin Luther King Jr. was assassinated in Memphis. I was saddened and upset and made a sign that I carried on campus the next day or two; it said "Long Live the King." By then I had become socially conscious. After I came back from the Yale Summer School, I was assigned a mentor, George Papcun. In his youth George had been a socialist, a coal mine union worker, and, later in life, an American labor organizer.

Because of his poor health, George and his wife, Alice, moved from Pennsylvania to Tucson in the mid-fifties. As a result of contracting black lung disease in the coal mines, he survived on one quarter of a lung. George worked in the mines from the age of twelve and eventually became a union organizer. In the 1930s and '40s he was a national labor organizer, an agitator. One time he told me that as he was crossing through East Texas, he tried to stop a lynching of a Black man by a white mob. The mob threatened to kill George if he didn't leave. The fact that a solitary white man tried to stop the lynching of a Black man—well, that's the kind of man George Papcun was. And the kind of man I wanted to be.

George had a profound impact on me. I had never met anyone like George Papcun before. I didn't know very much about economic, racial, and social justice. I mean, I knew what was happening in the South because we saw Jim Crow oppression and violence on television every night for years. I recall that 1963 was the year that the Sixteenth Street Baptist Church was bombed in Birmingham, Alabama, killing four young Black girls. This was also the year that the city's police commissioner, Bull Connor, instructed policemen and firemen to attack peaceful Black protesters with vicious dogs and powerful firehoses. I saw all of that, but so did the whole world.[4] So I knew what was going on. George had been an agitator and a fighter for social justice when it wasn't cool or safe. George was my mentor for about two years.

FIGURE 6. George Papcun in the *Daily Worker*, March 31, 1928.
Illinois Library, University of Illinois at Urbana-Champaign.

His wife, Alice, had gone to college, I think. George had not. She had also been a labor organizer with him, and together they were like fire and steel, she the fire and he the steel. They were among the early founders of the NAACP and ACLU in Tucson. They lived very humbly. His gift to humankind was the power of his spoken word—when he spoke, mountains trembled.

After high school, I became an activist. I had a lot to be angry about, especially after the killing in Ajo of Phillip Celaya, a young O'odham man.[5]

The Death of Phillip Celaya

I don't remember how we found out that Phillip Celaya had been killed in the parking lot of an Ajo bar. The story we heard was that he had been causing a disturbance in the bar and that it had moved outside to the parking lot. A Pima County deputy sheriff showed up and fired his weapon at Phillip as he tried to run away. The first shot hit him on the back of one of his hands, causing him to spin around. The second shot was to his front, causing him to fall and die. Situated in Pima County, the sheriff's department has law enforcement jurisdiction in Ajo.

Robert Cruz, a Tohono O'odham friend and former colleague at the Yale Summer School, was my activist collaborator at the time.[6] We were working out of the Indian Center in South Tucson. He was very concerned because he had heard that there had been a rash of killings of Native men by law enforcement agencies in the Tucson area. I forget how many he said, maybe five or six, and nothing had been done about them. We were really pissed off when we heard about Phillip Celaya.

Some of Phillip's family members were living in South Tucson, and they used to come in and out of the Indian Center. We got to know them there; maybe that's how we heard about his death. I don't know if Robert had a connection with the American Indian Movement (AIM), or if there was a local chapter in Tucson. Teresa Chico and Pam Evans, two young O'odham women still in high school, may have been members, the movers and shakers as I remember, of an informal AIM group. I don't know if it was them or Robert who contacted AIM and invited some of its leaders to come to Tucson.

Dennis Banks (Ojibwe), Cofounder of the American Indian Movement, Speech about the Death of Phillip Celaya

After 480 years of the white man robbing us, raping our women, we know who is really disturbing the peace! They say we are outside agitators—No Indian is from outside—they are the outside agitators! The longest undeclared war in world history is not Viet Nam, but the United States Government war against Indians. This struggle will continue from Ajo.*

*Ajo Copper News, July 27, 1972, http://ajo.stparchive.com/Archive/AJO/AJO07271972P02. php. The Ajo newspaper reports that there were also speakers from the National Indian Youth Council, the Afro-American Coordinating Council, and the United Farmworkers.

We held a press conference at the Tucson Indian Center to protest the killing. There was a lot of local coverage, and by the sheer force of AIM's celebrity status, Robert and I fell into the background. We were the ones who organized the press conference and then, later on, the protest in the Ajo Plaza and the march from there to Tom Childs' Ranch, where some of Phillip's relatives lived.[7]

After the Ajo protest and march, I realized that AIM was really a flash in the pan. It came, it grabbed all the media attention, and then it was gone. What good did it do? We were left behind to pick up the pieces and continue the fight. The protest and march were a big splash in the history of Ajo, my hometown. I'm glad they happened, but that was it. I don't think Ajo has had another protest or made the news again, until recently. This morning on National Public Radio there was a story about undocumented migrants being dropped off by the Border Patrol near the Plaza.[8]

We never got justice for Phillip Celaya or for his family. All we got was the one-sided version of the Pima County Sheriff's Department. How many people of color were killed by law enforcement before Phillip and how many more since?

The Path to the US Army

I wanted to go to college, not knowing that I was academically unprepared. I enrolled at the University of Arizona but didn't do well. I had a full-time job at St. Joseph's Hospital working as a kitchen aide, taking out trash, washing huge pots and pans, taking food up to the wards. I was a working family man and going to college, where I struggled and failed at algebra. I don't know if I ever took high school algebra, but the state requirement for a diploma was two years of math. I probably took two lower-level math classes. I had attended the Yale Summer School and had been offered a scholarship to an elite prep school. So why was I such a failure now?

The summer school was designed for inner-city, reservation, and barrio kids like me. Social scientists and teachers understood that if you gave these kids a chance to succeed, well, they could do something. This was the era of President Lyndon Johnson's War on Poverty.

And the faculty and students, wow. So many people of color. I had never known Black and Jewish intellectuals until then. I mean, we were reading *Crime and Punishment* by Dostoevsky and *Invisible Man* by Ralph Ellison! I wasn't reading those authors at Pueblo High School! But those were the times when children of color, poor children, and the sons and daughters of the working class were doomed to a second-class education because of their second-class citizenship in America. And somehow the National Science Foundation, the summer school's funder, must have understood that society had to give opportunities to *everybody*. "We'll invest this money and hire university professors and graduate students who look like these students." There were about a dozen Native American kids from tribes throughout the country. I had never known so many brilliant students of color, absolutely brilliant.

To go from that experience to struggling at the University of Arizona was heartbreaking. High school had been easy because I was taking general education classes. I thought that was all there was, not knowing that I too was floating in a sea of mediocrity. I never felt challenged or the need to study. I don't know if my high school offered AP courses, but if there were I know that I wasn't in any of them. Never took chemistry. Never took calculus. Never took trigonometry.

But that's what a barrio kid did, survive. Not excel, just survive. Your mother is cleaning houses and your father is doing yard work, so what's your vision? Your vision is no higher than what you see around you. That's all you know because that's all you see.

Laura, Joseph, and I were living next to her parents. They had a large front house and three small apartments in the back. We were living in one of those, rent-free, but it was still a struggle. My father-in-law was José Cruz Sr. His mother fled Mexico during the revolution, came north, and settled in Barrio Viejo, a predominantly Mexican American barrio. She bought the property from an O'odham woman and built one house and then gradually built the other little houses for rentals. We lived in one of those tiny apartments. The two of us and a newborn. It was comfortable. I wasn't prepared for fatherhood or being married, but I knew I had to do it. I was willing to try, and so was Laura. We stayed married for twenty-two years.

Two of our children were born in Tucson: Joseph, as I mentioned, in 1968, and then María Eliza (Lisa) in 1971. Our last child, Cecilia Maria (Ceci), was born at Fort Bragg, North Carolina, in 1975. They attended first grade through high school on Fort Bragg and in Fayetteville, North Carolina. Fayetteville is where they call home.

I was failing at the University of Arizona and working a dead-end, menial job at the hospital. I made the decision to join the army and signed up for two years.

Joining the Military (the First Time)

The Vietnam War was still going on. The first time I enlisted was September 29, 1970, and I was in for eighteen months. I was assigned to a signal company, Company B, 426th Signal Battalion, in Fort Bragg. I wound up getting out six months early because by 1972 Congress had mandated a reduction in force since the US military was winding down its mission in Vietnam. The US Army had to cut 200,000 troops within the next year. We were told by our first sergeant that if you had legitimate grounds, you could get out six months early. The basis for my "early out" was that I was going back to college.

I wasn't particularly gung ho in the Signal Corps. I found it very boring sitting in a metal cubicle in the back of a truck. It was also a very demoralized unit with a lot of drug use. It just didn't feel like a professional army. When I returned to Tucson, I went back to the University of Arizona, but I was *still* not academically prepared. I had a family to take care of now with two kids. When I was discharged from the army, my father-in-law got me a job at Pacific Fruit Express (PFE), cleaning out empty railroad cars as they came in. The cars would transport fruits and vegetables from the distributors to the marketplace. Once they were unloaded, they would return to Tucson for cleaning and maintenance. We would go in the empty cars and sweep and hose them out before they left to pick up their next loads.

I didn't see a future there.

One day I was helping my father-in-law put up a car porch. We were putting on a sheet metal roof. I was on a ladder, and as I leaned to my right the ladder began to slide. As I reached up to grab the roof to try to break the fall, I caught an edge of the sheet metal with my left hand and slashed my palm. The PFE was a subsidiary of Southern Pacific Railroad, which had a hospital, Carl Hayden, in Tucson. I went and got stitched up. A week later, I got a medical bill in the mail. I thought to myself, *Wait a minute. I work for Pacific Fruit Express, which is a subsidiary of Southern Pacific Railroad, and Carl Hayden is a company hospital.*

I walked to the hospital for an explanation. The biller explained to me, "Yes, but your accident was not related to work. You didn't cut yourself on the job, so we're not paying for that." I asked, "If I have no medical coverage for myself after 5 p.m. when I leave the railroad yard, what about my family?" I had thought, because this was a company hospital and I worked for the company, that I automatically had medical coverage for myself and my family. He said, "No, they're not covered either." I was so disgusted with PFE that I told Laura I would rather go back in the army for twenty years than put in two more hours at PFE. It was that slash on my left palm that made my decision. I was so angry that I pulled the sutures out with my teeth!

Soon after I went back to the army recruiter and took the ASVAB (aptitude) test. I scored high, 97 out of 99.[9] I asked the recruiter, "What do I qualify for?"

He replied, "With your score, anything you want."

"I want Special Forces."

"You've got it."

Returning to the Military: Special Forces

During my first enlistment, my squad sergeant, Sergeant David Rounds, told me, "I see a lot of potential in you. Why don't you polish your boots and put some starch in your uniform? And get a good haircut?" That's all it took. Within twenty-four hours I was doing all those things. I guess he was my mentor. He was like my high school teachers who had seen something. "This kid has potential. If I can just turn him around and give him a kick in the pants, he'll do much better." I took Sergeant Rounds's remark as a compliment, and I did something about it. I put starch in my uniforms. I got that close haircut. I spit-shined my boots. I became an exemplary soldier in appearance and in attitude. But that still didn't keep me in once I knew I could get an early out.

When I first told Laura of my plan to leave the army, she told me, "Mike, I don't know why you're getting out. You'll be back in within two years." My army buddy Herman McCoy had told me exactly the same thing when I told him that I was getting out. Apparently, they knew me better than I knew myself.

I went back in on September 29, 1973. Several months prior I saw live TV footage of American POWs being released from North Vietnam and returned to the United States. As they came out of the aircraft and down the ramp, they were received by military dignitaries. I remember there was one POW who was identified as one of the longest-serving POWs; he was a Special Forces soldier who had been imprisoned for about five years. There was a Special Forces detachment that received him, and one of them handed him a green beret. For me, that was a very symbolic gesture. It was more powerful than generals receiving him and saluting him. I didn't care if it had been the president of the United States who had been at the bottom of the ramp. It didn't compare to the image of a Special Forces detachment receiving one of their own. I said to myself, *That's where I belong.*

I didn't like what I had been doing during my first enlistment. I didn't want any part of *that* army because the army was in transition to a peacetime army. It was downsizing. Morale was low. It was the effect of being at war for almost ten years. It was a political war, and it was a losing war. I didn't want to go back into *that* army. I told myself, *Well, I'm going back in, but I'm gonna go back in for Special Forces.*

A Product of the Cold War

Why did I go in then, in that moment, knowing the politics of the era? Well, I was a product of the fifties and sixties, and I guess I was a product of that Cold War era. I experienced the American propaganda about communist incursion in the Americas. I lived through the Cuban missile crisis of October 1962. That was very real to me. I saw heavy bombers coming in and out of Davis-Monthan Air Force Base as I walked to Safford Junior High in the mornings. I saw bomber after bomber coming in low, and that's what really terrified me. News reports about the Cuban missile crisis made it crystal clear that the Soviet Union had long-range nuclear-tipped missiles in Cuba. As a seventh grader, I feared we were on the brink of a nuclear war. I thought if an American city was wiped out by a nuclear strike, then bombs would start falling like rain, here and in the Soviet Union.

I was aware of other struggles in this country, particularly those of poverty and civil rights, but I had a hope that we could fix those issues. But what we could not fix was communism.[10] My fear was that because Russia had a foothold in Cuba, it would use Cuba as a stepping stone to support "wars of national liberation" in the Western Hemisphere. I reenlisted as an anti-communist, without having a clear understanding of Marxist doctrine but having a gut feeling that something bad was going on.

Yes, I had been part of the anti-war protests of the sixties, including the Moratorium to End the War in Vietnam in 1969, where I marched and wore a black armband. I knew it was a political, losing war. But I also knew in my heart that Vietnam was part and parcel of a global Cold War. Korea, North Vietnam, South Vietnam, and now Cuba. What's next?

I reenlisted as a freedom fighter. And it was confirmed on the Special Forces crest: there is a dagger and two crossed arrows and a scroll inscribed *De oppresso liber*, "free the oppressed."[11] The genesis for this motto was in the early fifties when Special Forces was officially formed as a separate combat arms branch of the army. Following World War II came the fall of Eastern European countries to Soviet domination. The Special Forces mission was to "free the oppressed" in Eastern Europe. And that struck me. I thought, *I'm against oppression, whether here or overseas.* That motto clarified the feeling that I had made the right decision.

I was clear about that. And I remember thinking, *You know what? I am anti–Vietnam War. I don't like war. But who's going to fight for the world? Who is fighting for Hungary? Who is fighting for Poland? Who is fighting for Czechoslovakia? And all those countries in South America?* The political Left of this country was criminalizing the 1950s CIA operations in Latin America for supporting dictators like Fulgencio Batista in Cuba and Rafael Leónidas Trujillo in the Dominican Republic. I agreed with their criticisms because they were legitimate and true. But where was the liberal Left when Czechoslovakia fell? Where was the liberal Left when Russia invaded Hungary with tanks in 1956? And I still ask those questions now.

Yes, the United States has a sordid history in Latin America, but I was looking specifically at the fall of Eastern Europe behind the Iron Curtain. These countries were devastated and weakened economically, politically, and militarily by World War II. Russia took advantage. I didn't want communism to take hold in the Americas. As repugnant as the CIA was and can be, I said, "Well, I will take democracy, warts and all, any time, any place." And that continues to be my philosophy. Democracy is beautiful and ugly. It is an ongoing human experiment in self-government. It's imperfect, but it's a hell of a lot better than a totalitarian system.

My Father's Military Experience

I grew up under the roof of my father's military service. My father, José Vavages Wilson, not only was a veteran of World War II but had been an infantryman.

As a child, even until my preteen years, we would listen to his war stories when he came home from the bars. His stories were graphic, fascinating, and intriguing. He came from that Tohono O'odham storytelling tradition and would describe long, drawn-out narratives of his experiences during the war. I grew up in that listening tradition. Children of World War II veterans—especially those of us who were products of the 1950s—were living proof that the United States saved the world. My father would extend his hand and say, "Shake the hand that shook the world." I sensed his tremendous pride in having been a fighting warrior, an infantryman.

I view my father as one of those humble heroes who came off the reservation in December 1941—probably not even fluent in English—and went to war. He enlisted three days after Pearl Harbor. He saw combat in North Africa, fighting Nazism, and saw action in Sicily and Italy, fighting Nazism and fascism. And then combat in southern France, where he had his right calf blown off. I grew up under this banner of honorable military service. At this time, America considered people of color as second-class citizens. I felt that my father paid for his and his children's American citizenship with his blood.

I believe that most Native American veterans have a sense of profound loyalty. However, I don't think there is a conscious loyalty to the US government. Yes, we serve under the American flag and take the Oath of Allegiance to protect the Constitution. But for Native people, it is a higher, spiritual obligation to protect the land, the sacred Mother who bore us. Our umbilical cord is never severed from her; we're always connected.

There is a Tohono O'odham creation story that tells us that we are made of mud. I'itoi, Elder Brother/Creator, scooped soil into his palms and then added spit to make mud and from this formed our ancestors. We are of the soil and water and the land. In many Indigenous creation stories, First Peoples emerge out of the land or out of water. O'odham creation stories follow that narrative.

In many North American tribes, veterans are esteemed. It's that common bond where active duty and veterans are seen as being part of a warrior class that protects its people and its lands. I think non-Native military members consciously serve to uphold an oath to protect the Constitution of the United States. Theirs is an effort to defend the idea of land, a vernacular "homeland," but they don't mean the "sacred soil." I think there is a difference. There is a spiritual difference, a cultural difference. It is a different worldview.

I understood, even at an early age, the necessity to go to war to put an end to holocaust, tyranny, and fascism. I certainly didn't have the vocabulary then, but sitting at my father's feet, I understood the horrors of global war and of the contributions the United States made to put an end to it. I had always been interested in the history of World War II and understood that eventually it would be my duty to answer America's call to arms. To those of us baby boomers, products of the 1950s, military service was an inherited moral obligation.

It was one of those points of entry into manhood for young Tohono O'odham men, and I think for many Latino people also. There was an expectation that you would serve your country honorably. I remember one Mexican American classmate who dropped out of Pueblo High School, Paul Rodríguez. I saw him several months later in the high school parking lot in his US Marine Corps uniform, looking very sharp and very proud. He was shipping out to Vietnam. Within six months, he was dead, killed in action. If you were Brown, Black, or poor white and dropped out of high school, you were going to the meat grinder, Vietnam. Decades later I visited the Vietnam Veterans Memorial in Washington, DC, and made an etching of his name.

Through junior high and certainly through high school, there was the expectation that if you were drafted, you would go. No questions asked. I grew up in that tradition. It was never said verbally, but I understood what was expected of me. My dad's younger brother, whom I am named after, was a paratrooper with the 82nd Airborne Division during World War II. I saw military service as noble and expected.

I heard war stories, like the story from my dad about him being in northern Italy when Benito Mussolini, the fascist Italian dictator, was killed by his own people, by resistance partisans. My dad was in Milan and saw the battered bodies of Mussolini and his mistress being pissed on by civilians. What a great end to fascism. Stories like this were what I heard as a child. Brick by brick, they laid the foundation for a warrior mentality. It was the magic of his storytelling, through the lens of the oral tradition, that formed the foundation. It was my time to fight communism.

I went to Fort Bragg to start Special Forces training. I thought of my uncle, the World War II paratrooper. I thought of my dad, a World War II infantryman. I saw two sets of boot prints in the sand. They were two role models for soldiering, and I wanted to do it. I was anxious to do it. I'm not going to say that training was easy, but just the fact that I grew up doing manual labor by age twelve, working ten-hour days to help put food on the table, chopping cotton and picking cantaloupes—I knew that I was prepared for anything I would go through physically.

My proudest moment, other than the births of our three children, came when I graduated from the Special Forces Qualification Course in 1975. Several years later, while home on leave, I picked up my father in Tucson and I took him through Sasabe, Sonora, to Ce:dagi Wahia (Pozo Verde), his ancestral village. He wanted to go there for the weekend. My dad didn't talk a lot; he was normally very quiet. But on the drive he started talking to me using military vocabulary from the 1940s, from his days in the "Brown Boot army." He asked me, "So, are you home on furlough?"

"Yeah, I'm home on furlough."

"I heard you're a commando." He paused. "What outfit are you with?"

"Company A, Third Battalion, Fifth Special Forces Group."

He was honoring me with the wartime language that he knew. For him to speak to me using these archaic terms—furlough, commando, outfit—I felt I had been accepted into his warrior clan. It was a sense of brotherhood and privilege. Soldier to soldier. This is the power of the spoken word, from archaic to sacred. Hard work and discipline were not new to me or my family. In fact, you could go back two generations to my grandfather, my father's father. He was one of the first O'odham children to go to the Carlisle Indian Industrial School in Carlisle, Pennsylvania.

Manifest Destiny 2.0: The Carlisle Indian Industrial School

My grandfather was named Juan Vavages. There are still Vavages on the west side of the reservation, and I am sure we are related. We may also have relatives in Nogales, Sonora, primos (cousins), who spell their last name Babagi. My cousin Art Wilson tells me that the name Babagi comes from the O'odham word for a medicinal plant.

According to my father, my grandfather's name was changed to Harry Wilson after he was sent to the Carlisle Indian School in Pennsylvania, the first government boarding school for Indians. At Carlisle, my grandfather was "issued" the name Harry Wilson as part of "civilizing" him. It was part and parcel of the process of racial extermination and cultural genocide of Native Americans. The Indian School's mission statement was "Kill the Indian, save

FIGURE 7. Studio portrait of Juan B. Vavages and Thomas Kenay, c. 1900. Photograph by John N. Choate.

the man." This is what I call "Manifest Destiny 2.0," successor to the original westward expansion period known as Manifest Destiny, 1812–67.

Let me just give you some historical background of the Presbyterian church in the Tucson area, because I think it may make sense of how this ties in. The Presbyterian church had a boarding school in Tucson, the Tucson Indian Training School, that opened on January 4, 1888, near the University of Arizona.[12] Once the University of Arizona opened in 1885, adjacent real estate, on which the Indian school campus sat, became prime real estate.

The school was moved to the vicinity of South Tenth Avenue and West Twenty-Third Street, near the present site of Southside Presbyterian Church. In 1907, the school was moved once again to Ajo Way, where it remained open until 1960. By then, the school was popularly referred to as "Escuela." It was always outside the Tucson city limits. Indians are always pushed out.[13]

That Presbyterian zeal spilled over onto tribal lands where a series of small chapels were built in the Baboquivari Valley. There was even a day school at San Miguel. That little one-room day school still stands, and even the chapel. I used to preach there during my ministry on the reservation.

Maybe for my grandfather Juan Vavages/Harry Wilson, that schoolhouse was the Presbyterian and the Carlisle Indian School connection. It was certainly my dad's Presbyterian connection, because he went to the San Miguel day school through the fifth grade. I don't know how, if voluntarily or by force, my grandfather ended up in Carlisle.

Race in the Military and Experience in the Americas

During my first enlistment, I was in the Signal Corps with a lot of Black and Latino people, where I felt a sense of camaraderie. When I reenlisted in 1973, Special Forces did not have that ethnic diversity; it was mostly white. That's the first thing I noticed, but that was beside the point. I didn't sign up for the diversity; I went in to earn the Special Forces shoulder tab and to wear the green beret.

I never felt out of place at Fort Bragg. As a matter of fact, I felt that I belonged in the army. I was walking in the boot prints of my father and his brother, who opened the doors for me.

I was very impressed by the caliber of my Special Forces colleagues. Many of us had some college. But it wasn't only the academic smarts; it was the commonsense type. It was problem solving, outside the textbook. *That* kind of smarts. People with imagination. People who wouldn't take no for an answer and who were willing to take risks to get the mission done. And it didn't come from sitting in the classroom, even though there was a lot of emphasis on classroom instruction. I think the strength of a Special Forces soldier was, and is, the combination of the classroom instruction, his real-world experiences, and problem-solving skills. It may appear obvious, but you do what you have to do to get the mission done. I think that's what makes a Special Forces soldier a head above the others.

I also saw the common man. A lot of poor southerners. A lot of poor Mexicanos from Texas, California, Arizona, New Mexico. They may not have finished high school, but they found their place in Special Forces and *excelled*. I saw that over and over and over again. They were just *dynamic*.

There was a Chicano brother from Texas, Roy P. Benavidez, who won the Congressional Medal of Honor during his service in Vietnam. According to the citation, Benavidez engaged in hand-to-hand combat with North Vietnamese soldiers as he attempted the rescue of a twelve-man Special Forces patrol that had been surrounded by a North Vietnamese battalion. Under intense enemy fire, he went back several times from the helicopter to retrieve wounded and dying teammates. Despite being shot numerous times and having to resort to fighting hand-to-hand, he carried them to the helicopter and saved eight of his fellow soldiers. He was the common man from Texas, not one of your elites. Folks like him earned their PhDs from the barrios.[14]

The only disappointment of my military career was that I never saw combat. In Special Forces and throughout the army, the ultimate badge is the Combat Infantryman Badge, and I never earned it. Although I was in a combat zone in El Salvador, we were prohibited by Congress from participating in any type of combat operations.

I was mentally prepared to go to Vietnam. I actually *wanted* to go to Vietnam. My fear was of communism in the Americas, and this was before the fall of South Vietnam in 1975. I knew that South Vietnam had a history of French colonialism. But it goes back to the question: Which is worse? French colonialism? American colonialism? Soviet-style totalitarianism? When I look at North Korea, is there anything worse than *that* totalitarian state? You know that's Marxism to the tenth degree.

Would any government in the world *want* that kind of socialism? Again, communist countries called themselves socialist democracies. When East Germany was part of the Soviet Bloc, it called itself the German Democratic Republic. North Korea calls itself the Democratic People's Republic of Korea, a *democratic* republic. It's neither democratic nor a republic. Which is worse? I know that North Korea is an extreme model. But what's worse? A totalitarian North Korea, or a military dictatorship on the model of El Salvador?

Kill Juan Vavages, Save Harry Wilson?

Militarism and Activism in Indian Country

JOSÉ ANTONIO LUCERO

This chapter of Mike Wilson's story begins with joyful recollection of the dances at the Indian Center; it ends with a contemplation of the Cold War anxieties over democracy and dictatorship. His stories reveal a dialectic of hardship and joy from which springs a life full of meaningful encounters with friends, family, politics, and mentors. His urban Indian friend takes a character from Charles Dickens and transforms it into an O'odham rock band. A remarkable set of elders leave their mark on Mike's life, like O'odham community leader and military veteran Ella Rumley, whom he credits for creating spaces for Native urban young people like himself, and non-Native radical labor leader George Papcun, whose lungs were destroyed by Pennsylvania mines but whose political commitments remained strong during his twilight years in Arizona. In these memories, one begins to catch glimpses of the young Mike Wilson, "always on the move," clearly bright and charismatic, looking for his place in the world. One also sees the ways that Mike moves in and out of institutions like American Indian cultural centers, schools, churches, and the US military. In providing some contexts for these moves, this interlude will pay special attention to the historical connections between his narrative and the traces of the "civilizing" violence of Manifest Destiny. Intertwined with that story, one can also sense the complex and entangled histories of Native military service and political activism.

Battlefield and Classroom: The Shadow of Carlisle

> We make our greatest mistake in feeding our civilization to
> the Indian instead of feeding the Indians to our civilization.
>   —Richard Henry Pratt

I had known Mike for years before I found out that his grandfather had been among the students who had attended the (in)famous Carlisle Indian Industrial School, the first US government–run, off-reservation boarding school for Native children. This effort, as Mike put it, was part of "Manifest Destiny 2.0," an element of the state "solution" to the so-called Indian problem. As Mike and I were discussing how to approach this chapter, he told me almost casually the story of his last name. "Wilson," he said, replaced the family surname of Vavages two generations back, at Carlisle. That sent me to the Carlisle Indian School Project, a digital archive, hosted by Dickinson College, which contains a handful of records, newspaper accounts, and a photograph related to Juan Vavages, the person Mike believes is his paternal grandfather.[1]

Given the history of his relationship with his father, discussed in the previous chapter, it is understandable that stories about his paternal grandfather were not closer to the surface of his memories. Yet, that family connection with the first off-reservation, government-run Indian boarding school in the United States raises some crucial connections between Mike's family history and the project of termination, connections that link three institutions that loom large in Mike's life: military, church, and school.

Carlisle Indian Industrial School holds a central place in the rich, painful, and complex literature on Native boarding schools in the United

States.[2] While the story is well known, it is worth recalling the infamous speech given by the founder of the school, Captain Richard Henry Pratt (later promoted to the rank of brigadier general):

> A great general has said that the only good Indian is a dead one, and that high sanction of his destruction has been an enormous factor in promoting Indian massacres. In a sense, I agree with the sentiment, but only in this: that all the Indian there is in the race should be dead. Kill the Indian in him, and save the man. . . .
>
> When we cease to teach the Indian that he is less than a man; when we recognize fully that he is capable in all respects as we are, and that he only needs the opportunities and privileges which we possess to enable him to assert his humanity and manhood; when we act consistently towards him in accordance with that recognition; when we cease to fetter him to conditions which keep him in bondage, surrounded by retrogressive influences; when we allow him the freedom of association and the developing influences of social contact—then the Indian will quickly demonstrate that he can be truly civilized, and he himself will solve the question of what to do with the Indian.[3]

Carlisle represented a kind of "'experiment' to test white society's belief that Indians could be turned into humans," one based on Pratt's previous efforts to reform Arapaho, Cheyenne, Comanche, Caddo, and Kiowa prisoners of war at Fort Marion in Florida.[4]

Lower Brule Sioux historian Nick Estes insightfully observes that the very title of Pratt's autobiography, *Battlefield and Classroom*, encapsulates how US policy "transposed the Indian wars from the frontier to the boarding school."[5] Pratt, Estes reminds us, was not only a Civil War veteran and Indian killer but also a Methodist lay minister: "A cleric and a soldier, he wielded two powerful instruments of colonization, a Bible and a gun."[6] Pratt also maintained that the institution of slavery was a more "humane civilizer" than Indian reservations, since what Indian and Black people needed was not separation but to learn "life's first lesson, to obey."[7] It is hard not to see Pratt, as he emerges from the historical archive (and almost from central casting), as the very embodiment of settler-colonial violence. At the same time, it is also important not to exceptionalize him as especially devious but instead to see him as a representative figure of the impulses that created a system of schools that would spread over the territories of the United States and Canada.

I write these lines during a hot summer of reckoning. In May 2021, the remains of 215 Native children were found in a mass grave in British Columbia, on the site of the Kamloops Indian Residential School, which operated from 1890 until the late 1970s; then in June, members of the Cowessess First Nation in Saskatchewan found the remains of 751 people, most of them likely Indigenous children, at the Marieval Indian Residential School, not far from the provincial capital, Regina.[8] Although the Carlisle Indian Industrial School was in operation for a shorter time (1879–1919) than the schools in Canada, one can also find the gravestones of almost 200 children in an Indian cemetery that lies at the entrance of Carlisle, which is now the US Army War College (battlefield meets classroom, again). These graves are grim monuments to what David Wallace Adams aptly calls "education for extinction."[9] This location at a military base also illustrates a long history of militarization of Indian Country that goes back to the colonial founding of the United States.

While this history is important for understanding the ongoing work of settler colonialism in the United States, there is also something critical in the fact that Mike's reference to the boarding school experience emerges late, almost as an aside, in this chapter of his story, one that begins with joy, dances, and mentorship. The conceptual point Mike makes implicitly and I would like to underline is that there are good reasons *not* to center boarding school violence in histories of Native lives.[10] I do not mean to minimize the intergenerational damage or historical importance of these schools. This "horrible history," to use the expression of Chief Rosanne Casimir (Tk'emlups te Secwepemc First Nation), however, is far from the whole story. Red Lake Ojibwe historian Brenda Child, the granddaughter of people sent to Carlisle and Flandreau boarding schools, observes that those institutions were never the "defining chapters in our larger family narrative."[11] Despite the unquestionable damage of boarding schools, we should not confine accounts of Native lives to an accounting of damage to Native life. Building on decades of research on Native boarding school experiences,[12] Child explains, "Narratives of boarding school life include students who found happiness or refuge in the schools, while clearly others were abused and suffered and so we have learned that there is a wide-ranging continuum of Indian experiences. As Philip Deloria has suggested, Indian people do unexpected things in unexpected places. Indian people in American history continually made the best out of socially ambiguous situations."[13]

K. Tsianina Lomawaima (Mvskoke/Creek, unenrolled), who with Child is among the leading scholars of the Native boarding schools, observes that just as boarding schools were "crucibles of empire designed to eliminate the Native," they also "forged Indian identity, resistance, resilience, and commitment to our peoples, cultures, and languages."[14] Lomawaima made this observation during a presentation to the National Native American Boarding School Healing Coalition in which she was discussing the experiences of her father and uncle, Curtis Thorpe Carr and Robert Carlisle Carr, respectively, at the Chilocco Indian Agricultural School. In that conversation, Lomawaima was asked by one of the participants about her father's and uncle's names, both of which seem to refer to Carlisle (Carlisle is her uncle's middle name, while Thorpe, her father's middle name, seems to refer to Jim Thorpe, the most famous Native American athlete and also a student at Carlisle).

Lomawaima replied that her grandfather, who "did not have a reputation for telling the truth," claimed to be a student at Carlisle, despite the fact that the archives at Carlisle show no evidence that he ever attended. Yet, he chose to name his sons in ways that would connect them to Carlisle. Why? Lomawaima explained that there was a kind of status, "a badge of honor," associated with being a student at Carlisle. Whatever the veracity of Lomawaima's grandfather's claims, the names he gave his sons are indicators of the importance of Carlisle in Indian history and are one example of how Native peoples can find creative ways to rewrite often painful histories. Child's and Lomawaima's insights about the ways Native people "made the best" of ambiguous situations is a useful reminder about how Native peoples have long navigated experiences like relocation, missionization, and military service.

The Indigenization of Military Service

Mike's story illustrates how the decision to join the military is often influenced by the necessities of life. For Mike, who was young and married and had two children to support, joining the military made economic sense. It was a decision his father had also made. Yet, decisions to enter the military are almost always more complex. In Indian Country, Mike explains, "Veterans are honored, are esteemed in our traditions." American Indians enlist in the armed services at the highest rate of any demographic group in the United States.[15] In the academic literature, one finds many echoes of Mike's story. Oral histories with Native veterans have provided multiple accounts of the ways in which military service has been woven into long traditions of a "warrior" ethos and connected to Native defense of Native lands.[16] In Washington, DC, the National Native American Veterans Memorial, inaugurated in 2020 and located prominently on the National Mall by the National Museum of the American Indian[17] and in view of the US Capitol, serves as a public reminder of how generations of American Indians have, as Mike puts it, fought for the "rights and responsibilities" of citizenship and the protection of "sacred soil." That fight, of course, was and is a long one, one in which Native veterans acquired more responsibilities than rights. Despite the fact that Indigenous soldiers have participated in every conflict in US history, American Indians did not have full access to the franchise until the second half of the twentieth century, and even now the promise of citizenship feels elusive as American Indians face disproportionally high rates of incarceration, disease, and early death.[18] Mojave poet and scholar Natalie Diaz, reflecting on the impact of militarization on her family, observes, "America will sacrifice my brothers' and sisters' bodies on a battlefield in the same way they will sacrifice them in an agricultural field or a field of play, or on any street of any town or city in this country."[19]

Despite that high price, American Indian veterans have reframed and re-narrated their military service in powerful ways. Consider this scene described by Dakota historian John Little of a 2019 Lakota graduation ceremony at Sinte Gleska University on the Rosebud Sioux tribal community, emceed by Butch Felix.[20] It is worth quoting Little at length:

> The drumming slowly came to an end and the lead veteran of the honor guard shouted, "Order, halt," and each of the veterans stopped their movements. Felix asked all in attendance to give the graduates a round of applause, asking all the dignitaries to take their seats on the stage. Felix then requested that Fred Little Bald Eagle present a traditional prayer for the graduates before continuing with the agenda for the day. After the prayer, Felix returned to the stage and announced that a flag song would be sung to "pay tribute to the red, white, and blue that flies over the land, where the bones of our ancestors

are buried." Before the song, Felix told a story about Sinte Gleska or Spotted Tail, the namesake of the university, who went to treaty negotiations in the 1860s. As American cavalry soldiers struggled to erect a flagpole in the center of the treaty negotiations to hang the American flag, Sinte Gleska asked the soldiers to wait. He then took out an arrow and tied an eagle feather to it, raised the bow and shot the arrow and eagle feather into the top of the flagpole, stating, "Now they can put their flag up there. That feather is our flag of our common People."

Felix [reminded] . . . people that in 1876 after the Battle of the Little Bighorn, the grandmothers picked up the American flag from the ground claiming it as theirs and vowing that it would never again touch the ground. "Many of us, you can see here, we all served in the armed forces. World War I clear up to the present day to preserve this flag and protect the land and the freedoms that we so freely enjoy." After his comments, the great-great-grandson of Sinte Gleska, Charlie Spotted Tail, came up and sang the Lakota Flag Song. As Spotted Tail began the Wapaha Olowan or Flag Song, the lead honor guard yelled, "Order, ten-hut, present arms," and every Native veteran in the honor guard raised their flags. Per Lakota tradition, after the Wapaha Olowan, the Red Leaf Singers began immediately singing a Veteran's Song, while the honor guard lowered and tilted their flags, dancing in place. Felix asked any individual in the audience if they had a veteran—a father, uncle, auntie, grandfather—to dance along as well. Almost everyone in the auditorium moved along with the beat. After the Veteran's Song, Felix asked the audience to sit. He then announced each of the veterans by name, their military branch, and where they served. Each of the veterans proudly raised their flags as Felix announced their name. The veterans' service ranged from the Korean War and Grenada to Iraq and Afghanistan with a majority of the veterans being veterans of the Vietnam War.[21]

The importance of this kind of ceremony was especially clear during times when many Native customs and ceremonies were officially prohibited by federal law. Native peoples could use these kinds of officially sanctioned ceremonial spaces to "navigate colonial oppression" and creatively express "sovereignty, agency, and resilience."[22] Native peoples, who had created various kinds of warrior societies long before contact with Europeans, continue to create their own warrior societies up to the present, ones that sometimes take place within the machinery of US militarism and also often against it.[23] Native veterans not only have been important in military conflicts but also have been protagonists in social movements that have been associated with the "sacred soil" of places like Wounded Knee, Alcatraz, and Standing Rock.

American Indian Veterans and Political Activism

In 1968, Mike was in his last year of high school. Although he was on the cusp of marriage and fatherhood, he nevertheless took part in the protest politics of the decade. He remembers 1968 clearly as it was the year the Reverend Dr. Martin Luther King Jr. was assassinated. Mike made a protest sign that read "Long Live the King." That same year, a Native leader named Mel Thom (Walker River Paiute) addressed US government officials with his own words of protest: "We ask to be heard—not just listened to and tolerated. In World War I, World War II, and the Korean Conflict, American Indians had the highest volunteer turnout per capita than any other ethnic group in the country. Now some American Indians are becoming dissatisfied with rather than proud of their country and are going to jails rather than serving this country in battle. The inequality and dissatisfaction that is evidencing itself cannot be taken lightly. The oppressed can only be oppressed for so long."[24] Thom's observation anticipated the high-visibility radicalism of the next few years when many Native veterans of the Vietnam War emerged as leaders of Red Power organizations like the American Indian Movement and the Indians of All Tribes.[25]

The 1960s was a decade for many spectacular moments of Indigenous resurgence that can be only briefly summarized. A crucial background condition that united disparate struggles was a rejection of the US federal policy of previous decades that has been accurately described as "termination era" federal policies as they explicitly had the goal of eradicating Indian nations as sovereign entities. American Indians had enjoyed a brief moment of autonomy and federal support during the administration of Franklin Delano Roosevelt and what became known as the "Indian New Deal." However, the presidency of Harry S. Truman represented a dramatic change: "Within the first decade of the termination era, policies that Truman supported terminated more than 100 tribes, severing their trust relationships with the federal government."[26] Along with termination, federal policy also supported the "relocation" of Native peoples, especially to cities across the United States. Termination and relocation were seen as instruments of assimilation—or, more accurately, elimination. Those policies failed.

The movements of the 1960s helped usher in an era of Native self-determination that continues into the present and future. An early battle in this struggle took place over treaty-protected fishing rights in Coast Salish territory. In a set of actions known as the "fish wars," Native fishers disregarded Washington State limits on their rights to fish and then faced arrest by state police. In these struggles, they received high-profile assistance from Hollywood stars like Jane Fonda, Dick Gregory, and Marlon Brando, many of whom came at the invitation of the media-savvy leadership of the National Indian Youth Council. While the presence of high-wattage celebrities served an important purpose, it was local Indigenous activists who provided the most eloquent explanations of these events. When Sid Mills, a Yakima and Cherokee Indian from the small fishing community of Frank's Landing was arrested in 1968, he explained, "For two years and four months, I've been a soldier in the United States Army. I served in combat in Vietnam—until critically wounded. . . . I hereby renounce further obligation in service or duty to the United States Army. My first obligation lies with the Indian People fighting for the lawful Treaty to fish in usual and accustomed waters of the Nisqually, Columbia and other rivers of the Pacific Northwest, and in serving them in this fight any way possible."[27] Arguably the most visible Native face of the "fish wars" was Nisqually citizen Billy Franks Jr., who described his role succinctly: "I am not a policy guy; I am a getting-arrested guy."[28] The fish wars were won by Native peoples, and that victory was ratified in a famous legal decision authored by Judge George H. Boldt in 1974 (later upheld by the US Supreme Court) that found that the Nisqually and other tribes in the Northwest had a right to catch up to half the salmon in their traditional waters. This meant that Native peoples were now officially comanagers of the fishery.[29]

After the fish wars of the Pacific Northwest, American Indian social movements would gather more visibility with the takeovers of Alcatraz Island, the occupation of the Bureau of Indian Affairs, and the 1973 confrontation at Wounded Knee on the Pine Ridge Reservation that lasted seventy-one days. These and other related moments of American Indian protest, like the "Trail of Broken Treaties," have been discussed by a growing library of works.[30] In their own ways, each of these events shared a few common themes that connect to many parts of Mike's own story.

First, Native veterans were protagonists in the often-spectacular confrontations of Red Power, which captured media attention and invited US government persecution. For example, Dennis Banks (Ojibwe), a central figure in the takeover of the BIA offices and Wounded Knee (and who joined the protests that Mike had co-organized in Ajo, Arizona), had served in the US Air Force in Japan, an experience that he said had "changed the direction of his life."[31] Beyond the trauma of combat, military training provided many future Native activists with organizational and tactical skills that were important in feeding people and contending with police and military aggression. The Mohawk publication *Akwesane Notes* observed, "Young men defending Wounded Knee [were] militarily skilled and trained. Almost all [were] Vietnam veterans, and most of those were in the Special Forces—the Green Berets. In Southeast Asia they learned about guerrilla warfare, courtesy of the U.S. government, and now they are using what they learned for their people."[32] While much of the representation of Red Power foregrounds American Indian men, women have always been central to the movement. Grace Thorpe, for example, who was in charge of public relations on Alcatraz during the Indian takeover, was herself an army veteran. Her last name may be familiar; she was the daughter of the most famous American Indian Olympic athlete and Carlisle football player, Jim Thorpe. Women played crucial roles at Alcatraz, the fish-ins protests, and countless other movement events.[33]

Second, like Mike's experience with AIM during the Ajo demonstration after the murder of Phillip Celaya, there were tensions between the demands of local Native peoples and those of the pan-Indian organizers who often came from the outside. This was like the Ohlone of the Bay Area who were not consulted by the "Indians of All Tribes" who occupied Alcatraz,[34] or the Pine Ridge residents caught in the crossfire between AIM activists and US security forces.[35] There were also intergenerational tensions like the ones so palpable between the incrementalism of the

National Congress of American Indians ("Indians don't demonstrate") and the confrontational politics of the National Indian Youth Council and AIM.

Third, Native projects of self-determination and self-defense have been and continue to be connected to realities across scales, from local to global. Locally, activists have responded to the bordertown violence of settler colonialism, in which white men from towns next to reservations and Indian communities would take the lives of Native people with impunity. The murders of men like Raymond Yellow Thunder and Wesley Bad Heart Bull in South Dakota were among the sparks that led to the confrontation of Wounded Knee[36] and ignited protests across Indian Country, as illustrated by Mike's description of response to the police killing of Phillip Celaya in Ajo, Arizona. More recently, campaigns against an epidemic of missing and murdered Indigenous women reveal the gendered dimension that has always characterized settler-colonial violence.[37]

These movements also reflected local tensions between community members and their tribal leadership, the most infamous example of which was probably Pine Ridge tribal chairman Dick Wilson, whose corruption and violence led residents to invite AIM activists to help them impeach their tribal leader.[38] That local reality, of course, reflected a broader national context, specifically the federal policies that had created the framework for the governance of what Supreme Court chief justice John Marshall famously called "domestic dependent nations" in the nineteenth century,[39] nations that were the targets of termination and co-optation in the twentieth century. At the broadest scale, the 1960s and 1970s were a moment of global protest and decolonization. A generation of American Indians had witnessed US empire face a defeat in the jungles of Southeast Asia, and this created a new geopolitical sense of revolutionary possibilities. This was clear not only for the so-called radicals like Dennis Banks but also for the so-called incrementalists like Vine Deloria Jr., who observed, "An Indian doesn't have to know, or understand, anything about Kenya, or Burma, or Peru, or Vietnam. He feels the way they feel."[40] That shared feeling of solidarity would be tested by the events of the 1980s in Central America, which takes us to the next chapter of Mike's story and his time in El Salvador.

Chapter 3

El Salvador

The Roads to Sonsonate and Damascus

MIKE WILSON

I was very much an anti-communist.

This is something I can still feel, here, five decades later. You would think that as a human rights worker, I would be more tolerant of alternative views, alternative politics. On the other hand, things are never black and white. George and Alice Papcun taught me that. This former socialist was more Christian than many of the Christians I knew and know. Imagine, a white man traveling through East Texas trying to stop the lynching of a Black man? I remember thinking, *If that was a socialist, then I want to be a socialist.* And he was an atheist. His wife, Alice, came from a Russian Jewish background; she was also an atheist. They were both atheists who were doing very Christian things. I learned from them that nothing is black or white.

When I went to El Salvador, though, I was a cold warrior, and communism was the enemy. I was aware of what happened in Chile in 1973, a US-backed coup against socialist president Salvador Allende. I was aware, but I didn't care. I didn't believe that they were socialists. I thought socialism was the friendly face of communism. And I thought the same thing about El Salvador. As repugnant as that fascist state was, it was a fascist state against emerging communism.

I got to El Salvador in 1988. December 1988. We went as Special Forces military advisors. We were not there to engage in combat. As a matter of fact, we were *forbidden* from engaging in combat except in times of imminent danger and self-defense. Our instructions were very clear: we were not to engage in any combat activity. That was not our mission. We went on what were called military assistance missions, and we were the eyes and ears of the US embassy.

To tell you the truth, I was disappointed that I wasn't assigned to a combat zone. And the Salvadoran brigade commander where I was assigned didn't like any Americans in his command. But this was part of the terms set by Congress for American aid to the Salvadoran military, which in essence was a brutal military dictatorship wearing a democratic mask. The Salvadoran military was receiving tens of millions of dollars annually that was intended to be dispersed down to the brigade levels. The brigade commanders were receiving American money, but there was so much corruption along the pipeline that very little money reached the soldiers. They didn't want an American presence looking over their shoulders.

Pandemic Poverty: "Once the Bullets Stop Flying, You're Still Hungry"

I was struck by the extreme poverty. Not just extreme poverty but pandemic poverty. Everywhere. I thought I would see pockets of poverty. I'm sure there *were* middle-class communities, but I never saw them. I'm sure there were elite enclaves, but I never saw them either. What I mostly saw was extreme poverty in the cities and, of course, in the small towns and in the colonias (Central American vernacular for "shantytowns").

I had seen poverty like that in Honduras. I had been to Honduras on several short deployments. It was the same situation, and I came to the realization that military aid alone was not enough. Economic aid was needed. How do you provide the tools for an economic engine to move forward? How do you develop a robust economic base for any society, especially in a poor, predominantly agrarian society? How do you make that transition?

I don't think the main US interest at the time was economic aid. I think the prevailing policy was "We *can't* let this country fall to communism. This corrupt government *has* to win. And we can help make it transition to democracy after the war is won and over. But it *cannot* fall. We *cannot* have a Marxist state in Central America." It was that Vietnam-era fear—the theory of the domino effect, that if Vietnam fell, other countries in Southeast Asia would also fall, which has not happened. Nevertheless, I think that was the overriding fear in Washington. Who's next? El Salvador, Honduras, Nicaragua, Guatemala, Mexico?

There was talk that Daniel Ortega, president of Nicaragua who came to power after the 1979 Sandinista revolution, was threatening to invade Honduras, so we had gone down there to train the army to resist and defeat this invasion from Nicaragua. We had barely arrived in the country when the Iran-Contra affair broke, so our mission was stopped before it even started.[1] That was what was going on at the time in Central America: Central America was being seen as Vietnam revisited, and global communism was making its presence known again, this time in America's backyard. Unless we, the United States, stopped these insurgencies, we would have to deal with them on our southern border.

I knew that the ideology of the Soviet Union was that it would support foreign "wars of national liberation," which meant communist-inspired insurrections. As Special Forces, our mission was to stop these insurrections before they got a start. This was the post–World War II era; everything was in the context of this Cold War, this undeclared Cold War. Two irreconcilable ideologies were competing for world dominance—global communism versus global democracy—with each ideology seeing itself as the hope for humankind. As a Special Forces soldier, I saw us as the point of the spear in this Cold War.

I remember that poverty. It was regional poverty, not just national. I see that poverty literally walking through my front door today. When southern Mexicans, Guatemalans, Salvadoreños, and Hondurans walk through our front door into our house in Tucson, I see the faces of economic refugees.[2] That is the image that stays with me. During my deployment in El Salvador, I wore blinders and did not see the totality of the military violence. But I did witness the economic violence, which was profound. I think economic violence can be just as devastating as, if not greater than, military violence. Once the bullets stop flying, you're still hungry.

In El Salvador, I tried to do outreach with the rural schools. One day, I was with my bodyguard. All US military advisors were assigned bodyguards because

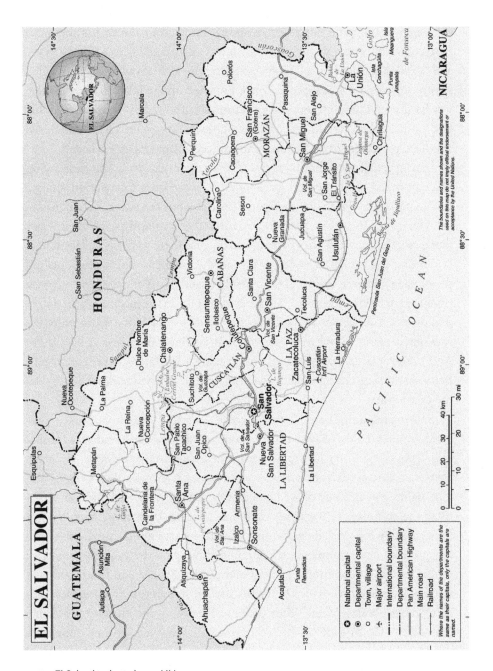

MAP 2. El Salvador, based on a UN map.
Sonsonate is in the western part of the country.
Courtesy of Wikimedia Commons.

there were bounties on our heads. My bodyguard and I visited a classroom in a rural community outside of Sonsonate. It was a classroom with a storage room, and that was it. They had a little first aid box with a red cross on it. They didn't have a nurse or a medical professional. I opened up the first aid kit, and there was hardly anything in there. I later returned with medical supplies from my first aid kit. I then rooted around in the little storage room and found an old overhead projector covered in dust and cobwebs. You remember those?

I learned that the school was built by the Peace Corps in the early 1960s. That overhead projector and transparencies were from that period and included botany and anatomy transparencies. This was the school's state-of-the-art technology in 1989 in rural El Salvador. The overhead projector was not being used because the bulb had burned out and there were no replacements.

When I got back to Sonsonate, I went to the high school that was behind the brigade. I knew a couple of teachers there and asked one of them, "Do you have a spare bulb?" She said, "Yes, we have a spare in the machine, plus there's one on the shelves. So, I'll give you that one." For lack of a spare bulb, the rural elementary school went without that overhead projector. A light bulb! And I also replaced the electrical cord, because it had been chewed on by rats. Between that and the light bulb, now that rural school had *some* technology in the classroom.

Sonsonate was my base. That was where the brigade was, in one of the noncombat zones. I didn't have a choice about being there. I believe every combat brigade in the country had to have an American observer/advisor. Officially we were trainers/advisors, but we were more eyes and ears. We were the human rights eyes and ears of the United States ambassador, and that was something the commander resented. He didn't want anybody there from the US military knowing what he was doing or what he was not doing. I don't have any proof of *how* commanders like him siphoned off the military assistance money, but it was common knowledge among the Special Forces advisors that these officers had their hands in the till, that the numbers in the brigades were inflated by "ghost soldiers." They could just make up the number of soldiers that were in the brigade so when the American taxpayers' money came in, it would be based upon those inflated headcounts.

In other words, leadership would skim off the top and provide very little for their soldiers, for whom the money had been intended as salaries. Those soldiers would send that money home to take care of their families, who were depending on it to put food on the table. Once they had been drafted, those campesino families had lost a breadwinner.

My view of the Salvadoran army was that it was corrupt. It was never a professional army. There was no *real* NCO (noncommissioned officer) corps comparable to ours. It had an officer corps, which was all-powerful. It did not have dynamic military leadership. What it had was a cult of personality, a caudillo, a strongman cult.

I wondered why the soldiers were buying cheap chrome-plated machetes and cheap knock-off tennis shoes. I learned from my bodyguard that they *had* to buy them. The corrupt officers were buying South Korean machetes and tennis shoes and forcing their soldiers to buy this junk, making an immoral profit off the backs of the American taxpayers. The soldiers had no choice. If they did not buy this crap, they would come up under disciplinary charges. It was referred to as "falta de espiritu militar," meaning "for lack of military spirit." So rather than being brought up on charges, they bought.

After a couple of months, I came to understand that this was a common practice throughout the army. All the military advisors would meet monthly at the US embassy in the capital, San Salvador. We would report on what was going on in our respective brigades. We reported on military activities, civic engagements, and human rights abuses. After our "official meetings," we would meet at night at a local bar. Over a couple of beers, we'd swap stories about the corruption in our brigades. Sure enough, we were disgusted at the extent of the corruption we were witnessing.

The other thing was about how Salvadoran soldiers were recruited. One of my bodyguards told me this story. He said that if you happened to go to the movies on any night, often the military would surround the theater, turn the movie off, and order everybody to exit single-file. If a young man did not have his military discharge papers on him proving he was a veteran, he was drafted back into the army for two more years. These were strong-arm tactics for recruiting.

The army had to keep its numbers inflated. When the United States Congress was determining the amount of military assistance to El Salvador, I'm sure legislators asked, "How big is the military? How many are we talking about?" The American taxpayer was paying the salaries of the rank and file and of the officer corps. The United States government was more focused on fighting communism than in rooting out corruption. For years, the US government tolerated the military's human rights abuses. By the time I got to El Salvador in December 1988, my perception was that there were fewer human rights abuses taking place, until the six Spanish Jesuit priests, their housekeeper, and her daughter were murdered by a death squad from the Atlácatl Battalion of the Salvadoran army in 1989.

There were also human rights abuses committed by the Marxist FMLN (Farabundo Martí National Liberation Front) through its military wings. They conducted political assassinations of mayoral candidates throughout the country. To me, it appeared the Marxist premise was, "We do not want democracy in El Salvador, and if we have free elections, it looks like democracy in action." I was stunned at some of the atrocities I heard from my colleagues who were stationed in the other departamentos.

The FMLN would have its military units organize a "paro," an armed roadblock on the main highways going into the cities. Now campesinos who sold their products in the cities could not get into the urban mercados (markets). The FMLN wanted to create economic disruption and chaos. It wanted to make the government *look* unstable, weak, and incapable of protecting the people. It would also dynamite the electrical transmission lines and knock out electricity throughout sectors of a departamento. This was another tactic it used to sabotage and undermine the central government. And for a while, it worked. But who suffered? The campesinos. They didn't have reliable electrical service. They couldn't sell their products in the urban mercados. If they ran those paros, they were machine-gunned. This information was coming from my Special Forces colleagues across numerous departamentos in the war zones. This economic terrorism was going on throughout the country.

I thought, wait a minute, didn't Mao say, "A guerrilla is like a fish. The guerrilla lives in the water and the people are the ocean"? The guerrilla fighter depends upon the people for his survival. If the FMLN continued its sabotage, it was going to lose the support of the populace. And guess what happened during late 1989? During the FMLN's "final offensive," when the guerrillas came out of the mountains and attacked the cities, it was expecting that a popular civilian uprising would join the offensive. But because the FMLN had terrorized its own people, that civilian uprising never took place.

As a matter of fact, its human rights abuses turned the civilians against the FMLN. Its sabotage of the electrical grid caused pumps for the water supply systems to be out for weeks at a time. Newborns were dying in their incubators because of the lack of electricity to the hospitals. Police protection in small towns like Sonsonate was very ineffective. In a civil war, among the first casualties are public services. I remember there were many days, in the small town of Sonsonate, when there was no garbage pickup. We take those public services for granted, electricity, water, police protection, and garbage pickups.

We're not even speaking about education yet. What about schools, if they don't have power? What about bus lines, if they don't have gas to get those kids to school? Who suffers? It's the campesinos. The FMLN alienated its campesino base, which, in a guerrilla war, it depends on. When the final offensive came, the guerrillas were effective for three days. But after three days, the army reorganized and mounted a devastating counterattack. The FMLN's expected uprising and revolution never happened.

The Final Offensive

When "La Ofensiva Final" came in December 1989, I was visiting another military advisor friend near the city of San Vicente. I was spending the weekend there, and I remember being at a fiesta in the town plaza. All of a sudden, I heard explosions and found out later that the guerrillas had blown up the bridges on the main highway. That was the beginning of the offensive nationwide. I quickly made my way back to the cuartel, a barracks area attached to the comandancia (brigade headquarters). My friend was out of town, and I was staying in his quarters. I could hear firefights outside the walls. I didn't know if the Salvadoran army could hold that comandancia. I was expecting the guerrillas to come to my door at any time and throw in hand grenades. I was prepared to fire in self-defense, but they never broke through the gates.

There were firefights throughout the city. The battle for control of the city raged on for two days. By day three, the strength of the guerrilla force withered, then collapsed, and the Salvadoran army went on a counteroffensive. It pushed the guerrillas out of town and back into the mountains, limping with their tails between their legs. So much for the People's Revolution!

After the firing stopped, they sent out soldiers to recover the bodies. The bodies were brought back in the bed of a two-and-a-half-ton truck, stacked like cordwood. They were then laid out in the open plaza of the cuartel. You couldn't tell the difference between the two sides because all were wearing camouflage uniforms and had been carrying the same kind of weapons, M16s. The bodies were so mangled and caked with dried blood and mud that I could not tell who was who.

The only way I knew the difference between the dead Salvadoran soldiers and the dead guerrillas was that the bodies of the guerrillas had little hands and little feet. This told me that they were dead child soldiers who had been recruited by the FMLN.

I had children back in Fayetteville, North Carolina. I knew what the hands and feet of children looked like.

I approximated that these children who had been sacrificed were twelve and thirteen years old. Some were missing lungs and hearts where M60 machine-gun rounds had entered their chests and exited through their backs, taking their hearts and lungs with them. When I looked at the exposed chest area of one of the dead children, I could see into the gaping cavity. All I saw were ribs on the back of the cavity wall. No heart, no lungs, just empty.

These were somebody's sons and daughters. The image still haunts me.

Part of my job was to know who the enemy was. I was expecting full-grown, adult combatants. When I saw the remains of children in camouflage fatigues, I thought, *I've got children; I've got a daughter this age.* What were these kids doing in this army? I knew they were FMLN because the Salvadoran army I worked with did not recruit child soldiers. They had young men but never child soldiers. Something else: the FMLN combatants had tied red ribbons on the tips of their M16s and wore red armbands on their sleeves to distinguish themselves from the Salvadoran army. When the human remains were recovered, the weapons still had the ribbons, but most of the armbands were missing. I thought, *What the hell are you doing?! Why are you tying red ribbons to your weapons!? You're showing the enemy where you are. You're pointing your weapon at them and they're going to see that red ribbon first.* It was suicidal political ideology over commonsense tactics on the battlefield.

A Changing Political Environment

In our conversations at the embassy, the US advisors also talked about the abuses of the government. I remember when a new ambassador came in. I believe his last name was Walker. At one of these monthly meetings, he told us our mission was changing and that we worked directly for him. Yes, we had our military command that we were responsible to at Fort Bragg, North Carolina. But in country,[3] we worked for the United States embassy and for him, in particular. He told us our mission was changing. We would continue to do advising and assisting, but we were going to be his "eyes and ears concerning human rights abuses." If we knew human rights abuses were planned by the Salvadoran military, we were to do everything we could to prevent them. If we came to find out they happened, we were to report those abuses immediately to him. This was a sea change.

My perception was that the Reagan administration's Salvadoran policy had seemed to be "Let's win the war now and deal with human rights abuses later." Now, I can't say categorically that this was the American policy. This new American ambassador, in effect, changed our mission statement. At the time I was thinking, *So, now we're into human rights abuses?* For Special Forces, as I far as I knew, human rights considerations had never been in *any* of our mission statements. That was the sea change. *Oh, so now I am a human rights advocate? Wait a minute, I thought we were special operators?* We thought we were gung ho, direct-action kind of guys. This change happened even before the six Spanish Jesuits and their housekeeper and her daughter were massacred at Central American University in 1989. This was an abrupt change of philosophy and direction. *Now we're going to be human rights observers? Yes!*

I welcomed that. I mean, that was so radically different. And I think many advisors welcomed that change. For those of us from US Special Forces, we were repulsed by the human rights abuses committed by the Salvadoran military's death squads. We were disgusted with the widespread corruption by the army's officer corps, taking American taxpayer money and living like royalty. This new elite class was buying properties and houses in Houston and Miami. Their sons were going to the University of Miami and the University of Houston, living like *princes* off the American taxpayer. And the sons of the underclass campesino were still being drafted, while the sons of the parasitic elite caste were hanging out at the discotecas in San Salvador. They never served a day in the military because they were exempt, an exemption that came through their families' political power and privileges.

I understood that there was an entrenched military hierarchy within the army. If we think of a pyramid, at the very top of that pyramid are the most senior generals. Everybody below was subservient to this military elite. The army was not loyal to a constitution or to democracy. Its loyalties were to this supreme leadership, which was called "La Tandona."

A "tanda" in Spanish was, I believe, what every graduating class from the military academy was called. This supreme leadership was from one of those classes. This was the *super* tanda, and it was referred to as La Tandona, the super graduated class. The army's loyalty was to La Tandona, which, in reality, was the military power behind the facade of a civilian democracy. I was aware of this deception.

Our colleagues in the El Salvadoran army knew what was going on. They saw the sons of the elites in San Salvador hanging out in the discotecas. Those sons didn't have to worry about being picked up without papers. *They* were not going to be drafted into the army, heaven forbid. When they were home for the summer they probably bragged, "Come September, I'm going back to Miami, where my dad bought property and a house. I'll be just fine, thank you very much."

The Road to Sonsonate

I was stationed in the town of Sonsonate, in the Departamento de Sonsonate. I forget the name of the brigade. Let me just refer to Sonsonate as being inclusive of the town and the brigade. I can't quite remember the name of the brigade commander, but let's just call him the colonel. When the new US ambassador arrived, this colonel did something that says a lot. There was a highway from the capital that came through Sonsonate and continued to the coast. Right off the highway, a Catholic priest from Boston had founded a vocational school for teaching trade skills like carpentry and plumbing.

I met the priest through some common Salvadoreño friends, a married couple. As a matter of fact, the husband grew up in San Diego and his wife in El Salvador. He spoke fluent English. He was a big Chargers fan, so sometimes he wanted to talk football. His father-in-law owned several hardware stores in Santa Ana and Sonsonate, and my friend was the manager for the Sonsonate store. They were a monied family. His wife spoke some English, and their daughters were fluent English speakers because they were raised in California. He was a supporter of the right-wing ARENA party.

I met the priest through this family. Let's call the priest Father Ernesto. I think he had been there twenty-eight or twenty-nine years. When I wanted to have a conversation in English or a break from my military duties, I could go visit him and my San Diego friend and his family and just be Mike for a couple of hours.

I had been in Sonsonate about six months when the US ambassador traveled to Sonsonate to visit Father Ernesto and see his vocational training campus that was all about social justice. So, here's what happened. I remember because immediately after the incident occurred, I was pulled out of Sonsonate.

My supervisor, a Special Forces army major stationed in Santa Ana, told me that the day before, the United States ambassador to El Salvador was in a convoy to Sonsonate to visit his friend, the priest. The ambassador traveled with a security team that included Special Forces operatives. The colonel knew that the ambassador was coming into town and had set up a blockade on the outskirts of Sonsonate, with a machine gun aimed at the ambassador's convoy. The colonel told the US ambassador something like, "You do not come into my departamento without my permission." The ambassador's security force was ready to respond with its own firepower. But the ambassador didn't want an armed confrontation with a supposed "ally."

To review: the Salvadoran brigade commander stopped the United States ambassador with a security force that included a M60 machine gun aimed at the ambassador. What happened? Well, the ambassador complied and returned to the United States embassy in San Salvador and most likely notified the US State Department. Soon thereafter, the colonel was on his way out of the country as the new military attaché to Chile.

You're outta here!!!

This diplomatic blunder between allies was symptomatic of the arrogance and assumed invincibility of members of the military class. It also demonstrated their sense of political power, which was extra-military by definition. It was above and beyond a military command. Yes, there was a civilian mayor of Sonsonate and a civilian governor, but in name only.

For this brigade commander, operating outside the boundaries of a military partnership, to stop and threaten the life of an American ambassador (and his security team) who represented the president of the United States and its Congress, who *were funding you* and all your cronies—well, this was stupid. It speaks of that sense of invincibility. That sense of accountability to nobody, no transparency.

I think that got back to the State Department. And the Tandona certainly must have known. I can imagine the high command saying, "Colonel, you are jeopardizing hundreds of millions of dollars that we are getting from the United States. By threatening the life of the ambassador and his security team, you dropped the mask of democracy and have threatened our pocketbooks." To protect the gravy train, the colonel was expendable.

A new brigade commander was coming in, and I was being replaced as the military advisor. I was transferred to another departamento, San Vicente. I was there when "La Ofensiva Final" started nationwide. I finished my deployment there. There was one other event in Sonsonate that transformed my life. It is what I call my "road to Damascus."

The Road to Damascus

I like to share this story because it still speaks to me over three decades after the fact. Some of the details may change as I tell the story over and over, but the spirit of the moment remains intact.

Again, this was in Sonsonate. I had been there several months. I was walking the street one day with one of my bodyguards, and I met a woman who had a pupuseria stand. It's like the Salvadoran version of a maize empanada, stuffed with meat or cheese.

She introduced herself saying, "My name is María[4] and I have been friends with many of your predecessors. I knew them well and I want you to know that you have a friend in El Salvador." And with that introduction, a friendship developed not only with her but with her husband and their three beautiful daughters.

A few months later, probably at her pupuseria cart, she said, "Mike, we've been friends since we met; why haven't you come over for dinner?"

"You haven't invited me!" I said. "What about this Friday evening?"

"Fine!"

As a counterinsurgency advisor, one of our dictums is that you have to win the "hearts and minds" of the civilians. You become friends with the civilian population and develop mission-support relationships. It's building acceptance, support, and respect. You win them over to your side, which will hopefully translate into the popular support of the government. She was my friend, but I understood this first and foremost within the context of winning the "hearts and minds." If we didn't do it, the Marxists would.

Friday came and it was early in the afternoon, and I was walking around town with my bodyguard. We stopped at an ice cream shop. I saw that they sold banana splits. I thought to myself, *You know what, I could use a banana split.* I ordered one banana split and my bodyguard had ice cream. I remember being charged what I thought was an exorbitant amount of money; I think I paid the equivalent of three US dollars and sixty cents. Standing at the counter, I felt very insulted. I thought the clerk had jacked up the price because she knew I was a gringo and that I had money to burn. And I did, but that wasn't the point. Insult turned to anger. I remember thinking to myself, *Don't they know who I am? Don't they know that I have come to save them from global communism?*

I was thinking within a self-righteous mindset. I was angry for the rest of the day. You know when something gets caught in your throat and you just can't cough it up or wash it down? It's there with every swallow you take. That's how angry I was. Then I reminded myself, *You know what? You've got a mission to accomplish tonight. You need to exploit this "hearts and minds" opportunity. This is a psyops mission (psychological operations), one person at a time, one family at a time. Una salvadoreña inocente. Una familia inocente.* It was pure exploitation. This was my mindset. This friendship was a means to an end. That was my job! This was Counterinsurgency 101.

I went to the house that evening, still angry about being jacked at the ice cream shop, but I had a mission to do. I put my anger aside. *You're going to a home of a poor family. You can do this. Take a six-pack of beer.* María had told me that her husband, José, worked late. He was a rural bus driver who drove one of those school buses, an American school bus, whose serviceability stateside had expired. When those buses die, they go to heaven in places like Central America to be resurrected as part of the public transportation system—in this case, as part of the rural bus system. José drove from village to village in the campo (countryside). María told me that he probably would come in late but to come over anyway.

I probably got there around six o'clock, and the girls were playing on the living room floor of their public housing apartment. María and I chatted. She said, "Why don't I feed the kids now, and when José gets home the three of us can sit down and have dinner together?" I said that would be fine because I knew the girls were hungry. They were active; they were being kids. They ate and went back to the living room.

We were sitting at the table, sipping our beers, trying to make them last until José came home. The food was prepared and sitting in pots on the stove. They didn't have a telephone, and this was 1989, pre–cell phone, so it's not like he could call and say, "Honey, I'll be home late; you and Mike have dinner. I'll catch up with you when I get home." Dinner was prepared; the kids had eaten. She said, "Let's eat. When he comes home, he can eat late. I don't want the food to get cold." So, we ate. It was a small, round table with a couple of chairs. We finished dinner and María cleared the table, and we were still finishing our beers, saving a couple for José.

José came home a little later and joined us in the kitchen. He was absolutely drained; you could see it in his face, mostly in his eyes. She said, "Sit down; I'll serve you a plate." He sat and I passed him a cold one. We were talking casually about whatever it was we were talking about. I noticed that he had brought a mason jar with a screw-on lid. He set it on the table. Sitting down, he put the mason jar in front of him. She served him his meal. I wondered why he put that mason jar full of coins on the table. It occurred to me that this is his salary. It hit me like a two-by-four between the eyes. This is the man's daily wages for himself, his wife, and his three children. He had been driving a bus all day and these coins were his wages. He was the salt of the earth.

As he ate, he unscrewed the lid from the mason jar. He tipped the jar over and shook all the coins out into a pile on the table. There were mixed denominations of only coins. From across the table, they looked like our equivalent of pennies, nickels, dimes, and quarters. He smoothed down the pile with two hands when he finished eating. He separated the coins by denominations, stacking them like poker chips. He stacked them one upon the other. At the end of his stacking, there were small pillars of coins. Then he moved these pillars, one by one, like you see on a poker table. He was counting his wage aloud.

At the end of his counting, I heard how much his day's wages were. I don't remember the final amount, but *I knew* that his wages were less than what I had paid for my banana split, three US dollars and sixty cents. After ten hours of driving a bus his wages were less than what I had spent on the frivolous luxury of a banana split!

Something was happening. I saw it. More than that, I felt it. When the scales fell from my eyes, I saw a system of economic oppression. I remember telling myself, *Mike, you are no longer at the kitchen table. You are now at the table of justice. Today, you spent more on your banana split than what José earned for a day's work.* I remember, distinctly, asking myself, *Which side of the table are you on?*

You American Green Beret. It's poor families like this one that the Salvadoran government is calling "the enemy." In your execution of Counterinsurgency 101, you are now a firsthand witness to injustice. You cannot excuse yourself from the table of justice, but Mr. American Green Beret, where do you sit? Are families like this the enemy?

I was humiliated to the bottomless pit of my soul. I was humiliated that I had brought anger into their house, anger because I thought I had been ripped off by the ice cream clerk. When I looked into the faces of human suffering, I saw my face reflected. I grew up poor, but never that poor. I had to look into myself and tell myself again and again, *Mike, you are now at the Communion table.* This table had been transformed from a *communal* table to a *Communion* table, in the most profound sense of the spiritual word (what we later called in seminary "Logos"). Whereas I had broken bread with the poor, I was now sharing the body and blood of Christ with them. I had been trained to suspect that they were my potential enemies, but I understood now that they were my brothers and sisters. This was my bright light on the "road to Damascus." On my way to Damascus, I had to walk through Sonsonate.

I was on the verge of tears; my heart was breaking. I was tearful because this was injustice, and I was complicit. *You are a witness to injustice to which your government is contributing.* Specifically at that time and place. That kitchen table became a sacred place. That mason jar became an economic injustice. I understood that my position at that table was a position of power derived solely from the power of the United States. José's and María's positions were positions of powerlessness. I had tried to impose my government's power over them. I was now humiliated. I hold onto that lesson and to those tears. And I honor that humiliation because it was my Pauline moment; it reminded me of the biblical story of Saint Paul.

Paul, before he was Paul, was Saul of Tarsus.[5] This is my understanding of him. Before Saul saw the light, some scholars suggest that he was a temple policeman in Jerusalem. He was on his way to Damascus to punish or retrieve heretical Jews. On the road, a light appeared and asked him, "Why are you persecuting me?" From this encounter, he was transformed into Paul, the disciple of Christ. That dinner in Sonsonate was a Pauline moment for me. Justice had spoken to me. It said, "Why are you persecuting me? Why are you persecuting my people?" That's the lesson I got out of that experience. Most of us on the left don't get that lesson. We are caught in our own tyranny of right versus wrong.

That moment changed everything. I began to question my government and my complicity. I looked at both sides fighting over, and supposedly on behalf of, the campesinos. It was a moment of self-doubt, self-criticism, self-accountability.

That Pauline moment at the table of justice—even after three decades—is what I hold on to. When I feel that my moral compass is off, I return to that kitchen table, and my bearings are corrected. When I put out water in the Sonoran Desert, I felt that pull toward justice.

A lot of time has passed, and yet that moment is ever present.

INTERLUDE 3

At the Table of (In)justice

Debates over US Policy in Central America

JOSÉ ANTONIO LUCERO

In 2011, I invited Mike to the University of Washington to share his story and perspectives with my students and colleagues. As part of his visit, he gave a guest lecture to my class on Latin American politics. To my surprise, he began by asking whether anyone in the class was from El Salvador. A young woman in the third row raised her hand and said that her parents were from El Salvador. Mike turned to her and apologized for what the US government had done in her country.

A few months after his visit, I was speaking with Mike and asked him why he felt the need to begin with that apology. He replied in a way consistent with the narrative he offered above. "Within the context of my human rights work," he said, "I acknowledge that as an American military advisor in El Salvador I was contributing to the continuation of an unjust war that was American-financed." He felt that he "owed the people of El Salvador an apology. Not for my government, but for myself."

I shared with Mike that the young woman whose family was from El Salvador told me that while she appreciated the gesture of apology, she could not forgive him. Her father had been part of the FMLN, and while he survived the war, he had been afflicted by chronic psychological struggles, including post-traumatic stress disorder. Mike registered no surprise. "Understandably so," he said. However, he went on to emphasize that such sentiments existed on both sides of the war. The FMLN, he insisted, was also morally culpable. He asked rhetorically, "FMLN, why are you machine-gunning campesinos who are going to the market? Why are you blowing up the transmission towers when it is the only electrification going out to the hospitals? Why are you cutting off the electricity to the hospital where newborns need their oxygen? Who apologizes for that? And these are the stories that are not being told because the perception is that the members of the FMLN were heroic freedom fighters. Yes, they were, but some of their tactics were equally terroristic."

In this pivotal moment in Mike's journey through the maze of life, one can almost sense him move in several directions at once. As he remembers his "road to Damascus" moment, he is pulled by a visceral anti-communism, by deep moral reservations about both the FMLN rebels and the US-supported right-wing government, and by a sharpening critique of the economic disparity that, as he says, flowed and flows from Central America to his doorstep in Tucson. As a career professional soldier, Mike views the corruption of the Salvadoran military with disdain. One gathers that the local military commander probably had a similar feeling about the US advisors who were the eyes and ears of the United States that came along with the hand that fed El Salvador's military budget. At the same time, Mike reserves some of his sharpest criticism for the FMLN rebels whose use of child soldiers and impact on local community livelihoods he finds to be just as morally objectionable as the brutal dictatorship it was fighting against. In this brief interlude, I want to put Mike's moral judgments in a broad historical and geopolitical frame.

El Salvador: A Long History of Suffering

There is a large and growing library devoted to the history of Central America and the pattern of suffering that we can only summarize here. Any summary would start centuries ago with the arrival of the Spanish to the lands of the Lenca, Pipil, Nahua, and Maya peoples and the creation of a colonial, feudal order, in which a relatively small number of Spanish families and their descendants were on top, while Native peoples faced the forces of genocide, dispossession, and exploitation. Yet, the forging of modern El Salvador (understanding that "modern" does not mean the end of "colonial") can be understood only by recognizing the importance of coffee. For many of us, coffee is simply the necessary caffeinated start of our morning. In Central America, however, coffee was a potent economic engine and a brutal force of dispossession.

In 1896, El Salvador's government, seeing the importance of this commodity to European markets, passed a law that mandated that at least two-thirds of all lands, much held collectively by Indigenous and mestizo rural peoples, were to be devoted to planting coffee. If communes did not comply, their lands were confiscated. Not long after this decree, the liberal Salvadoran government abolished communal property altogether. It also passed brutal "vagrancy laws" that forced the newly landless rural peoples to work on large coffee plantations. At the start of the twentieth century, El Salvador had the dubious distinction of having one of the most unequal distributions of land in all of Latin America, already one of the most unequal regions in the world. Power and wealth were concentrated in the hands of the infamous "fourteen families."[1]

Coffee connected the Central American isthmus to a world economic system that by the end of the nineteenth century was thirsty for new ways to fuel the wage labor of the Industrial Revolution. This meant a huge increase in demand for coffee and new incentives to concentrate on that commodity. Against the optimistic predictions of the economic theory of "comparative advantage," in which countries thrive if they focus on the factors of production they have in relative abundance, Central Americans paid a heavy price for the "prosperity" of the coffee boom. The logic of comparative advantage that told Central America to focus on land-intensive agriculture and low-wage labor resulted in a particularly brutal form of racial capitalism characterized by land dispossession, large plantations, and coercion-intensive forms of labor. The enclave coffee economies of Central America represent what could be the poster image of dependency theory, the account of underdevelopment that explains how the riches of a country bleed out, part of a global vampiric system in which local oligarchs, national security forces, and foreign capital feed off the misery of the poor.[2]

In 1929, Alberto Masferrer, the editor of the newspaper *Patria*, wrote with alarm about the "conquest" of the coffee industry over other traditional crops like beans and maize: "It extends like the conquistador, spreading hunger and misery, reducing the former proprietors to the worst condition. . . . Although it is possible to prove mathematically that these changes make the country richer, in fact they mean death."[3]

If things were already terrible at the start of 1929, they would get even worse with the onset of the Great Depression. Coffee prices dropped, and the oligarchy predictably made the decision to make the low wages even lower. Politically, however, this moment of economic distress coincided with a rare moment of democratic opening. In 1930, Salvadoran president Pío Romero Bosque declared that he would allow political parties and unions to exist as long as they did not threaten the existing order. When he learned that 80,000 rural workers had organized, however, he issued a decree banning rallies, demonstrations, and leftist propaganda. Hundreds of campesinos in the Department of Sonsonate, the same region where Mike Wilson was stationed almost six decades later, were arrested for signing a petition against the decree. The government ban on political activity backfired and ignited more mobilization. That, in turn, was met by more government repression. Thousands more were arrested, including an increasingly important communist leader named Agustín Farabundo Martí, a Salvadoran revolutionary who had spent years traveling the region working with other nationalists and leaders, including the Nicaraguan rebel Augusto César Sandino. Martí and Sandino led a life of transnational struggle, often interrupted by jail or exile. In 1930, Martí was expelled from the country but returned to El Salvador just after the election of a new president, who attempted to open the country politically even more than his predecessor.

In 1931, Arturo Araujo came to office as the first president in the country's history committed to allowing organizations from across the political spectrum to participate in public life. An emergent labor movement gained strength and included reformist, anarchist, and communist ideological currents. The worsening economic conditions served to increase the militancy of the movement. In an effort to reassure the armed forces and the oligarchy of his commitment to order, President Araujo named General Maximiliano Hernández Martínez as his vice presidential running mate. From the very first day of Araujo's administration, he faced growing unrest and instability. Just nine months into his term, the military and the oligarchy decided that order needed to be reimposed and staged a coup in December 1931. Things went from bad to worse.

Congressional and local elections in 1932 resulted in many leftist victories. The new military government refused to recognize the results of the elections. In response, leftist leaders like Martí began to organize a popular uprising in the western part of the country. The government learned of the Indigenous and campesino uprising; Martí and other well-known leftist leaders were arrested by the government. Despite these arrests, on January 22, 1932, a popular uprising went forward across various parts of the country. The day began ominously as the skies were literally darkened by the eruption of a volcano. Historians Jeff Gould and Aldo Lauria-Santiago describe it with cinematic detail: "As the darkness of the day turned to the darkness of night, the haunting whistles of conch shells echoed throughout the mountain valleys. On the outskirts of Ahuachapán, Sonsonate, Izalco, and Santa Tecla rocket flares shot up into the thick, smoky sky."[4] That announced the start of the insurrection, and Indigenous and non-Indigenous rebels attacked haciendas, military posts, and government offices. The uprising was a product of long-standing so-cial tensions, expressed through new and old forms of organizing. Union organizations, communist ideologies, religious cofradías, and Indigenous community were the mobilizing structures of the insurrection.

A ferocious government response followed. Martí and other leftist leaders, already in custody, were shot and then beheaded. José Feli-ciano Ama, one of the main Indigenous (Pipil) leaders in Sonsonate, was captured, tortured, and lynched. While the photographic record of this violence is thin, there is an iconic photo taken by a Canadian admiral of Ama's dead body, hanging from an olive tree in the main plaza. This graphic and macabre record speaks across the decades with brutal clarity of the anti-Indigenous racism of the violence.[5] Soldiers were authorized to take no prisoners and to kill anyone who looked "Indian" or fled from security forces. Many witnesses made the same chilling observation about the actions of paramilitaries and soldiers: "They killed all males from twelve on up."[6] The terms "communist," "Indian," and "barbarian" became interchangeable. One landowner proclaimed, "There is not one Indian who is not affiliated with the communist movement."[7]

Over the course of the next few days, the government killed between 10,000 and 30,000 campesinos. This massacre became known as just that, La Matanza of 1932, a bloody moment that left a permanent scar on the nation. Roque Dalton, the country's most famous poet, memorably described the impact of this massacre on his and future generations: "Todos nacimos medio muertos en 1932" (We were all born half dead in 1932).[8] The effect of such violence cannot be overstated. Public or even private mourning was made difficult as many families had no idea where the bodies of their killed relatives were. A newspaper account from February 5, 1932, recovered by historians Gould and Lauria-Santiago, provided this chilling detail: "At the moment in the department of Sonsonate, and in many places in Ahuachapán and some in Santa Ana, pork meat has become so discredited that it has almost no value. . . . All of this is the consequence of pigs eating in great quantities the flesh of corpses that have been left in the fields."[9]

The massacre, like so many massacres in Latin America and the Caribbean, was met with no international outcries.[10] One Salvadoran scholar notes that when one visits the National Archives in San Salvador, there are volumes devoted to the periodicals from almost every year of the nation's past, with one glaring omission: the volume from 1932.[11] The military government was able to instead narrate a story of terrible *yet necessary* violence. If the economics of coffee set the stage for the making of modern El Salvador, the violence of 1932 was the crucible that produced the longest period of continuous military rule in Latin America. While the oligarchy remained powerful, the military reigned supreme for the following decades. The forces that produced the uprising of 1932 did not disappear and would erupt once again like the volcanoes that stretch across the region.

Decades later, when news broke of another massacre carried out on the other side of the country, the echoes of the 1930s were impossible to miss. In El Mozote and five other hamlets in eastern El Salvador, the Atlácatl Battalion of the Salvadoran army, one of the many battalions trained at the US Army's School of the Americas in Fort Benning, Georgia, killed almost a thousand civilians, most of them children, over three days. Once again, despite the stories of eyewitnesses and early reports of the massacre, authorities in El Salvador and the United States denied that it had happened and covered up the violence. When asked about a report of the violence, the US ambassador to El Salvador said, "I certainly cannot confirm such reports nor do I have any reason to believe that they are true."[12] And like before, the truth eventually came out, even if justice for the victims remained elusive.[13] One could also hear the echoes of the 1930s in the very names of the rebel forces, such as the Farabundo Martí National Liberation Front and right-wing paramilitary death squads like the "Maximiliano Hernández Martínez Anti-Communist Brigade." Roberto D'Aubuissón, leader of the right-wing political party ARENA, went so far as to take as one of his 1984 presidential campaign slogans "Another '32."[14] In one campaign rally, D'Aubuissón reportedly declared, "If we had to kill thirty thousand in 1932, we'll kill two hundred and fifty thousand today."[15] While it would be wrong to say nothing changed in fifty years, histories of terror and counterinsurgency connect the 1930s and 1980s.

In 1979, a relatively progressive wing of the military staged a coup in the hope of moving the country in the direction of some agrarian reform and away from the increasing military repression that was already widespread in the country. This progressive military government was short-lived, and by 1980 the forces of revolution and those of military reaction were once again in open conflict.

Central America in the 1980s: Violence, Ideas, and Emotions of the Cold War

The story of the "inevitable revolutions" of the 1980s, fueled by endemic inequality and political repression, has been told well by many scholars.[16] Mike's reflections help bring to the fore the way that the violence of that decade was framed and felt by publics outside of the region. When Mike came to lecture in my Latin American politics class in Seattle, he realized that he had to explain to my mostly progressive students what the Cold War felt like:

> I am a product of the 1950s and 1960s. During these decades I understood there was a global war: the US had come out after World War II as one of two superpowers; the Soviets led the communist world and the US led what we used to call the "free world." You have to understand that this mentality made me who I was, during the 1970s and 1980s, as an American. Ask your grandparents what was up with this Cold War. For those of us who grew up here, served twenty-two years in the military, in Special Forces, the Cold War was still going on in the 1980s.

Mike's observations reflect the unmistakable grip of the Cold War. The Salvadoran military government was clearly bad, but so was the violence of the communist rebels. The United States, it seemed, had to choose the lesser evil. At the time, Mike believed that the lesser evil was a right-wing government, a view he has since reconsidered. In retrospect, Mike sees himself sitting on the wrong side of the table of justice, a finding validated by many post-conflict assessments, including a UN-appointed Truth Commission.

According to the Truth Commission, after twelve years of bloody war, most of the blood was on the hands of state officials. In thinking of the over 75,000 lives lost, the commission attributed 85 percent of the acts of violence to the agents of the Salvadoran state; approximately 5 percent of the acts of violence were attributed to the FMLN.[17] At the same time, Mike's recollections of the political assassination conducted by the FMLN are also accurate and confirmed in the final report of the Truth Commission. Similarly, the haunting images that Mike recalls of the corpses of child soldiers and the general practice of the recruitment of "child warriors" have been confirmed by accounts of other writers.[18]

To understand Mike's Cold War views, it is useful to examine some of the ideas that shaped the conversation around US foreign policy during the 1980s. If there was an "organic intellectual" of the aggressive Reagan foreign policy in Central America, it was Dr. Jeane J. Kirkpatrick, a professor of government at Georgetown University and later the US ambassador to the United Nations. Although a lifelong Democrat, Kirkpatrick saw in Reagan a politician who had an intuitive grasp of crucial distinctions that she sketched in a series of accessible and theoretically informed articles.

One key distinction that Kirkpatrick made was between traditional *authoritarian* states (like the military and oligarchic governments in Central America) and the *totalitarian* or "revolutionary autocracies" of the communist world. Both were offensive to American sensibilities, but the first were reformable; the second were not. In her view, "traditional authoritarian governments are less repressive than revolutionary autocracies, . . . more susceptible of liberalization," and "more compatible with US interests."[19] Mike translates these ideas well when he summarized the US view of the government: "This corrupt government has to win. And we can help make it change to democracy after the war is over."

Another influential contribution that Kirkpatrick made to the intellectual justification for US policy was a reframing of Central American history through the lens of Western political philosophy. In an unpublished but influential paper called "The Hobbes Problem: Order, Authority and Legitimacy in Central America," she took the ideas of seventeenth-century philosopher Thomas Hobbes to say that what Central America lacked was order. US policymakers, then, should abandon a foolish focus on human rights and endorse what she saw as the more culturally appropriate approach of the Salvadoran military's effort to impose order through repression, even if it meant the use of death squads. Kirkpatrick suggested that the political culture of El Salvador was founded on "strength, machismo, competition, . . . shrewdness, assertiveness . . . and a certain 'manly' disregard for safety." In its history, Kirkpatrick argued, El Salvador had heroes who should be emulated in the 1980s. "Hernandez Martinez is such a hero." He "ruthlessly suppressed the disorders [of the 1932 uprising], wiping out all those who participated, hunting down their leaders. It is sometimes said that thirty thousand persons lost their lives in this process. The traditional death squads that pursue revolutionary activities and leaders in contemporary El Salvador call themselves Hernandez Martinez Brigades, seeking thereby to place themselves in El Salvador's political tradition and communicate their purposes."[20]

Kirkpatrick's view was not an isolated one. A State Department official told the anthropologist Philippe Bourgois, who had witnessed and survived a massacre in El Salvador, that one had to contextualize such horrors in the "cultural history" of the country, which was one of blood and violence. Ordinary North American standards just did not apply. Bourgois noted that this had echoes of General William Westmoreland's infamous comments during the Vietnam War that one had to "understand the oriental mind" as it did not "perceive death and suffering the way we do." Such thinking, Bourgois observed insightfully, is not only racist but also obscures the self-defeating dynamic of such repression: it only fuels more armed resistance.[21]

As Mike noted above, Central America was "Vietnam revisited." Indeed, Vietnam was a central reference point for proponents and critics of US Central American policy. El Salvador in particular offered US military strategists an opportunity to "reverse the record" of counterinsurgency failure that the United States had faced in Southeast Asia. This meant efforts were made not only to strengthen the Salvadoran military but to professionalize it and move it away from the violent and corrupt practices that had been part of its history. Mike's account of the questionable behavior of military commanders represents evidence of the attempts to professionalize, and also the limited success those efforts had. For critics of US policy, this confirmed deep-seated fears of imperialism. As a popular bumper sticker put it, "El Salvador is Spanish for Vietnam."[22]

These ideas in Washington, DC, contributed not only to a set of foreign policy ideas but also to what we might call, borrowing from the literary critic Raymond Williams, a Cold War "structure of feeling." In times of global struggle, hard choices were required. As US military members thought about winning "hearts and minds," they also found their own hearts and minds shaped by the larger political and cultural logics. Part of those larger logics had much to do with different ideas of human life, made clear by the remarks of figures like Kirkpatrick and Westmoreland. To put it a little more philosophically, these foreign policy ideas were illustrations of what Achille Mbembé calls "necropolitics," a kind of sovereign power that fundamentally is about "the capacity to define who matters and who does not, who is disposable and who is not."[23] Yet, of course, ideas about who matters are not confined to the ones expressed in DC think-tank papers and government memos. Salvadorans also participated in the formation of these ideas and feelings. Responding to the voices that justified death and repression were also others that provided alternative moral frames for thinking about the lives of the majority of poor Salvadorans.

Religion in El Salvador

El Salvador. The very name of the country invokes "Our Savior" Jesus Christ and reminds us that the Catholic Church has a long and complex history in the Americas. While the church was (and is) undeniably part of the colonial order of things, it also often provided the infrastructure for grassroots organizing that was seen as a threat to the interest of oligarchs and right-wing leaders. Christian Base Communities, radio stations, and capacity-building workshops were tools for popular struggle. Clearly, we cannot give a full account of that political and religious organizing here. However, if there is one figure who is emblematic of that history, it is the archbishop of San Salvador, Óscar Arnulfo Romero y Galdámez, who was killed in 1980 and canonized by Pope Francis in 2008.

The story of Saint Óscar Romero is well known and the subject of numerous books and films.[24] In most of those works, the arc of his life has a Pauline quality to it. On his own road to Damascus, Romero went from conservative cleric to radical critic of repression. According to that narrative, Romero was selected as archbishop because he was seen as a traditionalist, unlike some members of the clergy who were more out-spoken in their criticism of the military. A cardinal in Rome close to the process reportedly said, "We don't want anyone who is going to oppose the government."[25]

Nevertheless, and again according to the conventional Romero story, global changes in the 1960s and the very local experiences of violence pushed him in more critical directions. After the Second Vatican Council (1962) and the Medellín meeting of Latin American bishops (1968), there was greater acceptance in the Americas for the central tenet of liberation theology, a "preferential option for the poor." Rather than preaching that suffering in this world meant salvation in the next, progressive currents in the church suggested that poverty and exploitation were theologically wrong, that they were not the will of God.[26] Additionally, the murder of Romero's close friend Father Rutilio Grande has often been named as the catalyst for Romero's radicalization. Grande had worked with other Jesuits to create grassroots Christian Base Communities (Comunidades Eclesiales de Base) and had become outspoken in his criticism of the government.

In one famous homily, Grande said that if Jesus himself crossed the border from Honduras to El Salvador, members of the military govern-ment would "not allow him to enter." They would accuse Jesus of "rebel-lion, of being a foreign Jew. . . . They will return to crucify him again." In that same homily, he told his congregants that no one should ever kill but that a Christian must be ready "to give his or her life in service for a just order."[27] Father Rutilio Grande did just that. On March 12, 1977, Father Grande and two traveling companions, a seventy-two-year-old man and a sixteen-year-old boy, were killed in their car by Salvadoran security forces.

Romero himself said, "When I looked at Rutilio dead, I thought, 'If they have killed him for doing what he did, then I too have to walk the same path.' Yes, I changed, but I also returned."[28] Eight days after the murder of his friend, and against the wishes of the government,

Archbishop Romero declared that there would be only one mass in that country, the misa única; over 100,000 people came to hear Romero celebrate mass and denounce the growing violence. Romero arguably became the most famous face of liberation theology. He appealed to US president Jimmy Carter directly to stop aiding the military of El Salvador. Romero also tried to communicate directly with the armed forces and appeal to their sense of morality.

On March 23, 1980, in a radio address, he implored the armed forces, "in the name of God," to stop the repression. He was assassinated celebrating mass the next day. One of the findings of the Salvadoran Truth Commission was that right-wing leader Roberto D'Aubuissón "gave the order to assassinate the Archbishop and gave precise instructions to members of his security service, acting as a 'death squad,' to organize and supervise the assassination."[29] US military aid continued to flow into El Salvador, despite Romero's pleas. Between 1980 and 1991, the United States provided over $1 billion in military assistance to El Salvador and nearly $6 billion in broader war-related assistance.[30]

Like all "roads to Damascus," the path that Romero took from conservative bishop to radical liberation is more complex than it may seem at first glance. Let me mention two issues that provide some nuance to this unquestionably important history. Without minimizing the moral shock that the death of his friend Father Grande had on him, we should take seriously Romero's statement that he not only "changed" but also "returned." As religious scholar Matthew Whelan persuasively argues, Romero "returned" to long-held beliefs about the injustice of inequality and land tenure in El Salvador. Indeed, for decades, Romero had made a deeply theological case against the land-tenure system that was one of the roots of injustice in his country.[31] This was certainly consistent with the message coming out of the reforms of Vatican II and the progressive currents of the Latin American bishops' meeting in Medellín, but it was also consistent with Romero's understanding of Catholic social teachings about land and property that can be traced back to an encyclical tradition that begins in 1891.[32] In other words, Romero's transformation was a return to long-standing commitment as well as an urgent response to worsening violence. Yet, as Mike notes above, the sources of that violence were and are economic. Viewed through the teachings of Jesus Christ or Karl Marx, it was clear that the misery of El Salvador had been in the making for a very long time.

Second, we should also underline the timing of Romero's work and death. While it is one of the better-known political assassinations in Central America, violence in the country would only get worse after his death. In some ways, his murder marks the start of the most brutal phase of a civil war that would take over 75,000 lives and displace countless more. Additionally, his death came before Ronald Reagan even entered the White House. While there were clear differences between Carter's and Reagan's foreign policies, it is important to note that in seeing US interests through the prism of anti-communism, there was a great deal of continuity between Democratic and Republican administrations.

Mike Wilson's service in Central America allowed him an intimate understanding of the long history of suffering that continues to this day. He also experienced there a crisis of conscience that shook the certainty he had previously felt about his Cold War political commitments. For Mike, El Salvador was a place that would forever change the direction of his life. And yet, like Romero, Mike both "changed" and "returned." As we will see, the next chapter of his life took him to reconsider some of the lessons he had first encountered with the nuns of Saint Catherine's in Ajo and the social justice struggles of the 1960s.

Chapter 4

Heroic Pioneers and Demonic Others

Seminary, Christianity, and Religion in Indian Country

MIKE WILSON

I retired from the United States Army on September 30, 1993, after almost twenty-two years of service. During my last two years of active duty, I was a noncommissioned officer instructor in the Reserve Officers' Training Corps program at the University of Alabama at Birmingham. During this period, I divorced and remarried. My wife and I then moved to San Antonio, Texas, where I got a job in the Army Junior ROTC program at Alamo Heights High School, in the township of Alamo Heights, next to San Antonio. All I knew about Alamo Heights was that it was a *very* wealthy community. Old money. A lot of old, white money.

I believe that under a court order the Alamo Heights Independent School District had to desegregate. The school district was forced to include Mexican American, Black, and poor white children. Where the San Antonio and Alamo Heights school districts touched, you had this whole swath of poverty right along the old Austin Highway corridor. Historically, there had been a cement plant in Alamo Heights and a Mexican American barrio called Cementville. Many Mexican American families still live there.[1]

As far as I know, Alamo Heights was against this court-ordered integration. It resisted this change. It had to take in a lot of these poor children. The Latino, Black, and poor white kids didn't have the same graduation rates as the more affluent white students. In an attempt to increase the graduation rate of its students of color, Alamo Heights High School introduced an Army Junior ROTC program.

This was a very elite school. Here's one measure of how elite the school was: the principal and possibly five faculty members had PhDs. Two PhDs that I knew of were the chemistry teacher and the math teacher. How many public high schools in the United States have multiple PhDs on their faculty? Any five of those PhDs could have been a university professor. But because it was a wealthy school district, they were probably getting good salaries as high school teachers. This was a *public* school.

Another measure of its academic prestige was that the high school had National Merit finalists every year. You mentioned "Alamo Heights" and people would just sort of turn up their noses, because that was the perception of that community. If you mentioned Heights, it was like the Harvard of high schools in the greater San Antonio area.

When I got to Alamo Heights, as a person of color, I saw two separate and unequal schools. One was an elite school for college-bound, predominantly white students who were taking the AP courses taught by the PhDs. And there was another school for the marginalized and poor children of color. One day I really noticed that disparity.

A teacher was coming in late, and the principal, Dr. Linda Foster, called me. She asked, "Mike, can you sub for the first hour this morning? So-and-so is coming in late. He'll be there, but could you take roll and just monitor the class? You don't have to do anything." It was an AP civics class. I took the roll call, looked up, paused, and asked the students, who were all white and mostly male, a question.

"What's wrong with this picture? Look around you; what's wrong with this picture?"

"Nothing, what?" someone asked.

"Where are the Mexican American students? Where are the Black students? Where are the poor white students?"

There was an embarrassed silence. Possibly, they had never been made aware of their white privilege. They had never been made self-conscious about it. Were all of those other AP classes all-white too? The students were embarrassed. And I'm glad they were. That told me that they had a moral conscience. And as much as I was concerned with increasing the graduation rates for students of color, I was equally concerned with the quality of their education.

I continued my college studies at the University of Texas at San Antonio and transferred those credits to the University of Alabama at Birmingham, where I completed my bachelor's degree with a major in Spanish and a minor in history. I started the Texas teacher certification program at UTSA because Dr. Foster told me that she wanted me to replace a retiring Spanish teacher. She encouraged me, "Mike, go back to school and get your teacher's certification. I want you back at this school." She saw the relationships I had with my students, with my cadets. Yet, despite the opportunity to teach at Alamo Heights, I wanted to return home, to Tucson.

My parents were getting older. I'd been gone for twenty-five years, and I knew that they weren't going to be around too much longer. So, I said to the principal, "I appreciate the offer, but I'm going home." The fact that she wanted me back meant a lot, coming from a person I respected very much. I did not tell her this, and maybe I should have, but as a person of color, I just felt an "otherness." When I walked in the halls, I felt as if I didn't belong in the school and that I didn't belong in the community. That's the way I felt. And if I felt that way, how did the students of color feel?

A few years ago, I saw a story on CBS News. The Alamo Heights High School basketball team played a team from San Antonio, one of the predominantly Mexican American schools. After the game, the Alamo Heights players and fans began yelling "USA! USA! USA! USA!"[2] That was the same Alamo Heights where I taught and lived. I asked myself, *What's going on?* Here was that undercurrent of racial tension I had felt years ago. When I heard the student body yelling, "USA! USA! USA!" I asked myself, *What are they saying? Are Mexican Americans the enemy? And do you know they're US citizens?* When you are looking for enemies, you often create your own.

Returning to Tucson, Becoming Presbyterian

I came home to Tucson in January of 1996. I was thinking about joining a church. I felt spiritually empty and disconnected from God and humanity. As a teenager I had grown up in the Pentecostal church, the Assemblies of

God. I didn't want to go back there because of its very narrow interpretation of scripture, its very conservative and oppressive theology. I had also been a member of the Unitarian Universalist Church (UU) in Birmingham, Alabama, for about two years, when I was stationed there at the UAB. When I moved to San Antonio, I attended a UU church for about two years. My disappointment with the Unitarian church was that it was inspiring only from the neck up, very intellectual. To listen to a UU sermon was to listen to a university lecture, no offense to university professors or to UU pastors. Nothing in those sermons spoke to my heart nor watered the roots of my thirsty soul.

After my return to Tucson, I shopped for a church. My O'odham aunt, Virginia Parvello, and her children had been lifelong Presbyterians at Southside Presbyterian Church. They had grown up in that church. Virginia's parents had been founding members when Southside was still a mission church. I said, "I'm going to go try Southside." I joined and stayed for ten years. I became active there and eventually became the youth minister by default.

At the time, I was working as the marketing manager at the Desert Diamond Casino, one of the Tohono O'odham Nation's casinos in the Tucson area. One evening, the casino was the sponsor of a "fan night" at a semi-professional baseball game in Tucson. As the representative of the casino, I had the privilege of throwing out the first pitch. But I didn't want to do it; I wanted a kid to do it. I asked my cousin if one of her grandsons, who played Little League baseball, would like to throw out the pitch. He said yes.

I picked him and his buddy up at my cousin's house in South Tucson. He and I walked to the pitcher's mound, and he threw out the pitch. Rather than take seats in the bleachers, we went to the grassy incline where we could sit and watch the game. It was me, him, and his friend. After a while, I could tell that they were restless and bored.

"We're gonna go walk around," he said.

"Yeah, fine, I'll be here."

The game was over, and they were still gone. As I was heading out toward the exit gate, I saw a police officer walking toward me. He asked, "Are these two with you?"

I said, "Yeah, why?"

"You need to come with me, all three of you."

During the time that they were "walking around," they had followed a kid into the men's bathroom, turned off the lights, threatened him, and took his money. They jacked him.

This was my cousin's grandson! The twelve-year-old Little Leaguer who threw out the first pitch! And this was our church kid. Eventually he was charged and had to go to counseling. Both of them were banned from the stadium.

As the representative of the Desert Diamond Casino and as a tribal member, I was embarrassed. I took him back to his grandma's house, and man, she read him the riot act. Once she finished with her ass chewin', he had tears in his eyes. I had to sit there at the kitchen table. Man, that poor kid didn't have *any* ass left.

Soon after, I went to our pastor, John Fife. I said, "John . . ." and I told him what happened at the baseball field. "This is one of our own, born and raised in this church, and he is getting into trouble. He's getting into trouble because there's nothing going on here to support our church kids. Southside has an international reputation for human rights advocacy.[3] But who's taking care of our children? Why are we solving the world's problems, but we aren't taking care of our own kids?"

John answered, "Mike, the squeaky wheel gets the grease. Guess what? You're the new youth minister."

He gave me a budget and a salary. "Now you've got the youth program," John said. And so, I did. I was the youth minister by default for a year and a half or two. That ministry put me on the road to seminary.

It took that experience at the ballpark to open my eyes. Our own kids, our own good kids, were doing stupid things. My biggest fear at the time was that some of them were involved in gangs or wanted to be. When I look back at the youth program, the girls did so much better. Of the three high school girls, one of them has finished her PhD, and the other two have finished their master's degrees. And the guys? One is serving twenty-two years in prison for second-degree manslaughter. He shot and killed a Navajo/Diné nursing student because she wouldn't date him. Another is a homeless alcoholic. Another is a career criminal serving time again in the state prison. This is the same kid who threw out the first pitch. Our program did some good, but not enough. How do you compete with the street?

Working with high school kids taught me a lot, though. They really needed structure, leadership, role models, education. And they needed the church. I decided to go to seminary to be ordained and get my master of divinity. In the Presbyterian church, the master's program takes four years, three years of academics and one for an internship. I planned on coming back to Tucson or to the reservation.

Entering and Exiting San Francisco Theological Seminary

I picked San Francisco Theological Seminary (SFTS), mostly for the location. It was close enough that I could drive to Tucson if I ever wanted to get back there a couple of times during the year. It was and is probably one of the more progressive seminaries in the Presbyterian church. So, I went.

Academically, seminary was not that hard for me. I was very surprised that I was doing so well. I hadn't been in school for many years, but I just took to seminary like a duck to a pond. During my first semester, I received three As and a B; I was on track. But then, you know, I had these creeping doubts: *What am I doing here?*

As a person of color, I struggled with SFTS. As far as I remember, I was the only Native American student there. There were some Chicanos and Chicanas who also claimed Indigenous ancestry but didn't identify themselves as Native American. Like me, there were other students who were questioning why we were even at seminary. There was a Black woman, a very dear friend of mine, named Clarissa. We had started seminary together. She was asking herself, "What am I doing here?" She realized she couldn't stay either. And there was a gay white man who came to seminary a year later. In our discussions, he once said, "There's no future for me in the Presbyterian church." At the time, the church did not ordain gay men. He ended our conversation by saying, "I might as well just go back to my law practice."

So, in my cohort, a gay white man, a Black woman, and myself, a Native American, all left SFTS about the same time. It was our shared struggle, the realization that there was no future or place for us in the Presbyterian church. That was the heartbreaking reality.

But it was a specific incident around a stained-glass window that finally brought everything down for me. Let me tell you that story.

I was in the Church Polity class. The classroom was next to the Stewart Memorial Chapel, a gothic structure with beautiful stained-glass windows. One day, as part of the lesson, the whole class walked next door into the chapel. SFTS had published a black-and-white pamphlet with narratives and drawings of all the twenty-eight nave windows, which represented the missionary expansion into the western states and territories.[4] SFTS was founded to train missionaries for the "uncivilized" territories and states. It was the only Presbyterian seminary west of the Mississippi River. In was part and parcel of the United States government's genocidal policy of Manifest Destiny. The

Presbyterian church realized that as the country expanded west, it needed more trained ministers.

The professor had cut out each narrative paragraph from the pamphlet, and there were enough students to read each one. The class moved down the sides of the chapel and stopped beneath each of the windows, where a designated student would read his or her assigned narrative that described the scene above. We had just come from talking about church history, so the professor probably thought this was an excellent opportunity to illustrate the lesson.

As we moved through the chapel and the students read their assigned narratives, the class members would look up in awe. I was assigned the second-to-last window, the S. Hall Young window. On previous visits to the chapel, I had noticed something unsettling in it. After reading the assigned narrative, I understood my discomfort and was appalled. There is a missionary, S. Hall Young, standing and holding an open Bible in his left hand. In his extended right hand, he holds a cross over a seated Native Alaskan. In the background, seated, are five more Natives. The Native seated in front of the missionary extends his left arm toward the cross.

I looked up at the window and saw an abhorrent scene. The Alaskan elder seated beneath the white missionary was possibly a shaman or medicine man. In the image he had fangs and horns coming out of his head, and what look like claws are on the tips of his outstretched fingers. With the light coming through the window, his face is pale green. To this Tohono O'odham, it was a scene of an exorcism. When we got to that window, I refused to read the Manifest Destiny narrative about the white missionary who apparently, with his Bible and cross, had come to save the "heathen savages" from themselves.

I was livid. I said to my classmates and professor, "If this is what white Christianity thinks of Indigenous people and Indigenous spirituality, then you need to ask yourselves: Why are there not more people of color in this seminary?" This was the tipping point of the doubt that I had about whether I should stay at SFTS.

The next Wednesday, like every Wednesday morning at nine, the entire campus community went to the Stewart Memorial Chapel to receive Communion. There was music and a short sermon, and then student leaders would move to the front of the chapel and administer the sacrament of wine and bread. Row by row, the congregation moved forward until the pews were empty. They then stood together at the front of the chapel, facing the nave, and in unison drank the cup of wine.

FIGURE 8. Medallions dedicated to S. Hall Young, Stewart Memorial Chapel. San Francisco Theological Seminary, *Stained Glass Windows*, 9.

As a matter of conscience, I refused to receive Communion knowing what was above me: this demonic portrayal of me and my people within this sacred place. I felt an aura of evil descend upon me from the window. That is how strong the impact was on me. I sat in the back, leaning forward with my face in my hands, weeping. I could hear, row by row, the shuffling of feet of the beloved community that I should have been a part of. I could feel the eyes of the congregation upon me as I sat alone in back. I had exiled myself from my God and my community.

As a Native American, I had to make a statement. As a Christian, as a Presbyterian, and as a seminarian, I could not in good conscience be a part of this faith community. As long as the church treats my people as the demonic "other," I could not participate.

My fellow students initiated a petition condemning the window and demanding its removal. Everyone in the class signed. Because donors had paid for the whole chapel and the windows, the matter had to go to the board of trustees; they had to decide how to respond. At their next meeting, they decided to take the window down. However, I had already decided to leave at the end of the semester.

By then, exams were coming up, and my mother had just died. I went to Tucson for her funeral and burial. When I returned to seminary, I struggled with my studies. Much reading was required, and yet nothing stuck. Not even a paragraph. It was as if the words evaporated as soon as they left my eyes. I knew I was in trouble. I went to my advisor and told her I was still mourning and that I could not study. I knew it was futile to stay.

Before I left SFTS, I met a Native elder from the Bay Area. She was a member of the Miwok Tribe. I told her about the window, and she was curious and wanted to see it. I also wanted confirmation from another set of Native eyes that what I was seeing was real. That is why I invited her. A few days later, she showed up with another friend, another Native woman elder, also from the Bay Area. I took them up the stairs on the outside of the chapel and onto the terrace. Standing at the window, they were terrified.

One of them took off her leather medicine bundle from around her neck and placed it on the windowsill. That's how scared she was. I suspected that the medicine bundle was to offer us protection against the evil coming from the window. It was in the afternoon, and the sunlight was strong. As it hit the window, it illuminated even more strongly the pallid green of the shaman's face. The fangs, the horns, and the claws became more pronounced. I felt the elders' fear. It was contagious. I was angry before. Now, I was afraid. I could almost smell sulfur in the air; I could almost taste it.

But I also felt relieved that they were there. I was grateful to the elder who put her medicine bundle on the windowsill to protect us from the evil. So that's what convinced me. *You're not the only one, Mike.* If these women could see and feel it too, it was a confirmation from my coastal elders that I didn't belong in seminary.

A Sense of Holocaust

One evening before all this happened, I stood on that same terrace with my back to the window, looking out over San Anselmo. I could see the coastal green hills, and I knew beyond them was the Pacific Ocean. I remember asking myself something to the effect of, *Amid all this spectacular beauty, where are all the Native people who lived here before European conquest? Where are my people? What have you, white America, done to them?* When I was in junior high, the public library was my sanctuary. I came across the book *Ishi: The Last of His Tribe.* It was a painful book to read. I remember how devastated I felt looking at the photos of Ishi, reading that he was the last of his tribe and that when he died the Yahi would be forever erased. What made it more painful was how similar Ishi's face was to my dad's. It made me think about my people. Would some anthropologist someday write about the last of the Tohono O'odham?

Now I was standing on the lands of the Yahi. I heard Yahi moving in the woods and the soft whimpering of women crying. Their spirits were out there. I heard them in the redwoods, but where are they now? *And why, church, are you here?*

I had this sense of a holocaust, of a spirit-killing Manifest Destiny, fulfilled at the edge of the continent. This was the emotional turmoil I was in. I struggled because I thought a person went to seminary because they were called by Creator-God. In this calling, there was a sense of purpose, obedience, and humility. I *now* asked my Creator-God, *Why did you call me if you knew this separation was going to happen? Why did I hear you call my name, "Michael," on my pilgrimage to Saint Catherine's in Indian Village in Ajo when I was making a decision?* I had shed tears of joy that I had made the right decision to attend seminary. And now, I was shedding tears of brokenness, sitting by myself in the back of the chapel.

Was I surprised that in the year 2000, this window was still in the chapel, this tribute to Manifest Destiny? Apparently, no one ever looked twice, or if they did, they didn't care. The chapel was built in the mid-1950s, during the era of the post–World War II white American triumphalism. Our World War II victory confirmed "our" moral authority as "heroic citizens." This legacy included the ongoing domestication and subjugation of Native Americans and Alaska Natives. "We" can subjugate "them" because "they" are the "demonic other" and conversely "we" are "heroic pioneers."

I learned that the board of trustees took down the window. Later, I went looking for it. It was in the basement of one of the dormitories, where the maintenance office and workshop were. The whole frame was there. It was on the cement floor, leaning against the wall. The trustees wanted to keep it in the basement until they figured out what to do. Down there, I met the maintenance supervisor, who had removed the window from the chapel. He said, "I'm glad you did this." Then he took a long pause. "I'm Cherokee from North Carolina." We looked each other in the eyes, Native to Native. With his words, I felt vindicated, as if *we* had won a Supreme Court decision.

He let me do something to record this historic moment. I wanted to make sure that what I was seeing was accurate. I placed white typing paper on top of the lead and glass, and I traced the face, including fangs and horns, as irrefutable evidence. I later thought of using that face as my personal letterhead at SFTS. I even considered using it as a tattoo on the inside of my left forearm, and on the inside of my right forearm I'd put another tattoo with the face of the suffering Christ. If someone asked, "Why do you have those tattoos?" I would respond, "America, who am I? The demonic Other or a follower of Christ?"

Back to Tucson

I left seminary and moved back to Tucson. I was embarrassed that I had not finished, but John Fife gave me the opportunity to address the congregation at Southside Presbyterian Church. The congregation understood.

At another Sunday morning service, a visiting O'odham woman told me her church on the reservation needed a pastor. The current lay pastor and his wife had medical problems and were moving back to the Phoenix area. I thought to myself, *You know, you don't want to burn any bridges should you ever decide to go back to SFTS and finish your master of divinity. Maybe I can use this one-year ministry on the reservation as my internship, an internship that is required for graduation.*

I accepted the position as the lay pastor and soon found my real calling. I realized this once I started putting out water on the lands of the Tohono

O'odham Nation for the thousands of undocumented migrants crossing tribal lands. Just as I was called to seminary, I was also called to my ministry putting out water in the desert. *That's* what I was called to do.

My church was the desert. And my sermon was putting out water. That was my ministry for twelve years. I never had the blessing of the organized church, but you don't need a PhD in theology to put out water where men, women, and children are suffering and dying. My ministry—my calling—was to put out water. Water is lifesaving. Water is the sacramental fluid of life. Water in the desert is the water of salvation.

INTERLUDE 4

Christianity and Indian Country

JOSÉ ANTONIO LUCERO

> Unless the Christian God is confined within the quasi-Gothic stone
> structure, He cannot operate. Needless to say, He does not do
> very well even within His real estate.
>> —Vine Deloria Jr., *God Is Red*

Let us begin with the image in that quasi-Gothic chapel and with that
window (see fig. 8).[1] This black-and-white sketch, reproduced from the
1955 seminary pamphlet, lacks what the unnamed authors of the pamphlet call the "jewel-like" color and light that give these windows their
translucent storytelling power, but it nevertheless conveys a remarkable
amount of information. The nave windows are described as telling the
"inspiring story of the Presbyterian Church in the West," representing "an
ever-glowing tribute in living light to the greatness and courage of the
early pioneers."[2] Contextualizing the central medallion image of S. Hall
Young, the Presbyterian missionary standing over the "demonic" Native
figure, the pamphlet tells us that Young had a "tremendous task" in his
work of bringing Christianity to the Alaska Natives, work that involved
learning to use a dogsled (pictured in the upper medallion), which gave

him the appellation of "the mushing pastor."[3] The accompanying images of the mortar and pestle, the scales of justice, and the miner's pick and pan tell a story about the labors that Young, a physician by training, had to do beyond his missionary work during the time of the gold rush.

Young arrived in Alaska at a time when "there were no doctors . . . or civil government." He thus had to act as both a healer and a judge to the Natives and "the miners and other white people streaming into the territory" with the gold rush. At the center of the window, however, we are reminded that despite the "progress" Young made in bringing Christianity to the Natives, "there were often serious lapses into the old ways." The image at the center of the window tells the story of one of those "lapses" and pictures a heroic missionary who had the courage to "march boldly into the council house, filled with frenzied Indians, and by the sheer force of his inspired argument was able to win his first real victory in eradicating the cruel native practice."[4]

Standing in sharp contrast to the "wicked superstition" of the Native shaman was the natural beauty of Alaska, an appreciation he shared with his friend, the naturalist John Muir, about whom he says much in a book titled *Alaska Days with John Muir* and in his autobiography.[5] Muir, a founder of the national parks system in the United States, had a famously negative view of Native peoples, whom he viewed as dirty. "The worst thing about them is their uncleanliness. Nothing truly wild is unclean," Muir wrote. For Muir, the "strangely dirty" Indians, as environmental historian Carolyn Merchant puts it, were the "polar opposites of the pristine lands in which he found them."[6] His aversion to the Native peoples he encountered in California sometimes even surprised him. "To prefer the society of squirrels and woodchucks to that of our own species must surely be unnatural," he wrote.[7]

I remember vividly the first time Mike described that stained glass missionary encounter with the "demonic Native Other." Mike and I were in Tucson, speaking at an open-air venue that was the location for a Borderlands Theater event. Mike was at the time president of the board of directors for this theater company. Taking advantage of some downtime before the fundraising event, we recorded one of the first oral history interviews for this project. As Mike and I spoke, he sketched a picture of that "diabolical" image from memory. I was shocked by the horns and fangs, and I remember wondering what the actual window looked like. Could such an outrageously racist depiction exist in a Bay Area chapel?

Several years later, I finally tracked down a copy of the 1955 seminar pamphlet that Mike mentions, the one with the descriptions of all the stained glass windows in the Stewart Memorial Chapel at San Francisco Theological Seminary. The image and the accompanying descriptions in the pamphlet were even more shocking than Mike's sketch. They are vivid illustrations of what the Osage theologian George E. Tinker has called "missionary conquest," the idea that in one way or another Christian missionaries of all denominations "were partners in genocide."[8]

Tinker's work helpfully clarifies how missionary work was (and is) entangled with the "political" dimensions of dispossession and violence. Missionaries were not only representatives of their denominations but also agents of imperial powers and projects. The governance of "Indian affairs" was often quite literally left to missionaries. The "care" of Natives took brutal forms across the Americas, including dispossession, forced labor, whipping, flogging, hobbling, sexual violence, family separation, and death. There were religious voices that spoke out against the abuse of Native peoples; perhaps the most famous and earliest example was that of the bishop of Chiapas, Mexico, Bartolomé de Las Casas, who described Spanish atrocities in his 1552 work, A Brief Account of the Destruction of the Indies.[9] Tinker reminds us, however, that even the "friends of the Indians," like Las Casas, were still agents of conquest. Tinker quotes Alfonso de Maldonado, a governor of Guatemala and contemporary of Las Casas, who described how through negotiations with the Natives, "Father Bartolomé de Las Casas and other religious here are succeeding in the peaceful conquest of this warlike territory."[10] This idea of "peaceful conquest" has had staying power.

In her award-winning Bad Indians: A Tribal Memoir, Deborah Miranda, a citizen of the Ohlone/Costanoan-Esselen Nation and of Chumash descent, writes eloquently about how the "Mission Mythology" sanitizes and euphemizes conquest. She gives as an example the seemingly innocuous fourth-grade "Mission Project," where young people learn how to make sugar-cube mission replicas, write stories of "Indian friends" who shared what they had with settlers, and find other ways to "think of Indians as passive, dumb, and disappeared."[11] "Can you imagine," Miranda asks, "teaching about slavery in the South while simultaneously requiring each child to lovingly construct a plantation model, complete with happy darkies in the fields, white masters, overseers with whips, and human actions? Or asking fourth graders to study the Holocaust by carefully designing detailed concentration camps, complete with gas champers, heroic Nazi Guards, crematoriums?"[12]

As I write, and almost on cue, my ten-year-old son, our in-house fourth grader, told me what he is learning in school. Practically walking out of Miranda's book, he told me that they were learning about the "Oregon Trail" in his progressive Seattle public school. He shared with me the narrative he wrote in response to the prompt he and his classmates received: "Imagine you are a pioneer traveling west in a wagon train on the Oregon Trail." To help students get started, the first sentence of the story is already provided: "I was ten years old when I woke up on a wagon train." My son's narrative is a lively one, full of deep rivers, rattlesnakes, and a tornado, all things that terrify him. I asked him if he had learned about the Native peoples whom the settlers encountered. "Not really," he replied. "Maybe later." Yes, indeed. We will talk about that later. But for now, I will stay closer to the stories told by the windows of San Francisco Theological Seminary.

Below, I use these chapel windows as portals into the history of missionary conquest, one of the oldest histories in the Americas. Almost as old, however, is the story of Indigenous negotiation, transformation, and resistance. It is fascinating to pause for a moment and think back to Mike's recollection of looking from the terrace of the Stewart Memorial Chapel and thinking of Ishi, arguably the most famous of California Indians.[13] Ishi's fame was largely produced by being labeled "the last wild Indian" in a popular book by University of California, Berkeley, anthropologist Theodora Kroeber. Ishi's story is usually told as a tragic tale, a Native person "discovered" by Western science who literally lived the rest of his days in a university museum, providing cultural knowledge to anthropologist Alfred Kroeber, Theodora's spouse.[14]

A lesser-known part of the story is that Ishi sometimes had a roommate: a Tohono O'odham man named Juan Dolores. Unlike Ishi, who stayed close to the museum, Dolores was a multilingual traveler who roamed widely across the West. Dolores liked to take Ishi on long walks in San Francisco. He spent time not only with Ishi but also with the Kroeber family. Novelist Ursula K. Le Guin, the Kroebers' daughter, has written fondly of the summers that Juan Dolores spent with the family at their home in Napa; she considered him an "Indian uncle."[15]

I mentioned this to Mike, who, of course, already knew the story. In fact, he told me, he was friends with one of Dolores's great-granddaughters, who told Mike of her memories hearing and understanding the recording of her grandfather speaking in the O'odham language.[16] James Clifford observes that Ishi's friendship with Dolores "opens a small window on the complexities of a changing California Indian life, in and out of cities. Today, Dolores serves as a kind of placeholder for unanswered questions of how Ishi's Indian contemporaries—emphatically not dying primitives—might relate to his predicament."[17] In this light, Mike carries on an O'odham tradition of travel and study and provides some compelling insights into these old predicaments.

With the examples of Juan Dolores and Mike Wilson in mind, I would like to emphasize that the aim of this interlude is both to convey a sense of the violence that came with Christianity *and* to refuse the temptation to narrate this simply as a story of Indigenous victimhood. Following the lead of Dolores, Wilson, and other Native intellectuals, I want to suggest that there are many moments in which violence and resilience are in dialectical tension, often producing unexpected outcomes.

Windows into Missionary Violence

I obtained a copy of the 1955 pamphlet about the Stewart Memorial Chapel through a loan from the library of Whitman College, an institution a few hours to the east of the University of Washington in Walla Walla. It is notable and, given the subject of this chapter, eerily appropriate that this college was named after the missionaries Marcus and Narcissa Whitman, who each have their own windows in the same seminary chapel. You can see the reproduction of the images from their windows in figures 9 and 10. There is a familiar mix of easily recognizable symbols for the gifts that the Whitmans brought out west: medicine, music, agriculture, wagon trails, and religion. In both windows, tomahawks also appear prominently, alluding to the violent end they met, something I will discuss below.[18] Before I say more about the end of their story, it is worth saying a word about the beginning, especially regarding the image in the upper medallion, described in the following terms: "The incident which actually decided him to embark on this work was the arrival of a delegation of Nez Percé [sic] Indians at St. Louis in the fall of 1831 with the request that white men come to their people and bring to them the Book which told how to live."[19]

There is considerable historical evidence that representatives from the Nimiipuu people (Nez Perce)[20] were indeed in St. Louis, visiting William Clark (of Lewis and Clark fame, superintendent of Native Affairs), whom they had met two decades earlier. Where the historical record gets murky concerns what exactly was said. According to various sources, there was no common language between the Nimiipuu and white authorities. A Catholic bishop who took part in some of the meetings with the four Native men (two of whom died in St. Louis) wrote in an 1831 letter, "Unfortunately there was no one who understood their language. . . . It was truly distressing that they could not be understood."[21]

Despite the problems of communication and translation, Protestants and Catholics were quick to transform the encounter into evidence that there had been a "Macedonian Cry" for religious instruction. The New York *Christian Advocate* produced an unbelievably eloquent oration depicting the Native delegation's request for the "White Man's Book of Heaven." According to some Catholic sources, the Indians even requested Jesuit Black Robes to celebrate mass. One Jesuit, inspired by the story, traveled to Montana to create a "New Paraguay," an allusion to the Spanish colonial "success" of the Jesuits in South America.[22] Missionary mythology seems to fill in the blanks of the historical record with remarkable ease and creativity.

The Whitmans are very well known in Washington State. In addition to the college named in their honor, one finds the Whitman name attached to a national forest, public schools across the state, countless streets, an upscale hotel, and several churches. Until it was recently renamed, there was a "Whitman Lane" located on my own campus of the University of Washington, located right behind wələbʔaltxʷ – Intellectual House, the UW's longhouse-style facility for Native students and the university community.[23] The fame of the Whitmans, it is safe to say, is mostly attributable to the circumstance of their deaths. On November 29, 1847, the Whitmans and eleven others were killed by members of the Cayuse Tribe near their mission at Waiilatpu ("place of the rye grass"), located close to present-day Walla Walla. That mission is a national historic site, as a quick visit to the National Park Service's web page vividly illustrates.

The digital story one encounters on the NPS website is a mix of good intentions, misunderstandings, white supremacy, and the cultural tensions that accompany contagions. As missionaries and waves of white settlers came through Cayuse land, new diseases like smallpox

FIGURE 9. Medallions dedicated to Marcus Whitman, Stewart Memorial Chapel. San Francisco Theological Seminary, *Stained Glass Windows*, 10.

FIGURE 10. Medallions dedicated to Narcissa Whitman, Stewart Memorial Chapel. San Francisco Theological Seminary, *Stained Glass Windows*, 10.

and measles decimated Native populations while mysteriously sparing settlers. Marcus Whitman, a physician like S. Hall Young, attempted to help the sick, both white and Native, but his efforts had uneven results. His treatments seemed to work in healing white children but not Native children. Noting this imbalance, the Cayuse came to believe that the Whitmans were poisoning Native people deliberately or releasing some form of evil. The Cayuse decided that the Whitmans had to be killed in order to prevent more Native people, especially children, from dying.[24]

In the immediate wake of the violence, however, settlers narrated the "massacre" of the Whitmans as confirmation of the worst fears about Native "savagery." Such stories only invited settler violence, which came swiftly and was deployed against the Cayuse and other Native peoples who were expelled from their land. A small group of Cayuse were found guilty of the "Whitman massacre" and sentenced to death by hanging. The Whitmans are remembered as truly pioneering agents in the story of "opening" the West. A National Park Service pamphlet from 1958 suggests that the Whitmans were among "the noblest of the pioneers colonizing the West. Their indomitable spirit, energy, and determination carried the American flag to remote regions and contributed to our national expansion."[25]

To this day (in 2022), a bronze statue of Marcus Whitman is displayed in the National Statuary Hall in the US Capitol; it was donated by Washington State in 1953. Wearing buckskin and holding a Bible in his right hand, the statue is Manifest Destiny and missionary mythology on full display. On the granite pedestal are words that could be the bumper-sticker version of Western expansion: "My plans require time and distance." In a sign that Washington State may be finally moving past violent mythmaking, the statue is scheduled to be replaced by a new statue of Nisqually tribal member Billy Frank Jr., one of the central Native protagonists of the "fish wars" and a historic figure in the efforts to strengthen treaty rights in Washington State and beyond.

The sense of holocaust that Mike felt years ago in the Stewart Memorial Chapel is powerful, and I would never seek to minimize or deny the terrible histories of violence that have come with Christianity. However, in the remaining pages of this interlude, I would simply point to the many contributions that Native scholars and communities have made to understanding the nuances in Indigenous and Christian encounters. The field of Native studies helps us rethink the place of Christianity in Indian Country

FIGURE 11. Marcus Whitman statue by Avard Fairbanks.
Photograph by Architect of the Capitol.

and also place Mike's complex relationship with Christianity in historical perspective.

Refusing Christian Impositions

There is a strong Native critique and even refusal of Euro-Christian worldviews. Vine Deloria Jr.'s influential argument in *God Is Red*, for example, suggests that there is a crucial difference between the *spatial* thinking of American Indian peoples and the *temporal* understanding of Euro-Americans. He writes, "American Indians hold their lands— places—as having the highest possible meaning, and all their statements are made with this reference point in mind. Immigrants review the move- ment of their ancestors across the continent as a steady progression of basically good events and experiences, thereby placing history-time in the best possible light."[26] This understanding of place comes with a sense of relationality that is very different from the expansionist logics of the Christian church that quite literally endorse the idea of conquer- ing new lands and peoples.

Osage scholar Robert Warrior, at the time a graduate student at Union Theological Seminary, crafted a well-known essay on the ten- sions between biblical and Native projects of liberation, "A Native American Perspective: Canaanites, Cowboys, and Indians." While African Americans, for example, have been able to find inspiration in the Exodus story of escape from oppression and slavery, that story has a very different resonance for American Indian peoples. In the Old Testament, Israelites flee the oppression of the Pharaoh in Egypt. As the chosen people, they are told by Yahweh to kill members of the nations in their way, including the Amalekites and Canaanites. Several chapters in the Old Testament (Numbers 13, Deuteronomy 20) describe the instructions that the Israelites received as they entered the lands of Canaan: "In the cities of the nations the Lord your God is giving you as an inheritance, do not leave alive anything that breathes" (Deuter- onomy 20:16). American Indians, Warrior suggests, read that story with "Canaanite eyes." This is not only a question of interpretation, of course, as those biblical passages were often literally invoked by Puri- tans and other Christians to justify extermination and the terrible work of Manifest Destiny.[27]

Another Osage scholar, George Tinker, has made a similarly forceful case against the imposition of Christian cognitive schemas that impose vertical forms of hierarchy, authority, and individualism that are out of place in Native traditions and practices. His essay "Why I Do Not Believe in a Creator" is perhaps the most succinct version of his argument against the "up-down" schema of Christianity (in which a "Lord" stands above and apart from all of creation), an image that goes against Indigenous visions of relationality, gender complementarity, and community. Acknowledging that many Native peoples do indeed speak of a Creator, Tinker notes that this "creator-language" is better understood as an accommodation that Native peoples have made in the face of intense colonial pressure and that such talk masks the importance of the "cosmic dualities" and "collateral-egalitarianism" across Indian Country.[28]

According to Tinker, even the progressive religious language of "liberation theology," like the one discussed in the context of Saint Óscar Romero in El Salvador in interlude 3, is an example of the impositions of European categories. While a "preferential option for the poor" may indeed be admirable, Tinker argues that Native peoples seek liberation not as "poor" individuals or even as a class of workers or peasants but rather as "national communities with discrete cultures, discrete languages, discrete value systems, and our own governments and territories."[29] In a word, Christianity imposes frameworks, worldviews, and structures of authority that, according to many Native critics, are not only different from Native traditions but incommensurable and destructive.

Terrible Ironies? Syncretic and Anti-colonial Possibilities

While there are good reasons to focus on these critiques that foreground the violence of missionaries and the tensions between Christianity and Indigenous worldviews, there are surprising and even anti-colonial dynamics that can emerge in religious interactions. Jace Weaver (Cherokee) notes that Tinker's account of missionary violence, though important, has the unintended drawback of minimizing the agency of Native peoples. In Tinker's understanding of missionary conquest, "Indians are not actors but are merely acted upon; they are not self-determined but are rather selves determined."[30] Interestingly, Weaver points to the example of S. Hall Young and his experience in Alaska. Beyond noting the disturbing elements of the heroic missionary narrative, Weaver reveals how the hagiographic view of the missionary's work obscures the fact that by the time Young arrived in Alaska, Native Alaskan communities were already literate, multilingual, "already Christian and theologically astute. In fact, the Aleuts had been sending their own missionaries to other tribes for generations."[31] There is, of course, a separate conversation one could have about Native people participating in Christian conversion, but what is clear from the historical record is that Indigenous people were not simply passive bystanders or hapless victims.

Indeed, for centuries Native peoples have been doing much more than unthinkingly reproducing European forms. Even in the most difficult and violent situations, Christian ideas and stories have been used for Native purposes and transformed by Native voices. Weaver, for example, notes that Christian hymns were sung on the Trail of Tears and other unexpected places. On December 26, 1862, in the aftermath of the US-Dakota War, thirty-eight Dakota men were led to the gallows to be hanged. As they awaited their fate in what would be the largest mass execution in US history, they sang the Christian hymn "Many and Great, O God" in the Dakota language. These examples may seem tragic, perhaps even further proof that Christianity is historically and hopelessly entangled with the destructive forces of colonialism. And yet, such a reading risks missing important parts of the story and minimizing the agency of Native peoples who have embraced Christianity for varied reasons. Native peoples have appropriated and adapted Christian forms for the purpose of Native survival, operating within a space that a Lakota nun described as the "terrible irony" of being Native and Christian.[32]

Tinker suggests that Native religious traditions and practices should be treated as their own forms of "old testament" faiths rather than be abandoned in favor of Christian practices. While Tinker advances this idea as a normative prescription for revalorizing Native traditions, this might also serve as an empirical description of what often happens as Native peoples combine various forms of religious ceremony and beliefs. Tinker himself notes the importance of the syncretic forms of Andean practices that take center stage during Carnival, when the "devils" or "tíos" of the underworld mines come to the surface for a few days and restore balance to the world.[33] Many scholars have observed (and debated) the myriad ways Native peoples have transformed Christian ideas.[34] Weaver recalls Warrior's advice to read Christianity with "Canaanite eyes," but rather than see this as a way to foreground conquest in the Christian stories, Weaver suggests that Native readers often "locate themselves and their perceptual experience in the story." He provides various Native rearticulations of Christianity:

> They report relating to Moses trudging up Sinai to meet the divine as one about to embark on a vision quest. They recognize Mary, the mother of Jesus, because she is *la Virgen de Guadalupe*, or White Buffalo Calf Woman, or Corn Mother, or *La llorona*, refusing to be consoled at the death of her child. They can chuckle knowingly at the exploits of Jacob because he is the trickster familiar to them as Coyote, or Raven, or Istomin. This is not the hermeneutics of the professional exegetes. Rather, it is the folk theology upon which Christianity at the ground level has always thrived as a living faith.[35]

On a more political and sociological level, religious institutions have often had an infrastructural power crucial to Indigenous social movements across the Americas. While one can agree with Tinker's critique of the philosophical terms of liberation theology, throughout the Andes and Meso-America, liberation theology and its related practices of community education and capacity building have been instrumental to radical and revolutionary movements like the Zapatista uprising in Chiapas and the "levantamientos" of Indigenous communities in what is today Bolivia, Ecuador, and Peru.[36] In Chimborazo, Ecuador, Catholic and evangelical Indigenous communities created their own political organizations that had different philosophies and goals but embraced both Christian and Native identities. The first intercultural bilingual education programs in the Andes were created by missionaries, and whatever their faults (and there were many), they helped strengthen thriving Indigenous linguistic communities that had access to print material, radio stations, and other forms of what we would now call information and communication technology. For example, the "popular radio schools" of Monseñor Leonidas Proaño, one of Ecuador's more famous liberation theologians, gave Kichwa communities in the 1960s the ability and capacity to transmit their own stories, music, and programming to address their own concerns and projects. While a revolutionary left-wing government began a program of agrarian reform in the 1960s, the radio schools arguably were just as important in breaking up the hegemony of the non-Indigenous landed elites who enforced a feudal system well into the twentieth century.[37] To put the point more broadly, Christianity can be both the language of domination *and* also the foundation for revolutionary change. This idea is captured powerfully in another part of the world, in the words of Zimbabwean nationalist Ndabaningi Sithole: "Europeans took our country, we fought them with our spears, but they defeated us because they had better weapons. But lo! The missionary came in time and laid explosives under colonialism. The Bible is now doing what we could not do with our spears."[38] Religion is not always anti-colonial dynamite, but neither is it always the opiate of the masses. Like so much of social life, it is complicated.

Sisseton Wahpeton Oyate scholar Kim TallBear recounts her own childhood on a Dakota reservation, encountering kind, "syncretic Presbyterians," Dakota ministers who gave sermons and sang hymns in the Dakota language and participated in Sun Dance ceremonies. "That's the kind of world I grew up in . . . and you kind of chose whether you wanted to go to ceremony or church. Some people do both. . . . Growing up in that kind of syncretic world . . . I was taught there are multiple ways to the Creator."[39] These complexities do not make these experiences any "less" Indigenous. On the contrary, they help us understand how Indigenous realities themselves are made up of innumerable tensions, contradictions, and possibilities.

Final Thoughts

Mike Wilson, in his own way, viewed the stained glass windows at the Stewart Memorial Chapel with "Canaanite eyes." He saw a clear and present history of violence, but he also located it within his own realities and relations. He came face to face with the horrible history of missionary violence in California and decided to leave seminary. Yet, as is fitting given the complex relationship between Native peoples and the church, Mike's exit from seminary led toward a new encounter with a religious community and a new sense of calling.

As we prepare to follow Mike's path back into the desert in the next chapter, I would like to conclude with a powerful poem by Hopi and Miwok poet Wendy Rose called "Excavation at Santa Barbara Mission."[40] The speaker of the poem is an archaeologist on a dig in Santa Barbara who finds human remains in the walls of an old mission. This poem is based on an actual excavation in 1977, perhaps something Rose learned about as she earned a PhD in anthropology at the University of California, Berkeley.

The poem begins with the speaker providing a description of the work and the thrill of discovery and even imagining herself as a Mission Indian:

> How excited I am
> for like a dream
> I wanted to count myself
> among the ancient dead
> as a faithful neophyte.

Then with the discoveries of marrow, fingerbones, and pieces of skull, her tone shifts from excitement to horror. She sees

> [s]o many bones
> mixed with the blood
> from my own knuckles.

The setting of this archaeological work becomes a long arc of historical violence:

> Beneath the flags
> of three invaders
> I am a hungry scientist
> sustaining myself
> with bones of
> men and women asleep in the wall.

The lyrical description of this work abruptly yields to a bracing final stanza:

> They built the mission with dead Indians.
> They built the mission with dead Indians.
> They built the mission with dead Indians.
> They built the mission with dead Indians.

Tony, This is the actual size of the demonic face/mask of the Alaska Native shaman. I traced this sketch from the S. Hall Young window that was removed from the Stewart Memorial Chapel at the San Francisco Theological Seminary. I made this sketch before I left SFTS in the spring of 2001.

Mike Wilson
14 June 2022

FIGURE 12. Mike Wilson's tracing of Stewart Memorial Chapel window. Photograph by Mike Wilson.

Deborah Miranda, a fellow Native California poet, observes, "This stanza stands on the page, in shape and intention, like an adobe brick."[41] We do indeed seem to hit that wall of final and unspeakable violence.

And yet, along the way we find a history and reality that is more layered and textured than the brute fact of apocalypse. Interestingly, that word, "apocalypse," comes from the Greek word ἀποκαλύπτειν, which means "to uncover, disclose."[42] Rose's poem functions as an archaeology of apocalypse, revealing at least two important horizons. First, there is a key point about the multiple intersecting identities that characterize Native peoples, illustrated by the changing voice of the speaker of the poem and perhaps even the poet herself, who speaks as an anthropologist, artist, Catholic, poet, and Native woman. Second, the form and style of the poem suggest an important lesson about the shapes that knowledge and culture take in Indian Country. The abrupt change in style may not be just one from lyricism to a brick wall of pain but a move from Western verse to Native song. Laura E. Donaldson proposes the following reading: "The ending's fourfold refrain—one repetition for each of the four sacred directions—also affirms the nascent identity and transformed epistemology of the narrator. Most American Indian songs make meaning through repetitive structures of intensification rather than Euro-American rhyme or meter schemes. These repetitions often have an entrancing effect and help to induce a holistic state of consciousness within the singer and her audience." Building on the work of Paula Gunn Allen, Donaldson reads this formal change in the last stanza of the poem as a recognition that "only a direct confrontation of colonization and its consequences allows any healing to emerge from such catastrophe." The poem's final stanza may actually be "a chant" that "works to inculcate within readers/listeners a deep integration of its disturbing message even as it administers a curative for Santa Barbara Mission's abyssal truths."[43]

Before he left San Francisco Theological Seminary, Mike had to examine the "abyssal truth" of missionary violence two last times: once with two Native elders from the area, one of whom left her medicine bundle as protection, and once to ask the Cherokee maintenance worker who had removed the nave window for the opportunity to sketch the outlines of the face of the "demonic" Native who stood in the path of the "inspiring story of the Presbyterian Church in the West."[44] Mike took the sketch back with him to the desert, where another landscape of death would provide him one more path to follow.

Chapter 5

Ministry in the Desert

Life and Death on the Border

MIKE WILSON

After seminary, I first came back to Tucson then to Sells where I worked as a lay pastor on the Tohono O'odham Nation (TON) for a year. I'd preach every Sunday, visit the hospital, and do family counseling and community work. Even though I am not in the church anymore, some people still call me "Pastor Mike."

I enjoyed living in Sells. Many people there knew my mother and father. Some were related to my father, so I had a lot of kin out there that I didn't know I had. Even members of my congregation were related to me. I was very comfortable; I had a salary and a house, called a manse, provided by the church. My work was challenging both spiritually and intellectually. I liked it. I would start writing my Sunday sermons on Tuesday nights. For me, that reflection, study, and writing were intellectually rigorous.

Prior to my arrival in Sells in September 2001, I had been an active volunteer with Humane Borders in Tucson. Humane Borders is a faith-based humanitarian organization whose mission is to maintain water stations along known migrant corridors in southern Arizona. Upon my move to Sells, my humanitarian efforts were redirected to the reservation. It didn't take a theologian to understand that I had a moral responsibility to respond to the migrant deaths and suffering on the Nation. Where death and suffering were occurring, that's where I needed to put water. I soon realized that my water ministry was in conflict with my church, but I knew what my priority was. I had to put out water.

The Deadly Costs of "Prevention through Deterrence"

To understand why there was so much death, we have to go back to the 1990s along the border, specifically 1994. Remember the militarization of the border in the San Diego and El Paso areas? It was about the same time as the start of the North American Free Trade Agreement. Of course, there was a relationship between NAFTA and migrant deaths! The Clinton administration and Congress knew that NAFTA was coming in 1994. There is documentary evidence that Immigration and Naturalization Service, the predecessor of Immigration and Customs Enforcement, knew that NAFTA was going to displace millions of subsistence farmers in Central America and southern Mexico.[1] The INS *knew* it was going to happen. And where were these displaced agrarian workers going to go for work? They were going to come north into the United States. Massive displacement *was expected* in INS strategic planning. As a result, the agency had to prepare for increased border enforcement. Under NAFTA, subsidized American grain exports, specifically corn, would replace the corn grown by campesinos, subsistence farmers. They could not compete with the heavily subsidized American grains that flooded their market. Even though the United States was responsible for displacing millions of farmers, we didn't want them coming here.

That's when the militarization began. It was a selective, proactive strategy to meet the expected "onslaught" of immigration that the US government helped create. The beefed-up military presence of Operation Hold the Line (1993) in El Paso, Operation Gatekeeper (1994) in San Diego, and other similar operations at other urban ports of entry channeled the migration flow into what the INS euphemistically referred to as "the western desert." It just so happens that part of the western desert in Arizona encompasses my tribal land, the Tohono O'odham Reservation. Through this policy of "prevention through deterrence," a migration corridor was created through the Tohono O'odham Reservation, by design! By the time I arrived in Sells, the Tohono O'odham Police Department estimated that *1,500 migrants* were crossing tribal lands *daily*.

Were we ever consulted? When in the *history* of the United States were we, as Indigenous people, ever consulted? Never! Since 1492, when have European colonizers asked *us*, "Well, what do you think?" And today no one was saying, "Don't you think it's a great idea that the US government is forcing migration through your tribal lands?"

That migrant you see in the documentary film *Crossing Arizona*, the one I helped on the side of the road, he was trying to get to Phoenix.[2] He had traveled from the southern Mexican state of Guerrero. He asked me, "How much further to Phoenix?" His coyote had told his group that Phoenix was only a couple of hours' walk once they crossed the border. He asked me again: "How many more hours do I have to walk to get to Phoenix?" From the Mexican border to where I met him, he had only walked seventeen miles, in three days! It is approximately 140 miles from the border to Phoenix. Seventeen miles in three days! And now he's asking me, how many more hours to walk to Phoenix?

I told him, "Días, mi hermano, días. No horas. Days, my brother, days, not hours. I cannot give you enough water for you to make it." I finally convinced him. "Walk out to the highway, my brother, and turn yourself in to the Border Patrol. Because if you walk north, you *will* die by the end of the day."

I saw what little dirty water he had left. He was down to the last drops in that one-gallon jug. He had no food. Now he had no water, and he was separated from his group and his coyote. The evening before, the Border Patrol had pursued his group with a Blackhawk helicopter.[3] The Blackhawk hovered over them in a tactic called "dusting." The downward blast of the rotor blades created such a violent dust storm on the ground that it panicked, blinded, and disoriented the group until they scattered and ran. Border Patrol agents, on the ground in vehicular or mounted patrols, would apprehend them one by one. This was why he was walking down the road, alone and scared. I finally convinced him not to keep going.

He said, "I will walk to the highway, because if I walk north, I will die." With tears in his eyes, he continued, "I don't mind dying. Because I know that if I die, I will die trying to feed my children. Which is worse? For me to walk north and die *trying* to feed them or for me to go back to Mexico and watch my three children starve to death in front of my eyes? My wife also needs surgery. I need money to pay for that." *This* was his dilemma. This is the migrants' dilemma, *still.* Do you die trying, or do you go back and watch your children die? This was the reality I was finding on the Nation.

Let me tell you about a migrant tragedy that an O'odham friend of mine shared with me. She was a member of the Baptist church in Sells. She said that one day there was a dead migrant at the back door of her church. He had crawled there and died for lack of water. Migrants were literally dying in our backyards. And nobody was doing anything to prevent their suffering and deaths, not the Nation's government, not any of the eleven district councils, not the hospital, not law enforcement, and not the churches. Nobody! And all around us migrants were dying. And everybody knew it. But nobody talked about it; nobody tried to prevent it. So that was the situation for my one year as a lay pastor at the Papago United Presbyterian Church.

Water Ministry

Many border crossers, like my brother from Guerrero, were lied to by their coyotes. They did not know how far they had to walk or how many gallons of water they had to drink per day to survive. We had that discussion at one of the early Humane Borders meetings I attended, probably late 2001. We were trying to make a medical assessment of how many gallons of water migrants needed, not per day but per hour. That was how meticulous our discussions were. Migrants were living hour by hour when it was 117 degrees. That was part of our calculations at Humane Borders, and it became part of my metrics when I started putting water out. Not understanding how much water they needed to carry to survive or the brutality of the unforgiving heat, not understanding the magnitude of the desert, migrants were walking themselves into death traps. *Nobody deserves to die in the desert for lack of a cup of water.* Crossing the desert should not carry a death sentence. God's children were dying in the Baboquivari Valley, this valley of death, within several miles of my church.

In the spring of 2002, I started putting out water in clusters of twenty-five to thirty-five one-gallon jugs along cattle trails that I knew the migrants were following. I determined the sites for my water stations after driving east on Baboquivari Mountain Road. I could see cattle trails strewn with dozens of empty plastic jugs, so I knew migrants were using those trails. That was my humanitarian aid work for twelve years. It was my ministry. And then my ministry came in conflict with church policy and tribal politics. By politics, I mean not only the main tribal government but also two of the eleven legislative districts within the Nation, the Sells and the Baboquivari Districts. The Baboquivari Valley became known as "the deadliest migrant trail in the country." You can see this on the death maps created by Humane Borders.

Initially, Humane Borders maps were called "Water Station Maps." Over time, these maps were overtaken by red dots indicating Border Patrol GPS locations of "recovered human remains," so we started calling them "death maps." On these death maps, you could see the cluster of migrant deaths that took place immediately east and south of Sells.

Humane Borders had received permission from land managers in southern Arizona to set up water stations in their jurisdictions. Those included the federal Bureau of Land Management, Pima County, the City of Tucson, and private property landowners. Humane Borders sought permission to put water out on the Nation. Reverend Robin Hoover, the head of the organization at the time, went to the Chukut Kuk District Council to request permission. According to Robin, he was kept waiting in the hall for four hours. When he was finally allowed entry, the council members spoke only O'odham among themselves and then told him in English that the district had denied Humane Borders' request. When Robin came back with that news, that was the catalyst for my water ministry. If Humane Borders can't do this, as a tribal member, I will!

Within months of my starting to put out water, I met resistance directly from the Baboquivari District Council. In June of 2002, the council passed the resolution "Disapproving the Placement of Water Stations and Water Jugs within Baboquivari District." I have a copy of the resolution from the district where I am an enrolled member.[4] I thought the resolution was anti-migrant, anti–human rights, and un-Christian. In spite of the resolution, I continued to put out water.

The Resistance from the Nation

I remember once traveling to service my four water stations in the Baboquivari District. I was driving east on Baboquivari Mountain Road through the Baboquivari Valley. I was heading toward my water stations, which I had christened Saint Matthew, Saint Mark, Saint Luke, and Saint John, after the Gospels.

As I walked to Saint John's, my last stop, I saw that the district council had posted two documents: a No Trespassing sign and a copy of the resolution! This was along the deadliest migrant trail in the United States! No one ever confronted me in person, but the sign and paper were placed in a very conspicuous location where they were clearly intended for me. The message was, "Tribal member, you cannot trespass!" Of course, the district cannot tell me I can't trespass. I'm an enrolled member of the Tohono O'odham Nation and can walk freely anywhere on the reservation. I didn't accept that any of the district councils had the legal authority to arbitrarily prohibit me from going anywhere on the reservation, and they certainly did not have the moral authority to prevent me from saving lives.

I've been asking myself this question for years: Do district resolutions have the legal authority of law? Because if resolutions are based on solid legal grounds, then they must show what laws are being violated and what the punishments are for violating each law. There were none cited. That made me question and disregard the validity of the resolution. The council was threatening me, but the threat was capricious, vindictive, and toothless. It was an administrative fig leaf to cover the stench of dead bodies.

Josue's Story

Let me tell the story of Josue Oliva, a child of God and a Honduran migrant whose remains we found in the Baboquivari District, northwest of my Saint John water station in 2011. On September 9, 2011, I was contacted by the Honduran consulate in Phoenix about a Honduran migrant who had been left behind on the Nation. I learned that Josue had been traveling with his brother and a group of migrants and a coyote. Soon after they crossed the border, he was struggling. Heavy-set, he was not in great shape, and his brother tried to convince him that they should turn themselves in to the Border Patrol. Josue would not listen. He was determined to get back to Oklahoma City, where his wife, Bethsebe, and two children were living. He never made it.

A woman in his group survived and eventually made it to Phoenix. She had the telephone number for Josue's wife. She called Bethsebe to say that the group had left Josue on a hilltop somewhere on the reservation. The group stopped to rest on the hill, and Josue started convulsing and vomiting. As he convulsed on the ground, the group formed a circle around him and prayed. After Josue died, this woman told Bethsebe that she closed his eyes with her fingers. Bethsebe, however, did not believe that her husband was dead. Her mother, whom Bethsebe considered a "prophet," kept telling Bethsebe that Josue had died but that God resurrected him, and he was waiting to be found in a cueva, a cave. Like Lazarus, whom Christ resurrected from the dead, Josue's ministry would be to tell the world of God's salvation.

Bethsebe and her sister-in-law, Elizabeth, drove overnight from Oklahoma City to the Honduran consulate in Phoenix to ask for help. When I spoke with the consulate, I was told that Bethsebe and Elizabeth were on their way to Tucson and would be staying at a hotel by Interstate 10. I had good working relationships with the Honduran, Salvadoran, and Guatemalan consulates. I told the consulate official, "Please call her and tell her that I am on my way to the hotel." By the time I got there, they were already in their room. I invited them to stay at Susan's and my house, because I knew a search would take a few days. They accepted my offer and came to stay with us.

Bethsebe's belief that her husband was alive gave her hope. Her hope was strong, but sadly, it was a false hope given to her by her mother. I didn't believe it, but I had to respect it. I told her that I would not give her false hope, but as long as she was in our house, Susan and I were here to support her.

Bethsebe was born in Miami, where her family had immigrated to from Venezuela. Bethsebe and Josue met and married in Miami and then moved to Oklahoma City, where they started a family. She told me how Josue got deported. He was in a car accident. He was not responsible for the accident but stayed at the scene and waited for the police, who asked him for his immigration documentation. He did not have any, so he was arrested and deported back to San Pedro Sula, Honduras. Soon, he began his journey back to Oklahoma City.

I called my friend Daniel,[5] a tribal member, for help. Daniel, Bethsebe, Elizabeth, and I drove to the Baboquivari District Council office to ask for permission to conduct a search for Josue. It just so happened that the council was meeting that day. They not only gave us permission, but some of the community members volunteered to help. I knew one of the volunteers, and I suspect she helped us get permission from the council. Now we could start the search.

I asked Bethsebe where she thought Josue's group had crossed the border. She said it was in the vicinity of El Bohio, Sonora, west of Topawa Road. That was my starting point. Knowing they were moving north from El Bohio, I estimated how far the group could have walked in two days. This goes back to my military training. In Special Forces, you live and die by your map-reading skills. I planned this search the same way I would have planned a military mission, and on the first day of the search, Sunday, September 11, we searched west of Topawa Road approximately seventeen miles north of the border. As we were walking on that first day, we saw migrants on the side of a hill. I think we startled them, and they ran north.

Here is something else I will remember until my last breath. It was hot, and we'd been searching for four hours. I said "Let's gather, drink some water, find some shade. I am calling it for the day." We were so tired, we just plopped down on the ground in the shade of a palo verde tree. I was sitting next to Elizabeth. At the same moment, she and I happened to see something behind her. She said in a calm voice, "Is that what I think it is?" It was a rattlesnake coiled, four feet behind us. We carefully moved away. The snake was doing what any wise reptile would do, resting in the shade. I vividly remember those migrants running and that coiled rattlesnake. That was how we ended the search on that first day.

On Monday night, September 12, after another long day of searching, Bethsebe was talking to the coyote again, pleading for more information. To our surprise, he sent to her phone a GPS map with pin coordinates of where Josue's body was left behind, and it also included another pin location nearby labeled "la parrilla"—Spanish for "grill." Susan, my partner, looked up the coordinates online and found they were in the Baboquivari District of the Tohono O'odham Nation. Finally, after two exhausting days of searching, we now had a map in hand that would lead us to Josue.

Before leaving the next morning from our home in Tucson, Susan pulled up the GPS coordinates and photo and showed the image to Daniel, who said, "I know where that's at." Pointing to the pin, he said, "That's a cattle guard." From the satellite photo, it does looks like a grill, "la parrilla." Daniel knew the exact location of the cattle guard.

That was September 13, 2011. We drove in our convoy, located la parrilla, and parked nearby. We walked in single file, with Daniel leading the way. I wanted him to be the one to find Josue. He agreed and went ahead.

We made it to the hilltop closest to la parrilla where I thought we would find Josue. Nothing was there. I was confused. This was the spot on the map. After looking at the map several times, it dawned on me. The GPS map did not show the contours of the surrounding terrain. As I looked north, I saw another hilltop. We were on the wrong hill!

Pointing north, I told Daniel, "He's on that hilltop. Stay way ahead of us. You go first, and I'll bring the rest of us slowly behind you." We headed for that hill and quickly lost Daniel in the mesquite. We got into the flatland when I heard his anguished voice, "Mike! Over here. Just you." Everyone heard Daniel. I told everyone to freeze. "Nobody comes forward!"

By that time, Josue's brother, Gerardo, Elizabeth's husband, had joined us. He had flown in from Oklahoma City the night before. I told the group—Josue's wife, brother, and sister-in-law and volunteers—"Do not follow me." They all stayed. I put Gerardo in charge. I had been deployed several times to Honduras, so I was able to establish a rapport with him quickly. I called him "catracho," which is how Hondurans affectionately refer to each other. "Catracho, quédate aquí, stay here."

I walked to the top of the hill and caught up with Daniel. He was standing with a very solemn look on his face. He pointed up the hill and said, "I think that's him." I was almost at the top of the hill. I didn't see Josue yet, but I found a white tennis shoe. I was afraid that there was a human foot in it. I moved it; it was empty. I didn't want the group to see anything like that. I had a backpack with me, with a blue tarp in it. I knew we would need it.

There was a sense of fear and foreboding that set in my heart. I didn't want to see what I knew I was going to find. I had flashbacks to El Salvador. Remember those dead child soldiers in El Salvador? Those children with gaping holes in their chests—with no hearts or lungs. That image came back to me. I felt fear, anger, and revulsion.

As I walked closer, I saw something black on the ground, a black mass. I knew it was Josue. The closer I got to him, the more my fear dissolved. My next thought was of my own son, Joseph, who's about Josue's age and also has a young family. I felt a transformation, a sense of calm, peace. I thought, *What if this were my son?* Wouldn't I want the person who found him to show him as much love as he would show his own child? I stepped into what I can only call an aura of grace, a sacred bubble. My fear, revulsion, and anger dissipated from one footstep to the next as I walked toward Josue. It was as if a host of angels, facing outward, had surrounded us in a circle, touching wingtip to wingtip. They allowed me entry into their bubble of grace. That is how sacred that moment felt. My revulsion left me. That was the grace I felt as I approached. That moment, however, didn't last. The pungent smell of death broke the bubble.

I reached this blackened mass of clothing, flesh, and exposed bone. Daniel and I brought out the tarp, covered Josue, and put rocks around the edges of the tarp so it wouldn't blow away. I prayed for him and his family. I went back to the group and told them, "We found somebody; we don't know if it's Josue." I told the group to remain where they were, and I took Gerardo to the hilltop. When we got to the body, I pulled back the tarp, revealing just the lower half of the legs. He was lying on his stomach. Gerardo said Josue had had surgery on his right knee and that a surgical pin had been left in. He asked us to turn him

FIGURE 13. Josue and Bethsebe's family photograph. Bethsebe gave this photograph to Mike Wilson. With her permission, it was later used by Humane Borders to tell the story of the human consequences of border policies.

over so he could look for the pin to confirm this was his brother. I told him, "I would rather not. Forensics will identify him. Because you are family, your responsibility is to go back and comfort Bethsebe and Elizabeth." I covered him back up. Gerado went back down the hill and returned with the group. An O'odham search volunteer called the Tohono O'odham Police Department (TOPD). That was the protocol. They arrived and put up yellow tape, marking the area as a crime scene. We stepped back. The investigative team took photographs of some articles of clothing: shoes and a belt buckle. That buckle was very distinctive. When they showed the photo of the buckle to Bethsebe, she said yes, that was his. The whole time we were standing on this windy hilltop, surrounded by the stench of death, emotionally drained.

Bethsebe gave me a photo of the family. I still have it. You can see a proud father, an adoring mother, two angelic children on their laps. They are all wearing white T-shirts. It is a picture of an immigrant family on their way to the American dream. This is the family portrait that they would send back home, as if to say, "We are not there yet, but are on our way. And here is proof."

Because of my deployments to Latin America, I knew the poverty they were escaping. The lash of the pharaoh, extreme poverty.

The TOPD placed the remains in a body bag and then secured it on the back of a motorized cart, like a militarized golf cart. I went with the driver riding on the passenger side. I wanted to accompany Josue on his last journey. We returned to our vehicles and followed the TOPD back to Sells, where a deputy sheriff from Pima County transferred the remains to the medical examiner's office in Tucson.

The week he died, the temperature had probably reached 110 degrees in the Baboquivari Valley. How dare anyone tell me I can't "trespass" and put out water? And to return to where we started, Josue Oliva died just a few miles from 100 gallons of water at my Saint John water station.

And why did I name my stations after the four Gospels? Well, that has a history too. They were initially just numbered 1, 2, 3, and 4, from west to east. At each site, I had two blue 50-gallon barrels, side by side. They were mounted on steel frames and had blue stickers that read "AGUA." These were provided by Humane Borders. Hundreds of gallons of water were either stolen or sabotaged numerous times from each of the four sites. A total of 400 gallons destroyed or confiscated! I suspected that it was the tribal police or local ranchers. I replaced them all at least once. By the third time, I christened the water stations Saints Matthew, Mark, Luke, and John. My thinking was that if I baptized them in the name of the Father, the Son, and the Holy Spirit, maybe the tribal police or local ranchers might be hesitant to remove them. I wanted them to have a sense of moral guilt, something that might prevent them from committing a desecration, a crime against humanity.

It didn't work, though. When I returned the following week, the barrels again were completely gone. I went back to putting one-gallon bottles of water on the ground, this time in the shape of a cross. I placed anywhere from twelve to twenty-five gallons, depending on how many I had with me in the bed of my truck. The cross was for approaching migrants. My worry was that they would avoid a cluster of water, suspicious of a Border Patrol entrapment. My thought was that if I put water out in the shape of a cross, the migrants, who were probably Roman Catholics, would see the cross and feel safe in taking the water. My reasoning was both practical and pious. It did not make up for what was lost, but I just could not keep replacing the barrels after they were repeatedly confiscated or destroyed. Some had bullet holes in them, while others were drained after the valves were broken or left open so the water would spill

FIGURE 14. Water station in the Sonoran Desert.
Photograph by Alejandra Platt.

on the ground. So, I decided to leave gallons of the water on the ground, even though those gallons jugs were often destroyed too—slashed, punctured, or run over by a vehicle.

The opposition by the Baboquivari District Council had been consistent. The resolution against me putting out water in the Baboquivari Valley was signed in June 2002. At the time, I was the only Presbyterian lay pastor on the reservation. I served the main church in Sells and three other chapels in San Miguel, Topawa, and Santa Rosa.

This is where the political intrigue came in. The Baboquivari District Council chairman sent the resolution with a cover letter to my church in Sells. The Presbyterian Church (USA) is a very democratic institution. Every local church is self-governing; it doesn't need the permission or approval of any higher church body to hire or fire its pastor. As part of church governance, there's a monthly meeting of the church council, called the session. The elected members of the session are called elders. The session, working with the pastor, determines policy.

The Resistance of the Session

I need to explain how the monthly session meetings were run. As the pastor, I set the agenda and moderated the meetings. Included in the agenda was the Pastor's Report of the work that I had done for the previous month. It could have included visiting the sick and dying in the Sells hospital, giving sermons, and in general the pastoral duties performed. I told the session, and I was honest from the start, that I was putting out water for migrants in the Baboquivari Valley and along Ajo Road. The valley was a main migrant corridor, and we all knew that migrants were dying within a few miles of Sells. I told the session that I drove my truck out there and retrieved the empty and discarded one-gallon jugs. If they were serviceable and passed the smell test, I put them in garbage bags, threw them in the back of my truck, and returned to the church manse (house). At the manse, I rinsed them out and stored them in the shed until I had a truckload. I would then refill, recap, and return them to the water stations. At the time, I had as many as ten stations. I had been telling the session about my water ministry because I wanted the congregation, session, and community to know exactly what I was doing. I knew that it was controversial.

After a couple months I was asked by an elder at a session meeting, "Pastor, why are you aiding and abetting migrants? They're wetbacks. As our pastor, you should be a role model." In essence, he was saying that I should be modeling blind obedience to all tribal, state, and federal laws. For him (and probably the rest of the session), undocumented migrants were criminals. "Pastor, how can you do that?"

My response to his accusation of "aiding and abetting" was clear. "Session, I don't like saying it, but I must concede one point. I agree that because they come undocumented and are not coming through official Ports of Entry, they are breaking US immigration laws. However, if I have to decide between two sets of conflicting laws, one being US immigration law and the other a higher, moral, and universal law, *which you and I call God's law*, as your pastor, which law must I follow? As your pastor, I have no choice here. Which one am I bound to obey? Church, which one must I answer to?"

Well, the elders just looked away or down at their shoes. These were life-long church members—third- and fourth-generation Presbyterians. They had been Presbyterians decades longer than I had been. I told them: *Is God concerned with inhumane laws or more concerned with universal justice? I wish that I could do both. I wish that I could agree with you and honor federal immigration laws, but when people are suffering and dying—if I may sound preachy,*

Presbyterians—when God's people are dying in the desert, when our sisters and brothers in Christ are dying within five miles from here, there's only one law I must obey.

I told the session that I would continue to put out water not only in the Baboquivari District but, with the aid of the Humane Borders "death map," wherever migrants were dying. Well, by the time the next session met, the Baboquivari District Council chairman had sent the resolution and a cover letter to the session. The chairman sent it to the clerk of session (secretary), who was his niece. She and her mother were on the session. The clerk introduced the letter and resolution for discussion and a vote. There was a unanimous vote to uphold the resolution prohibiting me from putting water out. In response, I said, "I will continue to do God's work." I knew, as a matter of conscience, I would have to leave.

Maybe I should have stuck around and gone through the Inquisition and let them burn me at the stake. I was so disgusted. I told the session, "I don't know who you are, but you deceived me when you hired me. You deceived me because you led me to believe that this is a Presbyterian church, but it is not. I don't know who you are. I don't think *you* know who you are. You don't know if you're Assemblies of God. You don't know if you're Nazarenes. You don't know if you're Baptists. You don't know if you're Roman Catholics.[6] You don't know who you are, but you are certainly not Christians because Christians would not threaten to fire their pastor for doing God's will."

My biblical justification for putting out water was the Gospel of Matthew, 25:34–46. There, Christ tells his disciples, "I was hungry, and you gave me food. I was imprisoned and you visited me. I was sick and you looked after me. I was thirsty and you gave me water." And then, the disciples asked Christ, "When were you imprisoned that we visited you? When were you naked that we clothed you? When were you thirsty that we gave you water? We don't remember this!" His response to them was, "As you have done for the least among you, you have done unto me." I asked the session that night, "How many times had I preached that lesson? Those who walk in the desert, the least among us, are the most deserving of food and water. Elders, Christ walks with them, and he suffers with them. He walks to the barrels and drinks from those barrels marked 'AGUA.' That's why I put out water. Presbyterians, what don't you understand?"

Absolute silence.

Absolute silence, but silence is not a neutral position. Silence speaks volumes. Silence screams injustice. That's how I knew that I had to leave. I couldn't stay. I had a conversation with one of my church members shortly after this. She came over to the manse and we were having coffee at the kitchen table, where we were talking about the viability of the church. I told her that my biggest responsibility as the pastor was to save this dying church. Across the table she looked straight into my eyes and said, "Mike, this is not a dying church; this is a dead church." Somebody else had to tell me a truth I already knew. She hit the nail on the head. You cannot save or revive a dead church. The session's unanimous vote to prohibit me from putting out water was the church's own death certificate. I too would have been spiritually dead if I had stayed.

I think I had known that the church was dead even before. When I first arrived in Sells, I was active in cofounding the Tohono O'odham Domestic Violence Coalition. The session was even against my participating in that! Over the previous few years, seven O'odham women on and off the reservation had been beaten or shot to death by their male partners. My former academic liaison was one of those women murdered. When I was attending UT San Antonio, I was getting financial aid from my tribe. The woman who had processed all of my financial assistance paperwork and sent me my checks had been beaten to death with a baseball bat. That was the level of domestic violence. Her partner's brother shot another tribal member in Tucson with a shotgun. She and her two-year-old ran into the bathroom and locked the door. He fired through the door and killed them both. This was the level of domestic violence against O'odham women. There was a desperate need for a domestic violence coalition, and the session was objecting to my participation in it, let alone my being a coalition leader.[7]

An elder said it was none of the church's business. He said, "We don't do that. We don't have that problem," meaning that we Presbyterians are not abusers and that I didn't need to be involved. And this was the same session that voted unanimously, 9 to 0, to prevent me from putting out water on the Nation. I reflected on my friend's wise counsel: "Mike, it's a dead church."

Social Justice and Human Rights Work

Let me clarify one point. When I started putting out water on the Nation, I was acting strictly as a humanitarian aid worker. I had no concept of "human rights." I was just putting out water. It was my Christian duty to put out water for those crossing the desert. It was only within the past couple of years that I've come to realize that I am doing something bigger than providing humanitarian aid.

I am doing human rights work. My work is water, water justice. For me, this is a quantum leap, because now when I speak about water justice it is within the framework of universal human rights. It is no longer parochial work. My water justice is for Mother Earth, not only for southern Arizona. Water justice and water ministry became one and the same.

Recently, I went to an open forum at the University of Arizona's law school. James Anaya, the UN Special Rapporteur for Indigenous rights was present. For two days, Anaya listened to an unbroken narrative of victimization and historical trauma presented by Indigenous audience members. We talked about these traumas in relationship to the United Nations Declaration on the Rights of Indigenous Peoples. Indigenous peoples throughout the world use this document to advocate for their rights.

By the second day, I had a question for Anaya:

> Let me reverse this narrative and ask, What if we Indigenous people are now the human rights violators? My own Tohono O'odham Nation is committing crimes against humanity in several ways. (1) One of its districts has passed a resolution prohibiting me from putting out water in its district. (2) My water stations have been confiscated, sabotaged, and destroyed by the Tohono O'odham Police Department. And (3), the Nation has ignored the hundreds of migrant deaths on the reservation. I believe the Tohono O'odham Nation must be held morally accountable by this same UN Declaration. This Declaration that we are now claiming goes both ways. We have become paralyzed by our own sense of victimhood, even now, when Indigenous people are dying on Indigenous lands. We who were once the oppressed are now the oppressors.

That's what I wanted James Anaya to understand. This Declaration holds us fully and *equally* accountable. It does not just protect us or exempt us but holds us universally accountable for human rights violations.

I put water in the desert for twelve years. My work was and is human rights. I also think that one of my responsibilities is to point out the moral hypocrisy of some of those on the political left in Tucson. I'm a persona non grata in my own social justice community. I am talking about liberal activists. I ask them, "Why do you hold the United States Border Patrol morally and criminally responsible for thousands of migrant deaths in the Sonoran Desert and yet you do not hold the government of the Tohono O'odham Nation equally responsible when at least 50 percent of these deaths are on tribal lands? This is moral hypocrisy on your part. You seem to think that in your benevolent silence, you find a safe and neutral position."

Silence is not a neutral, safe position. Silence is not a sanctuary. Silence is a position. Not only does your silence not prevent suffering and death, but it also guarantees more suffering and death, certainly on the Nation. You're not willing to challenge the Nation or yourselves. That you don't hold the Nation responsible is an admission that you are morally derelict. In a democracy, we cannot have a dual, selective system of justice, one for white America and one for Native America. There's only one universal moral code. You can't treat the Nation as "less than" or hold it to a lower moral code. You cannot pontificate against the United States Border Patrol and not hold the Nation equally responsible for migrant deaths.

Let me tell a story that demonstrates this hypocrisy. I got a call from a young woman who said she was a volunteer with No More Deaths in Tucson and wanted to meet with me. We met at a coffee shop. She showed up with two other young women. They were sincere and cordial. The woman who called me said, "We want to ask you to come with us on the Baboquivari Mountain trail. We've been hearing stories that the migrants are walking the mountain trail to evade the Border Patrol. They're following the summit of the Baboquivari range, and they're coming north. We want to investigate those trails for future water drops because there are none."

"Well, where do I come in?" I asked.

"You know that the Baboquivari trail is a reservation boundary line—to the west is the Tohono O'odham Nation, and to the east are state, county, and private properties. So, if we're walking on this migrant trail and take one step to the left, we're in Tohono O'odham country."

I said, "Yeah, I know."

"Well, the leadership of No More Deaths doesn't want us going on the Nation to put out water drops."

I replied, "But that's where at least 50 percent of the migrants are dying. The mission of No More Deaths is to put out water in the desert to prevent migrant deaths; that is where you have to go."

"Well, we can't do that. Because the leadership of No More Deaths will get mad at us."

I thought to myself, *You know what? This is the tip of the revolutionary spear, these young anarchists, these young self-described revolutionaries, doing volunteer work for this social justice group that calls itself No More Deaths.* I wanted to ask the three of them, "What beer do you drink? Wait, wait, don't tell me—Anarchist Lite?"

This is social justice? Not only does white America not hold Native people morally accountable, but it also stoops to an apologist narrative that says, "Oh well, you can't criticize them because, you know, look what we've done to them." There's this sense of white privilege that allows these volunteers to grant a moral exemption to Native peoples. I find that attitude paternalistic and racist.

As John Fife, one of the founders of No More Deaths, has said publicly, "The Tohono O'odham don't need white people telling them what to do." I agree. However, which is a higher priority? Risk offending tribal and cultural sensitivities, or fulfilling No More Death's mission statement to prevent migrant deaths in the desert? That's the question. I go with saving human lives: men, women, and children. Saving lives trumps sovereignty. Although John and I disagree, we're still friends.

The Paradoxes of Sovereignty

But what about tribal sovereignty? Indeed, there is this myth of Native sovereignty. What we *claim* is absolute sovereignty, yet in reality what we *have* is limited sovereignty. I am always asked, "Mike, why is the Border Patrol on your reservation? I thought the Tohono O'odham Nation is sovereign." I explain that federally recognized tribal lands—reservations—are first and foremost federal trust lands granted by the US Congress. Therefore, we are dependent upon Congress to honor and maintain our limited sovereignty. Because the US Border Patrol is a federal law enforcement agency, it has senior law enforcement jurisdiction over all other law enforcement agencies on federal lands, including tribal. In essence, what we have is an army of occupation by the US Border Patrol in Indian Country. Its presence on the Nation denies and makes a mockery of our claim of sovereignty. This is not just limited to the Tohono O'odham Nation; it is a warning to every federally recognized tribe.

Don't get me wrong. This is O'odham land. As a Tohono O'odham, I will never concede that this land ever was or is Aztlán.[8] Because if I acknowledge that, what am I agreeing to? Do I accept Chicano imperialism—the notion of "You name it, you claim it"? You name it Aztlán; therefore you claim it as your own. What does that make me? A subject of Aztlán? Not a citizen, but a subject in my own Native land? In O'odham land? No, no, no, no. Never.

I don't put out water anymore. With a Mexican drug cartel in control south of the border and the militarization by the Border Patrol north of the border, large numbers of migrants were no longer coming through the Baboquivari Valley. Several years later, my partner, now wife, Susan, and I provided overnight shelter to asylum families. We hosted nearly 200 men, women, and children in our home under the auspices of Catholic Community Services of Southern Arizona. The youngest was four days old. She and her mother stayed with us for twelve days. When I see the refugees on television crossing the Mediterranean Ocean, I see those same faces that were in our home. It's the same suffering, the same pharaoh that they're running from, the pharaoh of extreme poverty.

Part of a Greater Story

I am one part of a greater story, the telling of the border tragedy. That tragedy must be a national and global story. It cannot be provincial. We are not moving the needle on immigration reform. The greater immigration debate is dominated by the opposition. I see my role as an educator, a public speaker. I have been in at least five documentaries and two feature films. Has any of that moved the needle? Hopefully, my work has not been in vain. Maybe ten years from now, someone will say, "Mike, the work you did, the young people you spoke to, well, it made a difference." I recently ran into a former student of mine from City High School, Andrés Cano. He is now a representative in the Arizona State Legislature. At our Pima County Democratic Party precinct meeting, he said, "I learned my social justice from Mike Wilson." That meant a lot.

My religiosity is shallow, but my faith is deep. Churchgoing, ritualized churchgoing, is religiosity. It's like the Christmas tree tinsel. It's what we wear on the outside for people to see and admire. It's how we bring attention to ourselves. So, I'm not into religiosity. I'm reminded of that every time I go to a Catholic funeral mass. I see the solemn religiosity of the mass. It is a beautiful ceremony, and society needs ceremonies. I focus on the Logos, the "word of God," which often gets lost in the pageantry. So, am I a practicing Christian? I'll let my work speak for itself.

INTERLUDE 5

Between Sanctuary and Sovereignty

JOSÉ ANTONIO LUCERO

As we come to the end of this work, let's return to the beginning. Before I had ever met Mike, I saw him in the 2005 documentary *Walking the Line*. I screen this often in my courses as I find it an excellent film about the complexities of borders. Additionally, as the filmmakers were still undergraduate students when they made it, the documentary provides my students with a good example of what they can do with a little time, technology, and care. The main focus of the documentary is the armed vigilantes patrolling the border who say they are there to protect the United States from an immigrant "invasion." The film, however, also casts a spotlight on the community members who come not with guns and intolerance but with water and compassion, people like Pastor John Fife and Mike Wilson. While the film does not describe the connections between Wilson and Fife, it is fitting that they are the two figures in the documentary who seek to change the conversation about border crossing from one of invasion and security to sanctuary and human rights. Mike's own account in this book reveals important connections between him and John Fife. For the purpose of this final analytical interlude, those connections serve to reveal the historical relationships between US foreign policy, faith-based social movements, and an increasingly deadly US approach to migration flows. It also shows the complex role of religion in activism that takes place at the intersections of sanctuary and sovereignty.

Sanctuary Movements: Old and New

Sanctuary is a very old idea and can be found in many religious traditions and geographic locations.[1] However, when we speak of the "sanctuary movement" as a social response to the crisis of Central America refugee flows, it has a very specific origin story. It began in Tucson, Arizona, and was first proclaimed on March 24, 1982—the second anniversary of the assassination of Archbishop Óscar Romero—by the members of South-side Presbyterian Church, led by John Fife. The story of the sanctuary movement has been told by many scholars and journalists, but it is essential to retell it, even in broad strokes.[2]

The story usually begins with Jim Corbett, a Quaker who was rais-ing goats in southern Arizona. Corbett was told by his Quaker friend Jim Dudley that the Border Patrol had just pulled Dudley over after he had picked up a Salvadoran hitchhiker on a desert road. The Salvadoran man, named Nelson, begged Dudley for help and told him that if he were deported to El Salvador he would be killed by US-funded death squads as part of a deadly counterinsurgency strategy. Dudley did not know what to do as the Border Patrol took Nelson away. When Dudley told Corbett, a brilliant nonconformist with a graduate degree from Harvard, Corbett decided to look into the matter. He found some local legal aid and learned how to begin the bureaucratic process to halt Nelson's deportation and, along the way, raised bail for other Salvadoran migrants he encountered in the deportation machine. Despite weeks of detective work and completion of all the legal steps to secure Nelson's release while his asylum case could be considered, Border Patrol agents ignored US and international laws and deported Nelson back to El Salvador. Cor-bett was enraged by this act and learned that this was hardly an accident. US immigration officials had systematically discriminated against Central

American asylum seekers. One immigration official told Corbett that this discrimination was a response to pressure coming from the State Department. It would make the United States look bad if it granted asylum to people fleeing governments that the US government was supporting with billions of dollars of military assistance. Beyond the optics, accepting the asylum claims of Central American refugees would have legal and political implications, as it would reveal that the administration was in violation of the Foreign Assistance Act of 1961 that forbids US funding of any foreign government that "engages in a consistent pattern of gross violations of internationally recognized human rights."[3] The statistics were revealing. Between 1983 and 1986, the United States had granted asylum to only 2.6 percent of Salvadoran applicants and 0.9 percent of Guatemalans. In contrast, during the same period the United States granted asylum to 60.4 percent of Iranians, 51 percent of Romanians, and 37.7 percent of Afghan asylum seekers.[4]

As I write these lines, a similar dynamic is unfolding as Ukrainian asylum seekers speed through a process that has kept Haitians, Central Americans, and other asylum seekers waiting in crowded camps on the Mexican side of the border. A political cartoon makes the geopolitical point clear: as a Central American family of migrants pass a sign that reads "El Norte," the mother says to the father, "At the border, tell them we're Ukrainian."[5] Then and now, geopolitics—not international law or morality—shapes and breaks US asylum policy.

Enraged by this reality in the 1980s, Corbett began working with other like-minded people in various religious communities to create a network of support for asylum seekers, many of whom Corbett himself was bringing across the border. He reached out to John Fife for help with the practical matter of where to house the growing number of Central Americans. Fife had already been an outspoken critic of US foreign policy and took the question to his church and its session. The elders of the church voted overwhelmingly to offer sanctuary, and Southside Presbyterian became the first church in the United States to officially declare itself a sanctuary for Central Americans. At the high point of the 1980s sanctuary movement, it had grown to a decentralized network of around 70,000 activists across the United States and Canada, involving over 500 churches, temples, and synagogues.[6]

As the movement acted in open defiance of US immigration policies, the government was quick to respond. It launched a covert domestic surveillance program called Operation Sojourner that, among other things, placed undercover agents and paid informants in various congregations. In 1985, the government indicted several of the activists; eleven faced trials. Looking back over the decades, John Fife recalls how the judge gave instruction to the defense attorneys that there could be no mention of religion, human rights, refugee law, international law, or conditions in Central America. With little choice, the defense opted not to present its case, but the defendants had multiple conversations with reporters outside of the courtroom for the duration of the trial, a period of seven months. The jury, inevitably, found this group of nuns, priests, pastors, and religious activists guilty of breaking the law. The judge, under extraordinary political pressure from the United States and abroad, made what he probably thought was a Solomonic ruling: the defendants would receive probation for five years if they signed a statement saying that they would stop their sanctuary work. Sister Darlene Nicgorski, a Catholic nun, was the first to be sentenced. According to Fife, she told the judge, "Judge, we have been here a long time, and you haven't listened, so listen now. If you let me out of this courtroom, I am going right back and doing sanctuary for Central Americans. I have to. It's my faith." Visibly upset, the judge removed the condition of giving up sanctuary and gave all the defendants five years of probation.[7]

In his own sentencing statement, Fife made the case strongly: "Good citizenship requires that we disobey laws or officials whenever they mandate the violation of human rights. A government agency that commits crimes against humanity forfeits its claims to legitimacy. . . . Sanctuary depends . . . on the capacity of the human spirit to respond to suffering."[8] Much more could be said about the sanctuary movement in the 1980s and its remarkable victories, including getting the United States to halt deportation of Central American asylum seekers and the creation of a Temporary Protective Status designation for asylum seekers.[9] However, for now we might notice that the language of the sanctuary movement is strikingly similar to the arguments Mike would make two decades later in conflicts with his own tribal government and church, when a new sanctuary movement emerged in the twenty-first century to take on a new set of immigration policies. The unanimous support that John Fife got from his church's session, or governing council, contrasts with the unanimous vote of Mike's session against his "water ministry."

Between Sanctuary and Sovereignty

The early aughts, when Mike was a Presbyterian lay pastor on the Nation, saw a significant rise in border crossings largely by Central American and Mexican migrants who had been funneled through the desert by aggressive Border Patrol policing that became known as "prevention through deterrence." Building on the "success" of operations with names like "Hold the Line" and "Gatekeeper" that blockaded urban points of crossing like El Paso/Juárez and San Diego/Tijuana, these measures intentionally forced migrants to cross through the "hostile terrain" of the Chihuahuan and Sonoran Deserts. A macabre metric of the success of that policy was a spike in migrant deaths.[10] A mapping project coordinated by Humane Borders found forensic evidence of 3,937 migrant deaths between October 1999 and July 2021 in the Sonoran Desert, the majority of the human remains were found on the officially demarcated lands of the Tohono O'odham Nation.[11] Wilson saw it as his duty to do something about it. For the next twelve years, he created and sustained, almost single-handedly, a series of water stations. As a tribal member, Wilson believed he had the authority to maintain these water stations, which had previously been requested by Humane Borders, a request that had been turned down.

The water stations were controversial because they were seen as encouraging more crossing. At the peak of migration, approximately 1,500 desperate migrants could cross tribal lands in a single day.[12] As migrants were often hungry, thirsty, and desperate, break-ins were not uncommon. Adding to the worries on the reservation, drug cartels also took advantage of the opportunity to create smuggling operations on Native lands. This created a serious challenge for a tribal government that did not have the resources to manage the security and humanitarian disasters that came with these flows. Understandably, the tribal government reached out to the US federal government for assistance. This resulted in a greater presence of US Border Patrol on the reservation, something that, according to press reports, was and remains controversial on the Nation.[13] Wilson was among the tribal members who disagreed with the increased Border Patrol presence and militarization. He also objected to the lack of respect for the lives of migrants, spurring him to create and maintain several water stations on reservation lands.

While Wilson argued that he had the legal status to put water out on tribal lands, he did not have the approval of his government or church.

Eventually, he was forced to resign his position at the church and move off of the reservation to Tucson. He continued his water ministry there for eleven more years and gained attention from journalists, scholars, and filmmakers (his work is featured in at least six documentaries so far, with others in the works).[14]

It is not my place to evaluate the internal conflicts on the Nation. Clearly, there has been a significant amount of media attention on this tribe at the epicenter of border wall controversies and conflicts over what to do with the migrants dying on tribal land. I offer no secondary analysis on the question of whether one should side with Wilson's call for water justice or the Nation's defense of its sovereignty. Nevertheless, it is an illustrative example of what the feminist philosopher Greta Gaard describes as tension between "ethical context" (here, the framework of Native sovereignty) and "ethical content" (the policy decisions that the Nation makes within that framework).[15]

More broadly, these controversies invite us to consider, even if we cannot fully explore, just how fraught and complex the history and idea of "sovereignty" is. While at first blush it seems to be simply another way of thinking about self-governance or self-determination, "sovereignty" has posed a challenge to politics from the very start. Vine Deloria Jr. explains that this "ancient idea" was originally a theological term "appropriated by European thinkers" to characterize the power of the king to wage war and govern over domestic affairs.[16] Long after the era of the divine right of kings had passed, the theological roots of the term remained strong as Catholic and Protestant churches shaped the theories of the "law of nations" and "civil government." For many canonical European political theorists, "civility was evidenced by the existence of reason, social contract, agriculture, property, technology, Christianity, monogamy, and/or the structure and operations of statehood." On this view, Joanne Barker (Lenape) explains, "Nations possessed the full measure of sovereignty because they were the highest form of civilization; individuals roaming uncultivated lands did not possess either civilization or sovereignty."[17] Within the context of so-called discovery and conquest, "civilization" required a "savage" other.

In the history of Native relations with the United States, sovereignty acquires its own particular complexities and contradictions. The US Declaration of Independence called out Native peoples as "merciless Indian savages," but the "founding fathers" nevertheless saw the "savages" to be sovereign "enough" for the sake of signing treaties that ceded land to the US government. As Indigenous nations lost land and were relocated to reservations, they continued to occupy a strange, liminal position in the US system, something the Supreme Court famously defined in 1831 as "domestic dependent nations."[18]

This is a long and strange history of the power of legal fictions. The central fiction that was (and remains) a foundation for US approaches to Native nations is the so-called doctrine of discovery. Chief Justice John Marshall wrote in *Johnson v. McIntosh* (1823), "Discovery is the foundation of title, in European nations, and this overlooks all proprietary rights in the natives. . . . Even if it should be admitted that the Indians were originally an independent people, they have ceased to be so."[19] Relying on the English philosopher John Locke's view of private property, Marshall told the story of Native peoples who used and roamed the land but did not make productive, agricultural use of it, as the settlers did. Thus, while Native peoples were on the lands first, they were not, legally speaking, the sovereign owners of it. The fact that most parts of this story are wrong did not prevent it from being ideally suited to the goals of Manifest Destiny and empire. It also injected a foundational ambivalence into US legal approaches that would see Native peoples as self-governing nations *and* "wards" of the federal government, as permanent units of the US polity *and* destined to disappear. These early moments of confusion and contradictions about the status of Native people led to some radical swings in US policy. Vine Deloria Jr. and Clifford M. Lytle suggest the following historical periods:

- discovery, conquest, and treaty-making (1532–1828)

- removal and relocation (1828–87)

- allotment and assimilation (1887–1928)

- reorganization and self-government (1928–45)

- termination (1945–61)

- self-determination (1961–present)[20]

Native peoples have been nations to conquer, populations to resettle, racialized others to civilize, subnational units to administer, dependent relations to be ended, and self-determined subjects with their own futures. The tricky thing about this useful chronology, however, is that the past haunts the present. Even though tribes live in the era of self-determination, sovereignty is an elusive thing within the settler regimes of the United States, Canada, and beyond.

Scholars in Indigenous studies have had serious discussions and debates over the meaning and utility of the concept of sovereignty. Mohawk political philosopher Taiaiake Alfred offers an influential Native critique of "sovereignty" as irredeemably Western, an idea so contaminated by non-Indigenous forces and thinking that it should be abandoned in favor of specific Native traditions. Taking a slightly different tack, Joanne Barker suggests that we should not throw out sovereignty altogether but instead understand that it has always been "historically contingent"—embedded in Native peoples' "multiple and contradictory political perspectives and agendas for empowerment, decolonization, and social justice."[21] A third view, summarized well by J. Kēhaulani Kauanui (Kanaka Maoli), suggests that "we must theorize Indigenous sovereignties and how they distinctly differ from Western sovereignty." She cites the work of Goenpul scholar Aileen Moreton-Robinson as an illustration of this view in the Aboriginal Australian context. Moreton-Robinson argues that unlike Western models of social contracts and centralized authority, "our sovereignty is embodied, it is ontological (our being) and epistemological (our way of knowing), and it is grounded within the complex relations derived from the intersubstantiation of ancestral beings, humans, and land."[22]

Rather than choose only one of these formulations—outright rejection, historical contingency, or Indigenous multiplicity—we might instead embrace ambivalence. In doing so, we enter what Kevin Bruyneel describes as the "third space of sovereignty": "Indigenous political actors work across American spatial and temporal boundaries, demanding rights and resources from the liberal democratic settler-state while also challenging the imposition of colonial rule on their lives. This resistance engenders what I call a 'third space of sovereignty' that resides neither simply inside nor outside the American political system but rather exists on these very boundaries, exposing both the practices and the contingencies of American colonial rule."[23] This is not a space of agreement or consensus but a zone in which Native peoples debate, discuss, and disagree over matters that are of importance to their Nation and survival. In the particular case examined in this book, however, the tragedy is that this contestation coexists with the gruesome desert deaths of migrants, many of whom are Native people themselves, on their own journeys, to whom this "third space" offers little comfort.

Some Conclusions, on Coast Salish Lands

The history of the sanctuary movement in the 1980s was about ordinary people telling their government that its policies were unjust. It reemerged in the aughts with organizations like Humane Borders, No More Deaths, and Samaritans; it once again sought to provide relief to the border cross- ers and critique US immigration policy. John Fife was a central figure in both the old and new sanctuary movements. Yet, Mike Wilson observes, Fife was silent as Mike performed his own kind of prophetic protest against his Nation's practices. Native sovereignty served as a limit for sanctuary work. Mike recalls Fife's silence that night and does not con- demn it: "As non-O'odham he wanted to keep out of it. And rightly so."

As a non-tribal member myself, I will keep out of it too. While by now it is clear that I think Mike's story is one that should be heard, I would say the same about all of the voices coming from the tribe, many of which are increasingly finding media platforms.[24] Rather than comment on the O'odham context, I would like to (briefly) share another example, one that has been covered in my local news, of the friction between social justice and tribal sovereignty. This one concerns the Duwamish Tribe and their so-far unsuccessful efforts to gain federal recognition.[25]

Seattle is one of the few major cities in the United States named after a Native person, Chief Si'ahl ("Seattle" is the anglicized version of his name). Chief Si'ahl was a leader from both the Suquamish and Duwamish peoples and was a signatory to the Treaty of Point Elliott, which ceded great amounts of Coast Salish lands to the settlers. In return, the tribes were promised fishing and hunting rights—rights that they would have to demand over and over well into the twentieth century. Through this and subsequent treaties, various reservations were created for Native peoples of the region. In some cases, the reservations were for a par- ticular people like the Suquamish, but in other cases, like the Muckle- shoot, which was originally the name of a prairie, various related Coast Salish tribes came together to form a new federally recognized entity. Meanwhile, a growing settler population was burning down and clearing forests, draining rivers, and in many ways creating unprecedented ecological destruction.

Duwamish tribal members faced a difficult decision. Snohomish historian Josh Reid describes the dilemma well: "Do you follow those kinship connections and take up citizenship at Lummi, at Tulalip, at Muckleshoot, or do we stay here and try to eke out an existence and hope eventually to get a reservation? Those are the devil's bargain decisions families are making, that is how different Duwamish families ended up at these different tribal nations, while others stayed here, . . . trying to make it as Duwamish in the greater Seattle area."[26] Some Duwamish members, including direct descendants of Chief Si'ahl, organized in 1925 as the Duwamish Tribal Organization (DTO). The federal government, however, has denied the request for recognition based on the finding that the Duwamish have not demonstrated that the tribe has been "identified as an American Indian entity on a substantially continuous basis since 1900."[27]

In recent years, the cause of federal recognition has been taken up by many social justice groups in Seattle. The official website of the DTO, duwamishtribe.org, urges people to support federal recognition and sign an online petition (with over 100,000 signatures as of June 8, 2022). Additionally, one can contribute to the online fundraising campaign, Real Rent Duwamish, launched in 2017 by non-Indian volunteers, which today counts 20,000 contributors. Contributions to the DTO have grown since Real Rent began and topped $1.5 million in fiscal year 2019.

Other tribes like the Muckleshoot and Suquamish, tribes that include Duwamish descendants among their official members, see the DTO move as nothing less than cultural appropriation. "It's such a catchy narrative especially if you are coming from a point of believing in social justice and doing the right thing: 'This poor beleaguered tribe, they were left without,'" said Donny Stevenson, vice chairman of the Muckleshoot Indian Tribe. "It is a far more complicated story than that." Tribal leaders note that Duwamish descendants enrolled in other tribes, like Muckleshoot or Suquamish, do indeed have federal recognition by virtue of being members of those tribes. Others note that federal recognition of a new tribe will likely bring new gaming enterprises that could compete with existing tribal enterprises. There are real questions about who gains and who loses. Historian Josh Reid summarizes these concerns: If the Duwamish do win their case for federal recognition, where is that reservation going to be, what happens when they begin to pursue economic development, and what cost will there be to the others? He concludes, "It's part of the colonial system that pits us against each other, and that is why it appears to be such an ugly situation."[28]

Reid's observation is the crucial takeaway. While one could take sides for or against the various positions taken by Duwamish (or any tribe's) leaders or their critics, the fundamental issue is that settler colonialism has shaped the very conditions of possibility for all of us. To paraphrase Audre Lorde, we have to think again about what is possible with the "master's tools."[29] The struggles discussed in this chapter reveal that decolonial futures must be shaped in ways unbounded by settler constraints. Border policies, federal recognition, and other elements of the US political system have incredible impacts, yet they should not serve as the horizons for our collective lives or the ways in which relations of care and reciprocity can be made.

With this in mind, it is striking to note that once Mike stopped the physically taxing work of maintaining water stations in the Sonoran Desert, he and his wife, Susan Ruff, began to practice their humanitarian work in a different way, hosting approximately 200 Central American, Mexican, and South Asian refugees in their Tucson home over several years. Along with this quiet work of sanctuary, Mike continues to work with filmmakers, journalists, and scholars who want to take a closer look at the effects of federal border policies. And he remains in contact with O'odham relatives and social justice community leaders, despite disagreements with many of them. In other words, he has found many ways to continue the conversation about sanctuary and sovereignty in both the intimacy of his home and in the unpredictable reach of multiple films. This may seem an unusual accomplishment for someone who appears to have a pattern of rather dramatic departures from multiple communities, like the Presbyterian church, the theological seminary, and the Tohono O'odham Nation. Rather than stay, he opts for exit. Or does he?

Late in his career, the legendary social scientist Albert O. Hirschman reconsidered his famous thesis that in the face of organizational decline, people choose either "voice" (to protest and try to change the organization) or "exit" (to cut one's losses and leave).[30] In one of his last books, Hirschman opens with an essay (appropriately enough, on migration) in which he suggests that the "voice and exit" options were and are not mutually exclusive: exit itself can be a kind of voice.

This, I think, is the case for Mike. Indeed, Mike never really leaves quietly! Each of his "exits" has constituted a dramatic performance of voice. Through the withdrawals from each of his communities, Mike made public calls for others to see the injustice that he saw. Each exit represented a border-crossing act that itself called attention to the costs and the legitimacy of boundaries and their exclusions. Moreover, in speaking with Mike, one gets the sense that he never completely left any of his communities or commitments. In many ways, he is still "Pastor Mike," he is a proud US Army veteran, and he will never stop being O'odham. He continues to speak and act from all of his experiences, identities, and relations. As Mike says, "Life is a journey. Nothing is black or white."

Epilogue

Who Killed Raymond Mattia?

MIKE WILSON AND JOSÉ ANTONIO LUCERO

RAYMOND MATTIA

23–1802

MEDICAL EXAMINER REPORT

PIMA COUNTY, ARIZONA

TOHONO O'ODHAM POLICE DEPARTMENT

AGENCY CASE # 230518045 MAY 19, 2023

According to investigative information, this 58-year-old man was shot by United States Border Patrol agent(s) at his residence. Death was pronounced at the scene. . . .

In consideration of the known circumstances surrounding this death, the available medical history, and the examination of the remains, the cause of death is gunshot wounds.

The manner of death is homicide.

—Paige A. Peterson, M.D., Medical Examiner, June 14, 2023

The 58-year-old was killed in a hail of gunfire last month, after stepping outside to find nearly a dozen Border Patrol agents and at least one tribal police officer advancing on his property in the dark. Late last week, a tensely awaited medical examiner's report ruled the case a homicide, finding that Mattia was shot nine times. Border Patrol body camera footage released at the same time confirmed that what the authorities thought was a gun was in fact Mattia's cellphone.

—Ryan Devereaux, *The Intercept*

As we finished this book, we got the terrible news about the shooting of Raymond Mattia. According to multiple reports[1] and body camera footage released by Customs and Border Protection, the Tohono O'odham Police Department had received a call saying that shots had been fired near Mattia's home; TOPD reached out to US Border Patrol to request assistance. Agents from the Ajo Border Patrol station came to Mattia's house. Border Patrol agents ordered Mattia to take his hands out of his pockets. He complied, took his hands out, one of which was holding his cell phone. Roughly thirty-one seconds later, he was shot multiple times and died steps from his front door.[2]

In this tragic event one can hear echoes of the death of another O'odham man, Phillip Celaya, at the hands of a Pima County sheriff, a death Mike protested decades ago. This death also reminds us of the growing list of lives lost to the violence of policing, militarization, and racism in the United States and beyond.

Mike Wilson on the Death of Raymond Mattia: Say His Name

Who Killed Raymond Mattia?
It was fear who bought the bullets.
It was racism who loaded the gun.
It was hatred who pulled the trigger.

The question is not what happened to Raymond Mattia. The paramount question is *why* was he killed?

The militarization of the Tohono O'odham Nation makes it a de facto war zone. There is no practical oversight. There is no transparency or accountability. The US Border Patrol writes its own rules of engagement. Victims like Raymond Mattia are collateral damage.

Mattia's killing was not a solitary, isolated act of state violence against people of color. It was and is evidence of the Border Patrol's history of human rights abuses on the Nation. Tohono O'odham citizens live in fear of the Border Patrol, America's largest law enforcement agency. Fear is necessary for the emergence of a police state.

What does this say about our sovereignty? What is the relationship between the Tohono O'odham Police Department and the US Border Patrol? Is the TOPD subordinate to the USBP? Is the Tohono O'odham Nation subordinate to the Department of Homeland Security? If the Border Patrol does have legal authority over the Tohono O'odham Nation, what does that say about our leadership's constant claim of sovereignty? We must ask, why is Border Patrol here? The test of sovereignty is this: Does the Tohono O'odham Nation have the right to expel the Border Patrol from the Nation's land? If the answer is "yes," then it has sovereignty. If the answer is "no," then it does not.

The Nation is the canary in the coal mine for Indian Country and the United States. The killing of Raymond is not just a local story. It is an example of the violence of militarization and policing. In many ways, the Nation is a microcosm of the larger threat of a police state. Of course, it is not the only place where we can see evidence of this clear and present danger.

Not long ago, I was in Minneapolis. Three activists, a Chicano brother and two Native sisters, took me to visit and pay my respects at the George Floyd Memorial. I did not imagine that just a week later Raymond Mattia would be martyred as George Floyd was. Now we have one more name to add to the list of those unjustly killed at the hands of police—a list that has already grown too long.

Say his name, Raymond Mattia!

José Antonio Lucero: Native Death and US Policy

Though we traveled for different reasons and at different times, like Mike I found myself in Minneapolis as we worked to finish this book. While in the city, I went with a group of Indigenous academic colleagues and students to the George Floyd Memorial. I, too, see clear connections between Raymond Mattia's killing and the murder of George Floyd.

When I heard the news of Mattia's death, it also reminded me of the death of another Native person on the border, a Q'eqchi' Maya girl named Jakelin Amei Rosmery Caal Maquín. Jakelin had turned seven just days before she died on December 8, 2018, from septic shock in a hospital in my hometown of El Paso, Texas. Jakelin was traveling with her father and surrendered to Border Patrol officers as they crossed through the Chihuahuan Desert into New Mexico. According to relatives, Jakelin's father had done all he could to stay in his country. But as statistics from the World Bank indicate, the Q'eqchi' people suffer from chronic malnutrition and are among the poorest people in Guatemala, which is among the poorest countries in the Americas.[3] Jakelin's father found no other way to provide for his family and decided to look for opportunity in the North.

I can clearly recall the day I learned of Jakelin's death. It shakes me now as it did then. She was the same age as our son. She died in the hospital in El Paso where my father had worked for decades as an emergency room technician. When she died, protests erupted quickly in El Paso and elsewhere as many charged negligence on the part of the US Border Patrol in getting Jakelin medical attention.

Writing about this child's tragic death, scholars Greg Grandin and Elizabeth Oglesby ask, "Who killed Jakelin?" They suggest an answer that demands reckoning with the consequences of militarized border policies that force migrants to cross through remote deserts, face inhumane conditions in immigrant detention centers, and contend with the long-term effects of US-backed policies that have displaced countless Mayan peoples. Their answer is simple, compelling, and relevant today. "Who killed Jakelin Caal Maquín? Decades of US policy did."[4]

Mike Wilson: Concluding Thoughts

As we compose these final lines and I talk with Tony about Texas, I am now thinking about Eagle Pass, Texas. The barriers that the governor of Texas has put in the waters of the Rio Grande, barriers with concertina wire, have already injured many migrants, including pregnant women and children.[5] Even some members of the US Border Patrol are saying that the Texas National Guard has gone too far.[6] Yet, this is a familiar story. This brutality against migrants and people of color is all too familiar; it is ongoing and escalating. Like Raymond Mattia, these victims whose hands and feet are cut by razor wire in the river are collateral damage. The Border Patrol has long acknowledged and accepted this. The Texas governor has now helped make this kind of cruelty into a successful conservative political strategy. Collateral damage is part of the strategy. It has become normalized. But it is not normal!

There is a pattern of human rights abuses, in particular in the Southwest, against people of color. I know we live in an imperfect democracy, but shouldn't we still try to make it a more perfect union? When violence and militarization are normalized and accepted, I fear for democracy.

And yet, I find myself optimistic—partly because we, Native peoples, are also part of this process, this experiment called democracy. We are First Nations, and we are also First Citizens. We can and must remind people of our shared rights and responsibilities under our Constitution. We can and must remind people that the arc of the moral universe, as Dr. King said, bends toward justice. We can and must keep moving toward the light.

Notes

INTRODUCTION

1. Levine and Van Soest, *Walking the Line*.

2. Levine and Van Soest, *Walking the Line*. To avoid reinforcing borders, we do not italicize words from non-English languages in this book.

3. "Hostile terrain" is the language of the US Border Patrol (USBP). In describing prevention through deterrence, a USBP policy document states, "The prediction is that with traditional entry and smuggling routes disrupted, illegal traffic will be deterred or forced over more *hostile* terrain, less suited for crossing and more suited for enforcement." USBP 1994, quoted in De León, *Land of Open Graves*, 3. De León provides excellent analysis of the consequence of this policy shift, as does Nevins, *Operation Gatekeeper and Beyond*.

4. De León notes that given the work of nonhuman actors like vultures and other scavengers, the number of border deaths is likely a significant *under*count. De León, *Land of Open Graves*. For a visual representation of the border deaths, see Humane Borders, "Migrants Deaths, Rescue Beacons, Water Stations 1999–2021," Humane Borders, accessed September 1, 2020, https://humaneborders.org/printable-maps-and-posters/.

5. The traditional homelands of the O'odham go far beyond the reservation's official boundaries. As the Tohono O'odham Hemajkam Rights Network notes, ancestral O'odham lands "span East to the San Pedro River, West to the Baja of Mexico, North to Phoenix and South to Hermosillo, Mexico. We are comprised of Five O'odham Sister Tribes, the Tohono O'odham to the South, the Akimel and Onk Akimel O'odham to the North (Phoenix /Casa Grande Area), Ak Chin O'odham to the Northwest and the Hia Ced O'odham to the West." Tohono O'odham Hemajkam Rights Network, accessed September 2, 2020, https://tohrn383.wordpress.com.

6. Perla Trevizo, "Tribes Seek to Join Immigration Reform Debate," *Arizona Daily Star*, June 14, 2013, https://tucson.com/news/local/border/tribes-seek-to-join-immigration-reform-debate/article_d4fe1980-46d4-5e90-b690-ce78c5453bf1.html.

7. See Miller, "How Border Patrol Occupied the Tohono O'odham Nation"; Molly Hennessy-Fisk, "Arizona Tribe Refuses Trump's Wall, but Agrees to Let Border Patrol Build Virtual Barrier," *Los Angeles Times*, May 9, 2019, www.latimes.com/nation/la-na-arizona-tribe-border-patrol-trump-wall-20190509-htmlstory.html; and Rivas, "Systematic System of

Destruction." For the Tohono O'odham government's official response to the border wall, see the Nation's website at www.tonation-nsn.gov/nowall/, accessed September 12, 2021.

8. For reasons of confidentiality, we use pseudonyms for tribal members on the reservation.

9. The following films are available: Levine and Van Soest, *Walking the Line*; DeVivo and Mathew, *Crossing Arizona*; MacMillan, *Man in the Maze*; Jimmerson, *Second Cooler*; and Van Leeuw, *The Wall*. One feature film is in production: *The Long Walk of Carlos Guerrero*. Wilson's work has also been covered by PBS NewsHour. See PBS NewsHour, "Tribe Divided over Providing Water to Illegal Migrants Crossing Indian Land."

10. Gramsci, "Study of Philosophy," 324.

11. Auyero, *Contentious Lives*. Unlike Auyero's work, in which he retains authorial control, our project is a coauthored work in which Mike Wilson is first author and has the final word on what goes in and what stays out.

12. *I, Rigoberta Menchú* is undeniably the most famous example of this genre and also emblematic of some of the controversies over the kind of knowledge that this form of story-telling represents. For more on those controversies, see Menchú, *I, Rigoberta Menchú*; Arias, *Rigoberta Menchú Controversy*; Tula and Stephen, *Hear My Testimony*; Barrios de Chúngura and Moema, *Let Me Speak!*; and Barnet, *Biography of a Runaway Slave*. For additional dis-cussion of the role of storytelling in various modes of Indigenous knowledge formation, see Archuleta, "'I Give You Back'"; Bird, "Indigenous Peoples' Life Stories"; Corntassel, Chaw-win-is, and T'lakwadzi, "Indigenous Storytelling, Truth-Telling, and Community Approaches to Reconciliation"; Goeman, *Mark My Words*; and Million, "Felt Theory."

13. As Mike, a former army paratrooper, joked as we revised these lines, "Tony, you hav-en't earned your airborne wings!" For thoughtful discussions on the dangers of "parachuting" social scientists and the importance and challenges of testimonio as a literary and political form, see Beverley, *Testimonio*; and Kohl and Farthing, "Navigating Narrative."

14. Cody Lestelle did the lion's share of the transcription work. Additional research assistance for the analytical interludes was provided by UW students Hannah Dolph, Marcus Johnson, Meghan Jones, and Manisha Jha. Manisha did "double duty," copyediting the entire manuscript. Julie Bush did an exemplary job with the final copyedits for UNC Press.

15. Tohono O'odham Code, Title 17, Chapter 8, Section 8102 Scope and Applicability, 2. This "research code" was enacted and codified as 17 Tohono O'odham Code, Chapter 8, by Resolution No. 13–165, effective May 23, 2013, Tohono O'odham Nation Research Code: Title 17 – Health and Safety, Chapter 8 – Research Code, www.tonation-nsn.gov /wp-content/uploads/2022/09/Title-17-Health-and-Safety-Chapter-8-Research-Code.

16. Personal communication, March 29, 2022. The IRB suggested to Wilson that he might be better served writing a single-authored autobiography. Mike Wilson, exercising his own intellectual sovereignty, strongly disagreed. In his reply to the IRB, Mike accused the board of attempted censorship.

17. Dunbar-Ortiz, *Not "A Nation of Immigrants."* Key works on the Tohono O'odham borders include Leza, *Divided Peoples*; Marak and Tuennerman, *At the Border of Empires*; and Cadava, "Borderlands of Modernity and Abandonment." Other important works on Native borders include Saldaña-Portillo, *Indian Given*; Simpson, *Mohawk Interruptus*; and Speed, *Incarcerated Stories*.

18. On "experience-near" and "experience-distant," see Geertz, *Local Knowledge*; for global treatments of settler colonialism and border imperialism, see Castellanos, "Introduction: Settler Colonialism in Latin America"; Singleton, "Not Our Borders"; Miller, *Border Patrol Nation*; Mezzadra and Neilson, *Border as Method*; and Walia, *Border and Rule*.

19. Among the crimes of King George III listed in the US Declaration of Independence: "He has excited domestic Insurrections amongst us, and has endeavoured to bring on the Inhabitants of our Frontiers, the merciless Indian Savages, whose known Rule of Warfare, is an undistinguished Destruction of all Ages, Sexes and Conditions." For a helpful overview, see Dunbar-Ortiz, *Indigenous Peoples' History of the United States*.

20. Walia, *Border and Rule*, xliv. See also De León, *Land of Open Graves*; Greg Grandin, *End of the Myth*; and Miller, *Empire of Borders*.

21. See Bruyneel, *Third Space of Sovereignty*; and Dennison, *Colonial Entanglement*.

22. Miranda, *Bad Indians*; G. Tinker, *Missionary Conquest*.

23. Hondagneu-Sotelo, *God's Heart Has No Borders*; A. Rose, *Showdown in the Sonoran Desert*; Brueggemann, *Prophetic Imagination*; Smith, *Disruptive Religion*. Chapter 5 examines this theme in more detail.

CHAPTER 1

1. For a short clip of a promotional video produced by the US Department of the Interior, "The CCC on Indian Reservations," see YouTube, accessed June 2, 2021, www.youtube.com /watch?v=JbKIPSdjlho&feature=emb_logo. The Indian Division of the CCC (or CCC-ID) has been characterized as part of the limited and often disappointing set of programs that were part of the "Indian New Deal." Vine Deloria Jr. once noted that, if nothing else, checks from the CCC-ID helped his people "climb from absolute deprivation to mere poverty." This is quoted by Eric Zimmer in his insightful reevaluation of the opportunities the CCC-ID provided for Indigenous agency. See Zimmer, "Building the Red Earth Nation." See also Morgan, "'Working' from the Margins."

2. Miscegenation laws were on the books in Arizona until 1962; Hardaway, "Unlawful Love."

3. We have been unable to find Mike's testimony on segregation in Ajo. However, we did find a transcript of the testimony Mike provided to a later hearing of the US Commission on Civil Rights in which he focused on the problems that American Indians were having with local law enforcement. According to research Mike was coordinating at the Papago Cultural Research Center, American Indians were arrested at "four or five times" the rate of whites. Mike asked for special attention into the killing of Phillip Celaya, an O'odham man killed by Pima County police. We will return to that story in the next chapter. For the testimony, see US Commission on Civil Rights, "Testimony," 133–48.

4. The artist Félix Lucero is identified in several sources as Native. SPACES, a preservation project, describes him as follows: "Felix Lucero was a self-taught Native American artist born in Trinidad, Colorado in 1895. Lucero was drafted into the army and fought in WWI in the trenches of France. As the story goes, he lay wounded and dying on the battle field [*sic*] when he started to pray and the Virgin Mary appeared to him. He pleaded with Mary to let him live and promised that as thanks for his life he would spend the rest of his days creating art devoted to the life of Christ." SPACES, accessed February 10, 2021, http://spacesarchives

.org/explore/search-the-online-collection/felix-lucero-garden-of-gethsemane/. According to another source, Lucero was a Mayo Indian. Griffith, *Hecho a Mano*. We will revisit the topic of sacred places in chapter 4.

5. Mike is probably right about this. See Barbier et al., "Effect of Heavy Metals on, and Handling by, the Kidney."

6. The University of Texas at El Paso began as the Texas State School of Mines and Metallurgy. As a tribute to this origin, the sports teams are known as the "Miners."

INTERLUDE 1

1. "Chicano" and "Mexican American" are, for many, synonymous. However, I list them separately because Chicano is a political identification, a position that rejects assimilation and foregrounds Indigenous ancestry and kinship. On the US side of the border, only a few of my cousins embrace Chicanx identities. Most elders in my family, on both sides of the border, would refer to themselves simply as Mexican.

2. As the city council debated the smokestacks' demolition, one local news outlet put El Paso's monumental achievement in this perspective: "The smokestacks, the tallest in the world when they were built, have been hailed for their height, which towers over the St. Louis Arch, the Seattle Space Needle and the Washington Monument." Curtis, "ASARCO Smokestacks Headed for Demolition."

3. Department of Ecology, State of Washington, "Tacoma Smelter Plume Project," Ecology .wa.gov, accessed February 1, 2021, https://ecology.wa.gov/Spills-Cleanup/Contamination -cleanup/Cleanup-sites/Tacoma-smelter; Riddle, "ASARCO Smokestack."

4. "Superfund" is the informal term used to refer the Comprehensive Environmental Response, Compensation and Liability Act (CERCLA), enacted in 1980. This act allows the EPA to clean up contaminated sites. It also forces the parties responsible for the contamination to either perform cleanups or reimburse the government for EPA-led cleanup work. See "What Is Superfund?," EPA, last updated November 1, 2022, www.epa.gov/superfund /what-superfund. Tacoma was one of the first Superfund sites. The El Paso remediation was part of ASARCO's bankruptcy proceeding. For more on Superfund sites in Tacoma and El Paso, see Department of Ecology, State of Washington, "Tacoma Smelter Plume—History & Studies," accessed February 1, 2021, https://ecology.wa.gov/Spills-Cleanup/Contamination -cleanup/Cleanup-sites/Tacoma-Smelter/History-studies; Burnett, "Toxic Century"; and Perales, *Smeltertown*.

5. The smelter is one part of the Superfund site, which also includes the former site of the Tacoma Tar Pits. For more on the connection between environmental racism and carceral capitalism, see Ybarra, "Site Fight!"; Nail, "Climate-Migration-Industrial Complex"; and Young, *Forever Prisoners*.

6. De León, *Land of Open Graves*.

7. Melamed, "Racial Capitalism," 77.

8. Guidotti-Hernandez, *Unspeakable Violence*, 131.

9. Kuhn, "Untold Arizona."

10. Melamed, "Racial Capitalism," 77, says,

Capital can only be capital when it is accumulating, and it can only accumulate by producing and moving through relations of severe inequality among human groups—capitalists with the means of production/workers without the means of subsistence, creditors/debtors, conquerors of land made property/the dispossessed and removed. These antinomies of accumulation require loss, disposability, and the unequal differentiation of human value, and racism enshrines the inequalities that capitalism requires. Most obviously, it does this by displacing the uneven life chances that are inescapably part of capitalist social relations onto fictions of differing human capacities, historically race. We often associate racial capitalism with the central features of white supremacist capitalist development, including slavery, colonialism, genocide, incarceration regimes, migrant exploitation, and contemporary racial warfare. Yet we also increasingly recognize that contemporary racial capitalism deploys liberal and multicultural terms of inclusion to value and devalue forms of humanity differentially to fit the needs of reigning state-capital orders.

11. Parkhurst, "Ajo Townsite Historic District," section 8, p. 14.

12. Rosaldo, "Imperialist Nostalgia."

13. Haraway, "Teddy Bear Patriarchy."

14. While not directly related to the Spanish-American War, the annexation of Hawai'i also took place at this same historical moment. As in other imperial moves, it represented a mix of economic, ideological, and political motivations. For an excellent account, see Silva, *Aloha Betrayed*.

15. Turner, *Significance of the Frontier in American History*; Grandin, *End of the Myth*.

16. Dan Nowicki, "Greenway's Heroics, Arizona Career Largely Forgotten," *The Republic*, February 11, 2015, www.azcentral.com/story/news/arizona/politics/2015/02/11/john-c-greenway-heroics-mining-career-largely-forgotten/23264813/.

17. McBride, "Bisbee Deportation in Words and Images."

18. McBride, "Bisbee Deportation in Words and Images," 66.

19. Parkhurst, "Ajo Townsite Historic District," section 8, p. 11.

20. Parkhurst, "Ajo Townsite Historic District," section 8, p. 11.

21. Ybarra, "Site Fight!," 4.

22. Ayres and Parkhurst, "Mining and Mining Towns in Southern Arizona," 77.

23. Ybarra, "Site Fight!"

24. Warren, "New Kind of Company Town."

25. For more on the "American Futures" project, see the City Makers: American Futures section on the *Atlantic*'s website, accessed February 1, 2021, www.theatlantic.com/projects/city-makers-american-futures/.

26. Fallows, "Ajo, Arizona, Is the Story of a Better America." There is a hyperlink in the original story to a promotional document put together by the Sonoran Desert Conference Center: https://static1.squarespace.com/static/569177ccd82d5eff6cbb5928/t/578c0c67d1758e37cc72176b/1468796008518/Ajo+Top+Ten+for+AOT.pdf, accessed June 2, 2021.

27. The story of art in Ajo is an interesting and important one. It has received a significant amount of media attention. See, for example, Sy, "Arizona Mining Town Reinvents Itself as an

Arts Destination." Interestingly, that profile makes no mention of the increasing presence of the Border Patrol in the town.

28. Chad Graham, "Border Agents Add New Life to Arizona Town," *Arizona Republic*, April 15, 2007, A1.

29. Quoted in Warren, "Across Papaguería," 415.

30. Warren, "Across Papaguería," 167–68.

31. US General Services Administration, "Final Environmental Assessment."

32. Warren, "Across Papaguería," 169.

33. See De León, *Land of Open Graves*; Warren, "Across Papaguería."

34. Morley Musick, "Meet the Boy Scouts of the Border Patrol," *The Nation*, February 3, 2021, 14, www.thenation.com/article/politics/scouts-border-immigration-trump/.

35. Associated Press, "Group Accusing US Border Patrol of Water Sabotage Sees Member Arrested," *The Guardian*, January 22, 2018. www.theguardian.com/us-news/2018/jan/22/arrest-no-more-deaths-border-patrol-water-sabotage-migrants.

36. Teo Armus, "After Helping Migrants in the Arizona Desert, an Activist Was Charged with a Felony. Now, He's Been Acquitted," *Washington Post*, November 21, 2019, www.washingtonpost.com/nation/2019/11/21/arizona-activist-scott-warren-acquitted-charges-helping-migrants-cross-border/.

37. Armus, "After Helping Migrants in the Desert."

CHAPTER 2

1. At the University of Arizona in Tucson, there is a plaza that honors important women from Arizona. Written by Virginia F. Holmes, the text for Ella Rumley recognizes her military service and especially her work for off-reservation O'odham: "Her community involvement was legendary." One can find the names of these women in memorial bricks at the University of Arizona. A virtual plaza can be found here: https://plaza.sbs.arizona.edu/honoree/2613. This entry on Ella Rumley by Holmes references two obituaries: Hackenberg and Hackenberg, "In Memoriam: Ella Gloria Narcho Rumley"; and Paul L. Allen, "Obituary: Ella Rumley, Tohono O'odham activist," *Tucson Citizen*, July 24, 2004.

2. Fagin is a fictional character in Charles Dickens's novel *Oliver Twist*. He leads a group of kids who are trained to work as pickpockets and carry on other less-than-legal activities. The band spells the name a little differently, but rock bands often take artistic license.

3. The Bracero Program was a "guest worker program" created through bilateral agreements between Mexico and the United States. From 1942 to 1964, approximately 5 million Mexican men came to the United States to work mostly in the agricultural sector for short-term labor contracts. Workers often experienced harsh working conditions, while growers benefited from cheap labor. For more on the controversial history of this program, see the Bracero History Archive, accessed June 1, 2021, http://braceroarchive.org.

4. On September 15, 1963, four Ku Klux Klan members planted dynamite at the Sixteenth Street Baptist Church in Birmingham, Alabama, and killed four young Black girls. While that attack stands out in history, such attacks were already stunningly familiar. Indeed, at the time of the bombing, the Alabama city was already nicknamed "Bombingham." David Graham notes that "between 1947 and 1965, white supremacists planted more than 50 devices

targeting black churches, black leaders, Jews, and Catholics." Graham, "How Much Has Changed since the Birmingham Church Bombing?"

5. The killing of nineteen-year-old Phillip Celaya and subsequent protests were covered by the *Ajo (AZ) Copper News* and the *Arizona Daily Star*. These reports quote Pima County sheriff's representatives as saying that Celaya had resisted arrest and attempted to shoot at deputies. By a strange coincidence, one of the sheriff's deputies was named Mike Wilson. See multiple articles in the July 27, 1972, edition of the *Ajo Copper News*: http://ajo .stparchive.com/Archive/AJO/AJO07271972P02.php. See also Alex Drehsler, "Killing of Papago Brings Protest by Group," *Arizona Daily Star*, July 3, 1972, A2, www.newspapers.com /clip/14731729/arizona-daily-star/.

6. Robert Cruz has gone on to become a specialist in O'odham language and culture. See Cruz, "Am T Ñe'ok et a:t o ce:ek T Do'Ibioda:Lik/In Our Language Is Where We Will Find Our Liberation."

7. The ranch of Tom Childs was also a source of controversy. At the protest, Martha Celaya, Phillip's mother, stated that the Bureau of Land Management had destroyed her family's house, which was on land claimed by the descendants of Tom Childs, one of the founders of Ajo. See "Indian Protesters March Peaceably All the Way," *Ajo Copper News*, July 27, 1972, http://ajo.stparchive.com/Archive/AJO/AJO07271972P02.php.

8. Siegler, "Why the U.S. Government Is Dropping Off Migrants in Rural Arizona Towns."

9. Armed Services Vocational Aptitude Battery. The highest score is a 99.

10. One finds similar anti-communist sentiments in the testimonies of other Native veterans. Lumbee marine veteran Delano Cummings, for example, states directly that he joined the marines "want[ing] to fight for [his] country, and help stop communism, to keep it from taking over the world." See Cummings, *Moon Dash Warrior*, 14. These tensions between Mike's political commitments at home and Cold War concerns abroad will be a major theme of the next chapter, which examines how these tensions came to a head in the context of US foreign policy in Central America. For excellent discussions of these tensions in the testimonies of Native veterans, see Little, "Vietnam Akíčita"; and Nguyen, "We Became the Cavalry."

11. Citing the Lewis and Short (1879) *Latin Dictionary*, the Wikipedia entry for this phrase notes, "A correct translation of the Latin phrase *de oppresso liber* would be 'from (being) an oppressed man, (to being) a free one.'" Wikipedia, s.v. "*de oppresso liber*," last edited September 8, 2023, https://en.wikipedia.org/wiki/De_oppresso_liber. The US Army provides the history of the crest as follows: "The Special Forces crest insignia was adopted in 1960 and approved as the Special Forces regimental designator in 1984. Its design reflects both the lineage and mission of Special Forces." "Special Forces Crest," United States Army Special Operations Command, accessed March 1, 2021, www.soc.mil/USASFC/SFCrest .html.

The same source continues, "In 1890, the crossed arrows were officially prescribed as uniform insignia for the US Army Indian Scouts who served in the American West from 1860 through 1939. In 1942, during World War II, a joint US/Canadian special operations unit was established to conduct operations behind enemy lines. Members of this First Special Service Force wore the historic crossed arrows as their branch insignia. In the current Special Forces crest, the intersecting dagger represents the V-42 dagger issued to each member of the force."

12. For more on this history, see Sonnichsen, *Tucson*.

13. Here Mike refers to the old and familiar colonial practice of settlers pushing Natives out of urban spaces and moving them elsewhere, either through the "reducciones" of Spanish colonialism or with the later spatial strategies of "reservation" and "relocation." Melanie Yazzie and colleagues note, "Settler colonialism lays down borders everywhere. . . . Every town is a bordertown because every town serves as a border that settlers must defend." Yazzie et al., "Burning Down the Bordertown."

14. I have been unable to find the specifics of this case, but beyond that, the emotional force in Mike's telling, which can only partially be conveyed here, is significant for what it expresses about the way indigeneity, class, race, masculinity, and politics come together in thinking about military service.

INTERLUDE 2

1. The title of this interlude was suggested by Mike Wilson. While he wants to make clear the connection to the violent history of Native boarding schools, he emphasizes that "Carlisle failed in both 'killing' Juan Vavages and 'saving' Harry Wilson." The uncertainty about whether Juan B. Vavages is indeed Mike's grandfather stems from a lack of access to family documentation and from the fact that Carlisle had two students by the name of Juan Vavages, both from Arizona, at roughly the same time. One was at Carlisle from 1895 to 1902; the second Juan B. Vavages was in residence from 1899 to 1904. They are both referred to as "Pima," rather than as O'odham or Papago, which does not necessarily mean that one or both were not Tohono O'odham, as the label Pima, Mike explained, was often used as a "catchall" category for Native peoples from southern Arizona, including Akimel O'odham and Tohono O'odham. Tucson and Ajo are both located in what is now called Pima County, Arizona.

2. For more on Carlisle, see Archuleta, Child, and Lomawaima, *Away from Home*; Fear-Segal and Rose, *Carlisle Indian Industrial School*; and Estes, "Severed Ties." The archives of most boarding schools are not easily accessible. However, some exceptionally good digital resources include Carlisle Indian School Digital Resource Center, http://carlisleindian .dickinson.edu; and Away from Home: American Indian Boarding School Stories, Heard Museum, Phoenix, https://heard.org/boardingschool/roisd/.

3. Pratt, "Advantages of Mingling Indians with Whites," 260–71.

4. Estes et al., *Red Nation Rising*, 85.

5. Estes, "Severed Ties," 18.

6. Estes, "Severed Ties," 18.

7. Quoted in Estes, "Severed Ties," 18–19.

8. Ian Austen, "'Horrible History': Mass Grave of Indigenous Children Reported in Canada," *New York Times*, May 28, 2021, www.nytimes.com/2021/05/28/world/canada /kamloops-mass-grave-residential-schools.html; Ian Austen, "With Discovery of Unmarked Graves, Canada's Indigenous Seek Reckoning," *New York Times*, June 26, 2021, www.nytimes .com/2021/06/26/world/canada/indigenous-residential-schools-grave.html.

9. Adams, *Education for Extinction*, 199. The US Army War College has returned the remains of several Carlisle Native children to their families. See Army National Military Cemeteries Staff, "Army Conducts Second Disinterment of Native Americans at Carlisle Barracks." Thanks to Manisha Jha for this reference.

10. Across many works of Indigenous studies, there is a growing move away from "damage-centered" accounts of victimhood toward accounts of the resilience and resurgence of Native peoples. An influential statement in support of this kind of research is Tuck, "Suspending Damage."

11. Child, "Boarding School as Metaphor," 51.

12. See, for example, Archuleta, Child, and Lomawaima, *Away from Home*; Child, *Boarding School Seasons*; Fear-Segal and Rose, *Carlisle Indian Industrial School*; Lomawaima, *They Called It Prairie Light*; and Johnston, *Indian School Days*.

13. Child, "Boarding School as Metaphor," 46–47. Child is referencing Philip Deloria, *Indians in Unexpected Places*.

14. Lomawaima, "Historical Trauma and Healing."

15. Gover, "American Indians Serve in the U.S. Military," 2.

16. See, for example, Holm, *Strong Hearts, Wounded Souls*; Carroll, *Medicine Bags and Dog Tags*; Bernstein, *American Indians and World War II*; Little, "Vietnam Akíčita"; and De León, "Preserving Values."

17. National Museum of the American Indian, https://americanindian.si.edu/visit/washington/nnavm.

18. In 1924, the US Congress enacted the Indian Citizenship Act, which granted citizenship to all Native Americans born in the United States. The right to vote, however, was governed by state law. Several states barred Native Americans from voting until 1957. For the text of the act, see National Archives Catalog, https://catalog.archives.gov/id/299828. On the health harms of incarceration, see Simon et al., "To Advance Well-Being in Indian Country, Limit the Health Harms of Incarceration."

19. Diaz, "Introduction: Bodies Built for Game," xxxv. For another searing critique of militarism, see LaDuke and Cruz, *The Militarization of Indian Country*.

20. For a video of the event, see "2019 SGU Graduation—47th Wounspe Wowapi Yusutapi 36th GED Wounspe Wowapi Yusutapi," YouTube, August 23, 2019, www.youtube.com/watch?v=Sl-Z-iUeY2U&t=1974s.

21. Citations have been removed from this excerpt. See Little, "Vietnam Akíčita," 1–2.

22. De León, "Preserving Values," 149.

23. For more on the history of warrior society, see LaDuke and Cruz, *Militarization of Indian Country*, chapter 1. For an enlightening exploration of the intersections of masculinities and militarism in Hawai'i, see Tengan, "Re-membering Panalā'au."

24. Quoted in Cobb, *Native Activism in Cold War America*, 168. Thom was a cofounder of the National Indian Youth Council (NIYC). Cobb provides an insightful discussion of the encounters between Native and African American social movements in this moment. Members from the National Congress of American Indians (NCAI), the NIYC, and other Native organizations met with Martin Luther King Jr. in March 1968. The NCAI and NIYC disagreed on participating in King's Poor People's Campaign. The NCAI, led by Vine Deloria Jr. (Standing Rock Sioux), opted for an incremental and legalistic approach and decided against participating in the march. Smith and Warrior describe a memorable banner from the 1967 NCAI that read, "Indians Don't Demonstrate." As if to provide a rebuttal, organizations like the NIYC and the American Indians Movement proved more than willing to join in protest politics. Smith and Warrior, *Like A Hurricane*, 37.

25. To be clear, the radicalism of the 1960 and 1970s was not "new." Indigenous resistance is perhaps the oldest story of the "Americas." Writing about the high-profile Indigenous takeover of Alcatraz, Smith and Warrior note that "the only new thing about Alcatraz was the press attention." Smith and Warrior, *Like a Hurricane*, 36. "Indians of All Tribes" was the name used by the Native activists who occupied Alcatraz. The similar sounding "United Indians of All Tribes" is the organization that later occupied Fort Laramie in Seattle.

26. Landry, "Harry S. Truman."

27. Quoted in Dunbar-Ortiz, *Indigenous People's History of the United States*, 181–82.

28. Quoted in William Yardley, "Billy Frank Jr., 83, Defiant Fighter for Native Fishing Rights," *New York Times*, May 9, 2014, www.nytimes.com/2014/05/09/us/billy-frank-jr-fighter-for-native-fishing-rights-dies-at-83.html.

29. To add one more connection to the Pacific Northwest, I should note the role of Senator Henry M. Jackson, the Cold War Democrat for whom the School of International Studies, where I work, is named. Jackson's early career shows much support for termination policies. Over the decades, though, he became an advocate of self-determination, a remarkable transition chronicled ably by Shoshone-Bannack journalist Mark Trahant in *Last Great Battle of the Indian Wars*.

30. Magisterial synthetic accounts of Native activism in these years include Cobb, *Native Activism in Cold War America*; Smith and Warrior, *Like a Hurricane*; Dunbar-Ortiz, *Indigenous People's History of the United States*; and Treuer, *Heartbeat of Wounded Knee*.

31. Mueller and Salt, *Good Day to Die*.

32. Quoted in Holm, *Strong Hearts, Wounded Souls*, 178–79. The tradition of Native veterans working for Native sovereignty continues in times of Standing Rock and #NODAPL. For an excellent discussion of militarization and the possibilities of post-military activism, see Red Nation, "Veterans' Day and the Demilitarization of Indian Country with Krystal Two Bulls."

33. Langston, "American Indian Women's Activism in the 1960s and 1970s."

34. Akins and Bauer, *We Are the Land*, 285–85.

35. Treuer, *Heartbeat of Wounded Knee*, 325–26.

36. Smith and Warrior, *Like a Hurricane*, 182–83; Estes et al., *Red Nation Rising*.

37. See "Missing and Murdered Native Women" on the National Indigenous Women's Resource Center website, accessed July 13, 2022, www.niwrc.org/resources/topic/missing-and-murdered-native-women; and Urban Indian Health Institute, "Missing and Murdered Indigenous Women and Girls" on the Urban Indian Health Institute website, accessed July 13, 2022, www.uihi.org/resources/missing-and-murdered-indigenous-women-girls.

38. Wilson had his own private auxiliary police force that he dubbed his GOONs, Guardians of the Oglala Nation. Smith and Warrior, *Like a Hurricane*, 196.

39. Cherokee Nation v. the State of Georgia, 30 US (5 Pet.) 1 (1831), 17.

40. Quoted in Cobb, *Native Activism in Cold War America*, 147.

CHAPTER 3

1. The "Iran-Contra scandal" refers to a covert operation that took place during a time in the 1980s when the US Congress had restricted US military aid to anti-communist forces in Central America. To get around this restriction, officials in the administration used arms sales to Iran for two purposes: to negotiate the release of hostages and to raise covert funding for

the Contra rebels in Nicaragua. In March 1987, President Ronald Reagan held a prime-time address on the scandal and disavowed direct knowledge of the efforts but recognized that these illegal actions had taken place. In a memorable passage recognizing his earlier disavowals, Reagan said, "My heart and my best intentions still tell me that is true, but the facts and evidence tell me is it not." For a full transcript, see "Iran Arms and Contra Aid Controversy," American Experience, pbs.org, accessed June 11, 2021, www.pbs.org/wgbh/americanexperience /features/reagan-iran-contra/.

2. From 2013 to 2017, Mike and his partner, Susan Ruff, offered hospitality to nearly 200 Central American and South Asian refugees in their home. These refugees had been processed and released by Border Patrol. This humanitarian assistance was provided under the auspices of Catholic Community Services of Southern Arizona.

3. "In country" is a common term military personnel use to describe their deployments in many places across the globe. Some scholars suggest that the term is actually an abbreviation of the term "Indian Country" and has its origins in the US Indian Wars. See Dunbar-Ortiz, "'Indian' Wars"; and Silliman, "'Old West' in the Middle East." Upon learning about this history, Mike suggested deleting the phrase. We have decided to keep it as it serves as a revealing linguistic artifact of a long history.

4. This and her husband's name are pseudonyms.

5. Acts of the Apostles 9:1–31 (New International Version).

INTERLUDE 3

1. Scholars note that the "fourteen families" is not a numerically accurate accounting, but that phrase has become shorthand to describe the unquestionably unequal distribution of land and wealth in El Salvador. See, for example, Booth, Wade, and Walker, *Understanding Central America.*

2. For a magisterial account of the relationship between coffee economies and political systems in Central America, see Williams, *States and Social Evolution.* The classic statement on dependency theory remains Cardoso and Faletto, *Dependency and Development in Latin America.* A more literary version of dependency theory is Galeano, *Open Veins of Latin America.*

3. Alberto Masferrer, "La crisis del maíz," *Patria,* January 18, 1929, quoted in Montgomery, *Revolution in El Salvador,* 33.

4. Gould and Lauria-Santiago, *To Rise in Darkness,* 171.

5. A fascinating interpretation of the Canadian photographs of Ama's lynching can be found in Leal Ugalde, "La ejecución de Feliciano Ama."

6. Gould and Lauria-Santiago, *To Rise in Darkness,* 212.

7. Quoted in Gould and Lauria-Santiago, *To Rise in Darkness,* 231.

8. "Todos" in Dalton, *Las historias prohibidas del Pulgarcito.* The case of Roque Dalton could serve as yet another "hyperlink" to explore the fractal-like dynamics of memory, history, and violence. This book is a direct descendant of a form that Dalton innovated when he produced one of the first examples of "testimonial" literature in his book on Miguel Mármol, a survivor of the 1932 massacre. Dalton, *Miguel Mármol.* Dalton, through his prose and poetry, made 1932 a site of inquiry that continues to be explored. Dalton's murder by his own comrades in the Ejército Revolucionario del Pueblo serves as a kind of Rorschach test

that illustrates (for the Right) the violence of the Left or alternatively (for the Left) a tragic example of the way that the revolution devoured its own children. For excellent discussions, see Lindo-Fuentes, Ching, and Lara-Martínez, *Remembering a Massacre in El Salvador*; and Iffland, "Roque Dalton."

9. Quoted in Gould and Lauria-Santiago, *To Rise in Darkness*, 244.

10. Massacres committed with impunity are sadly a familiar part of the history of the Americas. A similarly nightmarish massacre took place in 1937 on the border of Haiti and the Dominican Republic, in which an estimated 30,000 ethnic Haitians (many born in the Dominican Republic) were killed by state and paramilitary forces following the orders of the dictator Rafael Leónidas Trujillo. This conflict was resolved by a cash payment from the government of the Dominican Republic to the government of Haiti and without any international controversy. A few years earlier in Colombia, security forces killed thousands of union workers protesting the abuses of United Fruit Company in what became known as the 1928 "Banana Massacre." A fictionalized representation of the massacre appears in Gabriel García Márquez's *One Hundred Years of Solitude*. In chapter 15 of the novel, the military passes a decree declaring striking workers "subversives" ("malhechores") and authorizes the use of violence against them. After 3,000 workers are killed, the military leadership tells one witness, "Surely it was a dream. In Macondo nothing has happened, nothing is happening, and nothing will happen. This is a happy town." My translation. García Márquez, *Cien años de soledad*. On the 1937 massacre of Haitians, see Turits, "World Destroyed, a Nation Imposed."

11. Leal Ugalde, "La ejecución de Feliciano Ama," 89.

12. Quoted in Binford, *El Mozote Massacre*, 49.

13. Salinas Maldonado, "El Mozote: 40 years after the Worst Military Massacre in the Americas, Victims Still Calling for Justice," *El País* (English ed.), December 16, 2021, https://english.elpais.com/usa/2021-12-16/el-mozote-40-years-after-the-worst-military-massacre-in-the-americas-victims-still-calling-for-justice.html. Sadly, given the violence we have already discussed, this newspaper's claim that this was the "worst military massacre" in the Americas (or even in El Salvador) is probably wrong. For more on the massacre and its coverage, see Binford, *El Mozote Massacre*.

14. Skidmore and Smith, *Modern Latin America*, 346.

15. Quoted in Berryman, *Stubborn Hope*, 94.

16. For influential and accessible overviews, see LaFeber, *Inevitable Revolutions*; Montgomery, *Revolution in El Salvador*; and Grandin, *Empire's Workshop*.

17. Betancur, Buergenthal, and Figueredo Planchart, *From Madness to Hope*, 11–13.

18. The journalist Jon Lee Anderson recounts a conversation in the early 1990s with two young FMLN fighters, Sandra and Sabina, who were examining an issue of *Time* magazine that had a cover story devoted to "child warriors." Disappointed that they found no pictures from El Salvador, Sandra complained, "They went all over the world. . . . So why didn't they come to El Salvador?" Anderson, *Guerrillas*, 56. Anderson's observation suggests that most of the FMLN rebels he met were teenagers. The government, of course, also recruited young people. According to one estimate, 80 percent of Salvadoran military forces were under eighteen, while around 20 percent of FMLN were under the age of eighteen. See Child Soldiers International, *Child Soldiers Global Report 2001—El Salvador*.

19. Kirkpatrick, "Dictatorships and Double Standards." The online edition describes this article as "The Classic Essay That Shaped Reagan's Foreign Policy."

20. Kirkpatrick, "Hobbes Problem," quoted in Bourgois, "What U.S. Foreign Policy Faces in Rural El Salvador: An Eyewitness Account," 27.

21. Bourgois, "What U.S. Foreign Policy Faces in Rural El Salvador," 22.

22. See Grandin, *Empire's Workshop*, 100–101.

23. Mbembé, "Necropolitics."

24. See, for example, Morozzo Della Rocca, *Oscar Romero*. An excellent resource is the Romero Trust, whose web page (www.romerotrust.org.uk) provides lists of biographies, links to documentaries, and homilies by Monseñor Romero.

25. Quoted in Montgomery, *Revolution in El Salvador*, 93.

26. Lernoux, *Cry of the People*, 37.

27. Kelly, *Rutilio Grande, S.J.*, 120.

28. The original Spanish text reads, "Cuando yo lo mire a Rutilio muerto, pensé: si lo mataron por hacer lo que hacía, me toca a mi andar por su mismo camino. Cambié, sí, pero también es que volví de regreso." López Vigil, *Monseñor Romero*, 75–76.

29. Betancur, Buergenthal, and Figueredo Planchart, *From Madness to Hope*, 141–42.

30. Eldridge and Amaya, "Archbishop Óscar Romero Is Declared a Saint."

31. Whelan, *Blood in the Fields*.

32. Whelan discusses the long history of Catholic social teaching that goes back to Pope Leo XIII's 1891 encyclical *Rerum Novarum*. See Whelan, *Blood in the Fields*, 86–88.

CHAPTER 4

1. Cementville was a company town, like Ajo, where Mike grew up. By the time Mike got to San Antonio, Cementville was already gone; only the smokestacks were left as historical decor for new developments. On that site there is now a shopping center and the Quarry Golf Course. Mike still feels the force of the history that haunts this part of Texas. See "Smokestacks Are All That's Left; 'Cementville' Was Company Town for Decades," *San Antonio Express-News*, September 3, 2018, A12.

2. There are several accounts of this event online; see, for example, Johnson, "High School Basketball Fans Accused of Racism for 'USA' Chant"; and Prep Rally, "San Antonio Prep Hoops Fans Accused of Racism over 'USA, USA' Chant," Yahoo! Sports, March 8, 2012, https://sports.yahoo.com/blogs/highschool-prep-rally/san-antonio-prep-hoops-fans -accused-racismabover-usa-123930890.html.

3. Southside Presbyterian Church, under the leadership of Pastor John Fife, was often described as the birthplace of the sanctuary movement in the 1980s. This movement was critical of US foreign policy in Central America and also worked to provide support for refugees fleeing the violence in El Salvador and other countries in the region. See Coutin, *Culture of Protest*; Paniagua, "Sanctuary Movement"; O'Gara, "Southside Presbyterian, Birthplace of Sanctuary Movement, Honors Former Pastor"; and Crittenden, *Sanctuary*. We will say more about this history in chapter 5.

4. San Francisco Theological Seminary, *Stained Glass Windows*.

1. Professors Lydia Heberling, Josh Reid, and Chris Tirres provided invaluable bibliographic guidance for this interlude, for which we are grateful.

2. San Francisco Theological Seminary, *Stained Glass Windows*, 6.

3. San Francisco Theological Seminary, *Stained Glass Windows*, 9.

4. San Francisco Theological Seminary, *Stained Glass Windows*, 9.

5. Young, *Alaska Days with John Muir*; Young, *Hall Young of Alaska*.

6. Merchant, "Shades of Darkness," 382.

7. Quoted in Merchant, "Shades of Darkness," 382. Merchant provides an insightful discussion of the ironic and cruel logic of early conservationism that saw Native removal as a prerequisite for making "public" national parks. She reminds us that the 1964 Wilderness Act defined wilderness as areas where "man is a visitor who does not remain," writing Native peoples out of their own lands. Merchant observes that Muir's attitudes toward Natives were softened by his travels in Alaska with Young. Nevertheless, in the multiple editions of his works, Muir never revised any of his negative evaluations of Native peoples.

8. G. Tinker, *Missionary Conquest*, 4.

9. The full title is worth noting: *A Brief Account of the Destruction of the Indies. Or, a faithful Narrative of the Horrid and Unexampled Massacres, Butcheries, and all manner of Cruelties, that Hell and Malice could invent, committed by the Popish Spanish Party on the inhabitants of West-India, Together With the Devastations of several Kingdoms in America by Fire and Sword, for the space of Forty and Two Years, from the time of its first Discovery by them.* There are various translations, but Las Casas's famous work is available through the online Project Gutenberg, https://gutenberg.org/ebooks/20321.

10. G. Tinker, *Missionary Conquest*, 7.

11. Miranda, *Bad Indians*, xviii.

12. Miranda, *Bad Indians*, xvii.

13. Mike's observation that he is on "Ishi's lands" is certainly correct as we think of the large and complex homelands of California Native peoples. As Lydia Heberling notes, it is probably more precise to say that Mike was on the lands where Ishi was "removed to," as the traditional homelands of Ishi's people were closer to the Sacramento Valley (personal communication, June 16, 2022).

14. Kroeber, *Ishi in Two Worlds*. Theodora Kroeber is an important writer and anthropologist in her own right, and her fame is amplified by her familial relations, including her husband, the renowned anthropologist Alfred Kroeber, and her arguably much more famous daughter, the novelist Ursula K. Le Guin.

15. "One of them, Juan Dolores, was a Papago, or O'odham—he was a real family friend. And he would stay for a couple weeks or a month. So we sort of had this Indian uncle. Just having these people from a truly other culture—it was a tremendous gift." Le Guin, "Art of Fiction."

16. In addition to being a very witty interlocutor for anthropologists and government agents, Dolores was an important knowledge producer, providing some of the first studies of O'odham grammar. See his 1913 work published by the University of California Press, *Papago Verb Stems.*

17. Clifford, *Returns*, 116–17. In these pages, Clifford gives a sense of the liveliness of Dolores's mind and wit by quoting from a 1911 letter Dolores wrote to Professor Kroeber. Telling Kroeber about his encounter with a government agent who wanted him to stay put in Arizona, Dolores writes, "He wants me to get married, grow corn. But how can I afford to do that[?] . . . Anyway I'm a tramp, too attached to my freedom."

18. In the window dedicated to Narcissa Whitman, there is also a seemingly incongruous symbol of a pineapple—an allusion to the fact that Native Hawaiians, "brought from the Islands by the Hudson Bay company as laborers," were among the Whitmans' "first helpers." San Francisco Theological Seminary, *Stained Glass Windows*, 10. This is a reminder that Manifest Destiny did not end at the western coast of the United States but spread far into Oceania. On the campus of the University of Washington is a statue of George Washington that was created on the occasion of the Alaska-Yukon-Pacific Exposition, one of the many "world's fair" events that cities used to establish themselves as gateways to modernity. Like many such events, it was problematic for its unapologetic embrace of empire, made even more uncomfortable through its exhibition of Native peoples from Alaska and the Philippines. Revealingly, that statue of George Washington is facing West, toward the Pacific, a clear allusion to US expansionism, for which the statue has earned the disparaging but accurate moniker of "Imperial George." For images of the fair, see the Alaska-Yukon-Pacific Exposition, Special Collections, University of Washington, accessed May 2, 2022, www.lib.washington.edu /specialcollections/collections/exhibits/ayp. For an interesting "counter-map" and history of the University of Washington campus, see "A Peoples' Landscape: Racism and Resistance at UW," Divest and Demilitarize UW, accessed May 2, 2022, https://divestdemilitarizeuw .carrd.co.

19. San Francisco Theological Seminary, *Stained Glass Windows*, 10.

20. The name "Nez Percé" was the name given to the Nimiipuu by French traders for the mistaken belief that they had pierced noses. Nimiipuu means "the people" and is the term that tribal members use to refer to themselves. Nez Perce (without the accent), however, is how the tribe and reservation are federally recognized. See the Nez Perce Tribe website, accessed May 2, 2022, https://nezperce.org.

21. Letter by Bishop Rosati, in American Catholic Historical Society of Philadelphia Yearbook (1888), II, 188, cited in Haines, "Nez Percé Delegation to St. Louis in 1831," 77.

22. Addis explains that the "Macedonian Cry" is an allusion to the dream the apostle Paul describes in Acts (16:19) in which a man asks for Paul to come to Macedonia and help. Addis, "Whitman Massacre," 231.

23. In response to complaints from Native students, staff, and faculty, the University of Washington renamed Whitman Court "sluʔwił," a word in Southern Lushootseed language that means "Little Canoe Channel." Sudermann, "Renamed Campus Road Honors Indigenous History." My American Indian Studies colleagues have told me that the very location of wəɫəbʔaltxʷ – Intellectual House represents an anti-colonial intervention: it is located between Stevens Way (named for Governor Isaac Stevens, who oversaw the Treaty of Point Elliott, which dispossessed the lands of many of the local tribes), Whitman Court (named for the missionaries), and Lewis and Clark Halls (named after the Oregon Trail explorers). As one of the newer buildings on campus, wəɫəbʔaltxʷ – Intellectual House interrupts multiple colonial narratives and makes visible Native presence.

24. Banyard's *A Prophecy Fulfilled* is a twenty-five-minute film that explores what it calls a "tragic" history of this encounter between settler and Natives. For discussions of the impact of the story of the massacre on the working of Manifest Destiny, see Addis, "Whitman Massacre"; and Koening, *Providence and the Invention of American History*.

25. Quoted in Tate, "Whitman 'Massacre.'"

26. V. Deloria, *God Is Red*, 75–77.

27. Warrior, "Native American Perspective." Excellent responses to and discussion of Warrior's argument are provided by Donaldson, "Joshua in America"; and Weaver, "Premodern Ironies."

28. T. Tinker, "Why I Do Not Believe in a Creator."

29. T. Tinker, "American Indian Traditions," 340.

30. Weaver, "Premodern Ironies," 292.

31. Weaver, "From I-Hermeneutics to We-Hermeneutics," 6.

32. Weaver, "From I-Hermeneutics to We-Hermeneutics," 2.

33. T. Tinker, "Why I Do Not Believe in a Creator," 175. See also Nash, *We Eat the Mines and the Mines Eat Us*.

34. There is a vast literature, but good places to start include Vega, *Comentarios reales de los Incas*; Cleary and Steigenga, *Resurgent Voices in Latin America*; Gruzinski, *Mestizo Mind*; and Smith et al., "Native/First Nation Theology."

35. Weaver, "From I-Hermeneutics to We-Hermeneutics," 19.

36. There are many studies that explore this phenomenon. For an overview, see García and Lucero, "Resurgence and Resistance in Abya Yala."

37. Lucero, "Representing 'Real Indians.'"

38. Quoted in Maxwell, "Decolonization," 303.

39. TallBear, "Can a DNA Test Make Me Native American?"

40. The poem appears in W. Rose, *Going to War with All My Relations*, 6–8. I am grateful to Lydia Heberling, who introduced me to this poem and much of the critical literature around Wendy Rose and Deborah Miranda in her brilliant dissertation, "California Indians Dreamin.'"

41. Miranda, "Bones Speak," 293.

42. *Oxford English Dictionary*, 2nd ed., 1989, accessed May 23, 2022, www.oed.com/oed2/00010284;jsessionid=4424D83EACA3E638ADAF7B041AA00A8E.

43. Donaldson, "Joshua in America," 286–87.

44. As we reviewed this interlude, Mike emphasized the importance of this encounter with the Cherokee man: "He spoke with pride of being Cherokee from North Carolina. He represented a history of displacement and diaspora."

CHAPTER 5

1. The 1994 strategic plan of the Border Patrol makes this clear, with the "prediction" that border-crossers would be "deterred or forced over more hostile terrain." Quoted in De León, *Land of Open Graves*, 32. Six years after the publication of the strategic plan, former commissioner of INS Doris Meissner admitted that "we did believe that geography would be an ally to us." When asked if the policy was ever reevaluated in the face of the spike in migrant deaths,

she replied that the idea of stopping the policies "because of that consequence was not a point of serious discussion." Quoted in Cantú, *Where the Line Becomes a River*, 259. As Cantú, a former Border Patrol officer notes, border deaths were expected, accepted, and ignored.

2. DeVivo and Mathew, *Crossing Arizona*. For a similar scene, see Levine and Van Soest, *Walking the Line*.

3. The naming of military helicopters is another artifact of the history of militarism and what the US government calls "Indian Affairs." According to the Department of Defense, a US Army Regulation (AR 70–28) required that military aircraft be categorized with "Indian terms and names of American Indian tribes and chiefs." Names were provided by the Bureau of Indian Affairs. That 1969 regulation is no longer in effect, but the tradition continues. Lange, "Why Army Helicopters Have Native American Names."

4. Resolution of the Baboquivari District Council, "Disapproving the Placement of Water Stations and Water Jugs within Baboquivari District," Resolution 02-B-23, June 15, 2002, on file with the authors.

5. Again, we use pseudonyms for tribal members here. As Josue and Bethsebe's story has been shared publicly, we use their names and the name of the family.

6. Mike notes, "There were many fundamentalist missions on the reservation. In the Presbyterian congregation, you had a mixture of church histories. You could hear echoes of different kinds of fundamentalisms in this church. This was a sharp contrast with the progressive approach of Southside Presbyterian."

7. The crisis of missing and murdered Indigenous women has gained increasing attention in recent years. We cannot do justice to that topic here, but for important places to start, see the following online resources: MMIW USA, https://mmiwusa.org; Native Women's Wilderness, Murdered and Missing Indigenous Women, www.nativewomenswilderness.org/mmiw; Coalition to Stop Violence Against Native Women, www.csvanw.org/mmiw/, all accessed September 3, 2021.

8. In some versions of Chicano ideology, what is now the US Southwest was called Aztlán, the original homelands of the Aztecs. The presence of Mexican people in the US Southwest was thus narrated as a "return" to the homelands of the Aztecs. As Mike points out, this narrative is problematic in erasing the many other Native peoples who call these lands home, like the Diné, O'odham, Yoeme, Pueblo, and many other Native peoples.

INTERLUDE 5

1. For a helpful overview, see Rabben, *Sanctuary and Asylum*.

2. Excellent places to start include Davidson, *Convictions of the Heart*; Rabben, *Sanctuary and Asylum*; Cunningham, *God and Caesar at the Rio Grande*; García, *Seeking Refuge*; and C. Smith, *Resisting Reagan*.

3. Quoted in Valdes, "Their Lawsuit Prevented 400,000 Deportations."

4. This summary draws from Davidson, *Convictions of the Heart*; C. Smith, *Resisting Reagan*, 61–65; and Valdes, "Their Lawsuit Prevented 400,000 Deportations."

5. For the cartoon see Bramhall, editorial cartoon, *New York Daily News*, March 20, 2022, www.nydailynews.com/opinion/ny-bramhall-editorial-cartoons-2021-jan-20220110

-wtmocdmrkjearn62tqfkbixqdi-photogallery.html. Context on the contrasting treatment can be found in Eulich, "Will US Extend Speedy Ukrainian Refugee Welcome to Others?"

6. Kaganiec-Kamienska, "Sanctuary Movement," 1865–66.

7. Del Bosque, "Acts of Resistance and Faith."

8. Quoted in Davidson, *Convictions of the Heart*, 154.

9. For a lucid account of the history of TPS, see Valdes, "Their Lawsuit Prevented 400,000 Deportations."

10. See De León, *Land of Open Graves*; and Nevins, *Operation Gatekeeper and Beyond*.

11. Humane Borders, "Migrants Deaths, Rescue Beacons, Water Stations 1999–2021," Humane Borders, accessed September 1, 2020, https://humaneborders.org/printable-maps -and-posters/. As we have already noted, the traditional homelands of the O'odham are much greater than the official reservation borders.

12. Perla Trevizo, "Tribes Seek to Join Immigration Reform Debate," *Arizona Daily Star*, June 14, 2013, https://tucson.com/news/local/border/tribes-seek-to-join-immigration -reform-debate/article_d4fe1980-46d4-5e90-b690-ce78c5453bf1.html.

13. Opposition to US government policy has been vocal. Many tribal members have publicly voiced their condemnation of US Border Patrol and immigration policies. The tribal government has expressed clear opposition to the construction of the border wall through its lands but agreed to cooperate with other border control measures. See Miller, "How Border Patrol Occupied the Tohono O'odham Nation"; Molly Hennessy-Fisk, "Arizona Tribe Refuses Trump's Wall, but Agrees to Let Border Patrol Build Virtual Barrier," *Los Angeles Times*, May 9, 2019, www.latimes.com/nation/la-na-arizona-tribe-border-patrol-trump-wall -20190509-htmlstory.html; and Rivas, "Systematic System of Destruction." For the Tohono O'odham government's official response to the border wall, see the Nation's website, www .tonation-nsn.gov/nowall/, accessed September 12, 2021.

14. The following films are available: Levine and Van Soest, *Walking the Line*; DeVivo and Mathew, *Crossing Arizona*; MacMillan, *Man in the Maze*; Jimmerson, *The Second Cooler*; D'Hondt, *Inside the Labyrinth*; D. Smith, *Border Wars*; and Van Leeuw, *The Wall*. Mike is also involved in the making of one feature film on the border, *The Long Walk of Carlos Guerrero* (by Joseph Mathew). As of this writing, it is still in production. Mike's work is also discussed in at least two books, not including the current one: De la Torre, *Trails of Hope and Terror*; and Regan, *Death of Josseline*.

15. Gaard, "Tools for a Cross-Cultural Feminist Ethics."

16. V. Deloria, "Self-Determination and the Concept of Sovereignty."

17. Barker, "For Whom Sovereignty Matters," 2–3.

18. Cherokee Nation v. the State of Georgia, 30 US (5 Pet.) 1 (1831), 17.

19. Johnson v. McIntosh, 21 US (8 Wheat) 543 (1823), 568.

20. Deloria and Lytle, *American Indians, American Justice*, 2–21.

21. Alfred, *Peace, Power, Righteousness*; Barker, "For Whom Sovereignty Matters," 21.

22. Kauanui, *Paradoxes of Hawaiian Sovereignty*, 26–27.

23. Bruyneel, *Third Space of Sovereignty*, xvii.

24. See, for example, *Tohono O'odham Young Voices*, https://podcasts.apple.com/us /podcast/tohono-oodham-young-voices/id1460323371; and the September 16, 2021, and

February 10, 2022, episodes of *The Border Chronicle*, www.theborderchronicle.com
/p/under-occupation-a-discussion-with?s=r#details; www.theborderchronicle.com
/p/blockading-the-border-bulldozers?s=r#details. The official website of the Nation is
www.tonation-nsn.gov.

25. This discussion is based on a special report on Duwamish recognition that was
published in the *Seattle Times*. All quotations below about the Duwamish, unless otherwise
indicated, are from Lynda Maples, "'Real' Duwamish: Seattle's First People and the Bitter
Fight over Federal Recognition," *Seattle Times*, May 29, 2022, www.seattletimes.com
/seattle-news/real-duwamish-seattles-first-people-and-the-bitter-fight-over-federal
-recognition/. An excellent scholarly account is Thrush, *Native Seattle*.

26. Maples, "'Real' Duwamish."

27. Another possible complication concerns the BIA requirement that the "membership
of the petitioning group is composed principally of persons who are not members of any
acknowledged North American Indian tribe." The chair of the Duwamish Tribe is herself an
enrolled member of the Suquamish Tribe, and there are Duwamish enrolled in many of the
other Coast Salish tribes. For the BIA requirements, see Bureau of Indian Affairs, Criteria for
Federal Acknowledgment, accessed May 2, 2021, www.bia.gov/sites/default/files/dup
/assets/as-ia/ofa/admindocs/25CFRPart83_2015_abbrev.pdf.

28. Maples, "'Real' Duwamish."

29. Lorde, *Master's Tools Will Never Dismantle the Master's House*.

30. Hirschman, *Propensity to Self-Subversion*.

EPILOGUE

1. The Pima County Medical Examiner released the Paige A. Peterson report. It is available
from multiple media outlets, but we found it on the Spanish-language Telemundo website,
Telemundo Arizona, "Autopsia y video de cámara corporal revelan cómo murió Raymond
Mattia a manos de CBP en la Nación Tohono O'odham," accessed June 23, 2023, www
.telemundoarizona.com/noticias/local/arizona-ajo-cbp-tohono-oodham-raymond-mattia
-patrulla-fronteriza-estados-unidos-mexico/2324755/; Ryan Devereaux, "Border Patrol
Video of Killing Shows Native Man Had No Gun, Complied with Orders," *The Intercept*, June
26, 2023. https://theintercept.com/2023/06/26/border-patrol-killing-raymond-mattia/.

2. Devereaux, "Border Patrol Video of Killing Shows Native Man Had No Gun"; José
Ignacio Castañeda Perez, "Bodycam Footage Released in Fatal Border Patrol Shooting
of Tohono O'odham Man," *Arizona Republic*, June 22, 2023, www.azcentral.com/story
/news/politics/border-issues/2023/06/22/bodycam-video-released-in-fatal-shooting
-of-tohono-oodham-man/70348612007/.

3. Greg Grandin and Elizabeth Oglesby, "Who Killed Jakelin Caal Maquín at the
US Border?," *The Nation*, December 17, 2018. www.thenation.com/article/archive
/guatemala-refugee-crisis-jakelin-caal-maquin/.

4. Grandin and Oglesby, "Who Killed Jakelin Caal Maquín at the US Border?"

5. Mike has again identified a detail that has great historical significance. The concertina
wire used by politicians like the Texas governor is a variant of the original barbed wire used in

the nineteenth century, dubbed "devil's wire" by Native peoples. Historians have documented the importance of this technology to control human and nonhuman bodies in the process of westward colonial expansion. For a helpful political history of barbed wire, see Onion, "That Beautiful Barbed Wire."

6. Edgar Sandoval, Jay Root, and J. David Goodman, "Texas' Harsh New Border Tactics Are Injuring Migrants," *New York Times*, July 19, 2023, www.nytimes.com/2023/07/19/us /texas-border-migrants-abbott.html.

Bibliography

PRIMARY SOURCES

Archives and Museums

Alaska-Yukon-Pacific Exposition. Special Collections, University of Washington, Seattle. www.lib.washington.edu/specialcollections/collections/exhibits/ayp.

Away from Home: American Indian Boarding School Stories. Heard Museum, Phoenix. https://boardingschool.heard.org/roisd/.

The Bracero History Archive. https://braceroarchive.org.

Carlisle Indian School Digital Resource Center. https://carlisleindian.dickinson.edu.

Historical Publications of the US Commission on Civil Rights. Thurgood Marshall Law Library, University of Maryland, Baltimore, www2.law.umaryland.edu/marshall/usccr/.

Newspapers

Ajo (AZ) Copper News
Arizona Daily Star
Arizona Republic
El País
Los Angeles Times
New York Times
San Antonio Express-News
Seattle Times
Tucson Citizen
Washington Post

Books

Dolores, Juan. *Papago Verb Stems*. Berkeley: University of California Press, 1913.

San Francisco Theological Seminary. *Stained Glass Windows: Stewart Memorial Chapel*. Pamphlet. San Francisco: San Francisco Theological Seminary, 1955.

US Commission on Civil Rights. "Testimony of Reverend John Fife, Pastor, Southside Presbyterian Church, South Tucson, Arizona; Mr. Michael Wilson, Student, University of Arizona and Board Member, American Indian Association; And Wallace Baker, Esq., Attorney-at-Law and Part-Time Magistrate, City of Phoenix, Arizona." In *Hearing before the United States Commission on Civil Rights: Hearing Held in Phoenix, Arizona, Nov. 17–18, 1972*, 133–48. Washington, DC: US Government Printing Office, 1974. www2.law.umaryland.edu/marshall/usccr/documents/cr18p56.pdf.

Young, Samuel Hall. *Alaska Days with John Muir*. New York: Fleming H. Revell, 1915.

———. *Hall Young of Alaska, "The Mushing Parson": The Autobiography of S. Hall Young*. New York: Fleming H. Revell, 1927.

SECONDARY SOURCES

Adams, David Wallace. *Education for Extinction: American Indians and the Boarding School Experience, 1875–1928*. Lawrence: University of Kansas Press, 1995.

Addis, Cameron. "The Whitman Massacre: Religion and Manifest Destiny on the Columbia Plateau, 1809–1858." *Journal of the Early Republic* 25, no. 2 (2005): 221–58.

Akins, Damon B., and William J. Bauer Jr. *We Are the Land: A History of Native California*. Berkeley: University of California Press, 2021.

Alfred, Taiaiake. *Peace, Power, Righteousness: An Indigenous Manifesto*. Oxford: Oxford University Press, 1998.

Anderson, Jon Lee. *Guerrillas: Journeys in the Insurgent Worlds*. New York: Penguin Books, 2004.

Archuleta, Elizabeth. "'I Give You Back': Indigenous Women Writing to Survive." *Studies in American Indian Literatures* 18, no. 4 (2006): 88–114.

Archuleta, Margaret L., Brenda J. Child, and K. Tsianina Lomawaima, eds. *Away from Home: American Indian Boarding School Experiences, 1879–2000*. Phoenix: Heard Museum, 2000.

Arias, Arturo, ed. *The Rigoberta Menchú Controversy*. Minneapolis: University of Minnesota Press, 2001.

Army National Military Cemeteries Staff. "Army Conducts Second Disinterment of Native Americans at Carlisle Barracks." US Army War College News Archives, June 11, 2018. www.armywarcollege.edu/News/archives/13897.pdf.

Auyero, Javier. *Contentious Lives: Two Argentine Women, Two Protests, and the Quest for Recognition*. Durham, NC: Duke University Press, 2003.

Ayres, James E., and Janet H. Parkhurst. "Mining and Mining Towns in Southern Arizona." In *Cross-Cultural Vernacular Landscapes of Southern Arizona: A Field Guide for the Vernacular Architecture Forum 25th Anniversary Conference*, edited by Laura H. Hollengreen and R. Brooks Jeffery, 71–86. Tucson: Vernacular Architecture Forum, 2005.

Banyard, Rory, dir. *A Prophecy Fulfilled*. National Park Service, park film, 2012. www.nps.gov /whmi/learn/photosmultimedia/multimedia.htm.

Barbier, Olivier, Grégory Jacquillet, Michel Tauc, Marc Cougnon, and Philippe Poujeol. "Effect of Heavy Metals on, and Handling by, the Kidney." *Nephron Physiology* 99, no. 4 (2005): 105–10.

Barker, Joanne. "For Whom Sovereignty Matters." In *Sovereignty Matters: Locations of Contestation and Possibility in Indigenous Struggles for Self-Determination*, edited by Joanne Barker, 1–32. Lincoln: University of Nebraska Press, 2005.

Barnet, Miguel. *Biography of a Runaway Slave*. Willimantic, CT: Curbstone Press, 1994.

Barrios de Chúngura, Domitila, and Viezzer Moema. *Let Me Speak! Testimony of Domitila, a Woman of the Bolivian Mines*. New York: Monthly Review Press, 1978.

Bernstein, Alison R. *American Indians and World War II: Toward a New Era in Indian Affairs*. Norman: University of Oklahoma Press, 1999.

Berryman, Phillip. *Stubborn Hope: Religion, Politics, and Revolution in Central America*. New York: New Press, 1995.

Betancur, Belisario, Thomas Buergenthal, and Reinaldo Figueredo Planchart. *From Madness to Hope: Report of the Commission on the Truth for El Salvador*. New York: United Nations, 1993.

Beverley, John. *Testimonio: On the Politics of Truth*. Minneapolis: University of Minnesota Press, 2004.

Binford, Leigh. *The El Mozote Massacre: Anthropology and Human Rights*. Tucson: University of Arizona Press, 1996.

Bird, Stan. "Indigenous Peoples' Life Stories: Voices of Ancient Knowledge." *AlterNative: An International Journal of Indigenous Peoples* 10, no. 4 (2014): 376–91.

Booth, John, Christine Wade, and Thomas W. Walker. *Understanding Central America: Global Forces, Rebellion, and Change*. Boulder, CO: Westview Press, 2006.

Bourgois, Philippe. "What U.S. Foreign Policy Faces in Rural El Salvador: An Eyewitness Account." *Monthly Review* 34, no. 1 (1982): 14–30.

Brueggemann, Walter. *The Prophetic Imagination*. Philadelphia: Fortress Press, 1978.

Bruyneel, Kevin. *The Third Space of Sovereignty: The Postcolonial Politics of U.S.-Indigenous Relations*. Minneapolis: University of Minnesota Press, 2007.

Burnett, John. "A Toxic Century: Mining Giant Must Clean Up Mess." National Public Radio, February 4, 2010. www.npr.org/templates/story/story.php?storyId=122779177.

Cadava, Geraldo L. "Borderlands of Modernity and Abandonment: The Lines within Ambos Nogales and the Tohono O'odham Nation." *Journal of American History* 98, no. 2 (2011): 362–83.

Cantú, Francisco. *Where the Line Becomes a River: Dispatches from the Border*. New York: Penguin, 2019.

Cardoso, Fernando Henrique, and Enzo Faletto. *Dependency and Development in Latin America*. Berkeley: University of California Press, 1979.

Carroll, Al. *Medicine Bags and Dog Tags: American Indian Veterans from Colonial Times to the Second Iraq War*. Lincoln: University of Nebraska Press, 2008.

Castellanos, M. Bianet, ed. "Introduction: Settler Colonialism in Latin America." *American Quarterly* 69, no. 4 (2017): 777–81.

Child, Brenda J. *Boarding School Seasons : American Indian Families, 1900–1940*. Lincoln: University of Nebraska Press, 1999.

———. "The Boarding School as Metaphor." *Journal of American Indian Education* 57, no. 1 (2018): 37–57.

Child Soldiers International. *Child Soldiers Global Report 2001—El Salvador*. Refworld, 2001. www.refworld.org/docid/498805fe4.html.

Cleary, Edward, and Timothy Steigenga, eds. *Resurgent Voices in Latin America: Indigenous Peoples, Political Mobilization, and Religious Change*. Piscataway, NJ: Rutgers University Press, 2004.

Clifford, James. *Returns: Becoming Indigenous in the Twenty-First Century*. Cambridge, MA: Harvard University Press, 2013.

Cobb, Daniel M. *Native Activism in Cold War America: The Struggle for Sovereignty*. Lawrence: University Press of Kansas, 2008.

Corntassel, Jeff, Chaw-win-is, and T'lakwadzi. "Indigenous Storytelling, Truth-Telling, and Community Approaches to Reconciliation." *ESC: English Studies in Canada* 35, no.1 (2009): 137–59. https://ojs.lib.uwo.ca/index.php/esc/article/view/9788/7888.

Coutin, Susan Bibler. *The Culture of Protest: Religious Activism and the U.S. Sanctuary Movement*. Boulder, CO: Westview, 1993.

Crittenden, Ann. *Sanctuary: A Story of American Conscience and the Law in Collision*. New York: Weidenfeld and Nicolson, 1988.

Cruz, Robert. "Am T Ñe'ok et a:t o ce:ek T Do'Ibioda:Lik/In Our Language Is Where We Will Find Our Liberation." *Berkeley Raza Law Journal* 22, no. 1 (2012): 97–116.

Cummings, Delano. *Moon Dash Warrior: The Story of an American Indian in Vietnam, a Marine from the Land of the Lumbee*. Livermore, ME: Signal Tree Publications, 1998.

Cunningham, Hilary. *God and Caesar at the Rio Grande: Sanctuary and the Politics of Religion*. Minneapolis: University of Minnesota Press, 1995.

Curtis, Genevieve. "ASARCO Smokestacks Headed for Demolition." Recasting the Smelter, November 27, 2012. www.recastingthesmelter.com/?p=3081.

Davidson, Miriam. *Convictions of the Heart: Jim Corbett and the Sanctuary Movement*. Tucson: University of Arizona Press, 1988.

Dalton, Roque. *Las historias prohibidas del Pulgarcito*. 8th ed. México: Siglo XXI Editores, 1985.

———. *Miguel Mármol*. San José, Costa Rica: EDUCA, 1972.

De la Torre, Miguel A., ed. *Trails of Hope and Terror: Testimonies on Immigration*. Maryknoll, NY: Orbis Books, 2009.

Del Bosque, Melissa. "Acts of Resistance and Faith: An Interview with the Rev. John Fife on Founding the Sanctuary Movement, and the Ongoing Struggle for Human Rights in the Borderlands." *The Border Chronicle* podcast, April 19, 2022. www.theborderchronicle .com/p/acts-of-resistance-and-faith-an-interview?utm_source=substack&utm_medium =email&utm_content=share&s=r#details.

De León, Jason. *The Land of Open Graves: Living and Dying on the Migrant Trail*. Berkeley: University of California Press, 2015.

De Leon, Justin. 2020. "Preserving Values: Militarization and Powwows." *Borderlands* 19, no. 2 (2020): 131–56.

Deloria, Philip. *Indians in Unexpected Places*. Lawrence: University Press of Kansas, 2004.

Deloria, Vine, Jr. *God Is Red: A Native View of Religion*. 30th Anniversary ed. Golden, CO: Fulcrum, 2003.

———. "Self-Determination and the Concept of Sovereignty." In *Economic Development in American Indian Reservations*, edited by Roxanne Dunbar-Ortiz, 22–28. Albuquerque: University of New Mexico Press, 1979.

Deloria, Vine, Jr., and Clifford M. Lytle. *American Indians, American Justice*. Austin: University of Texas Press, 1983.

Dennison, Jean. *Colonial Entanglement: Constituting a Twenty-First-Century Osage Nation*. Chapel Hill: University of North Carolina Press, 2012.

DeVivo, Dan, and Joseph Mathew, dirs. *Crossing Arizona*. New York: Cinema Guild, 2006.

D'Hondt, Caroline, dir. *Inside the Labyrinth*. Brussels: Cobra Film, 2016.

Diaz, Natalie. "Introduction: Bodies Built for Game." In *Bodies Built for Game: The Prairie Schooner Anthology of Contemporary Sports Writing*, edited by Natalie Diaz, xv–xli. Lincoln: University of Nebraska Press, 2019.

Donaldson, Laura E. "Joshua in America: On Cowboys, Canaanites, and Indians." In *The Calling of the Nations: Exegesis, Ethnography, and Empire in a Biblical-Historic Present*, edited by Mark Vessey, Sharon V. Betcher, Robert A. Daum, and Harry O. Maier, 273–90. Toronto: University of Toronto Press, 2011.

Dunbar-Ortiz, Roxanne. "'Indian' Wars." *Jacobin*, September 16, 2004. www.jacobinmag .com/2014/09/indian-wars/.

———. *An Indigenous Peoples' History of the United States*. Boston: Beacon Press, 2014.

———. *Not "A Nation of Immigrants": Settler Colonialism, White Supremacy, and a History of Erasure and Exclusion*. Boston: Beacon Press, 2021.

Eldridge, Joe, and Kevin Amaya. "Archbishop Óscar Romero Is Declared a Saint: Can El Salvador and the U.S. Honor His Call for Justice?" Washington Office on Latin America, October 12, 2018. www.wola.org/analysis/archbishop-oscar -romero-declared-saint-can-el-salvador-us-honor-call-justice/.

Estes, Nick. "Severed Ties." *High Country News* 51, no. 17 (2019): 16–21.

Estes, Nick, Melanie K. Yazzie, Jennifer Nez Denetdale, and David Correia. *Red Nation Rising: From Bordertown Violence to Native Liberation*. Oakland: PM Press, 2021.

Eulich, Whitney. "Will US Extend Speedy Ukrainian Refugee Welcome to Others?" *Christian Science Monitor*, May 10, 2022. www.csmonitor.com/World/Americas/2022/0510 /Will-US-extend-speedy-Ukrainian-refugee-welcome-to-others.

Fallows, Deborah. "Ajo, Arizona, Is the Story of a Better America." CNN, December 6, 2019. www.cnn.com/2019/12/06/opinions/small-town-ajo-arizona-heal-divide-fallows/index .html.

Fear-Segal, Jacqueline, and Susan D. Rose, eds. *Carlisle Indian Industrial School: Indigenous Histories, Memories, and Reclamations*. Lincoln: University of Nebraska Press, 2016.

Frey, John Carlos, dir. *The 800 Mile Wall*. San Diego, CA: Gatekeeper Productions, LLC, 2009.

Gaard, Greta. "Tools for a Cross-Cultural Feminist Ethics: Exploring Ethical Contexts and Contents in the Makah Whale Hunt." *Hypatia* 16, no. 1 (2001): 1–26.

Galeano, Eduardo. *Open Veins of Latin America: Five Centuries of the Pillage of a Continent*. New York: Monthly Review Press, 1973.

García, María Cristina. *Seeking Refuge: Central American Migration to Mexico, the United States, and Canada*. Berkeley: University of California Press, 2006.

García, María Elena, and José Antonio Lucero. "Resurgence and Resistance in Abya Yala: Indigenous Politics from Latin America." In *The World of Indigenous North America*, edited by Robert Warrior, 429–45. New York: Routledge, 2014.

García Márquez, Gabriel. *Cien años de soledad*. Lima: La Oveja Negra, 1981.

Geertz, Clifford. *Local Knowledge: Further Essays in Interpretive Anthropology*. New York: Basic Books, 1983.

Goeman, Mishuana. *Mark My Words: Native Women Mapping Our Nations*. Minneapolis: University of Minnesota Press, 2013.

Gould, Jeffrey L., and Aldo A. Lauria-Santiago. *To Rise in Darkness: Revolution, Repression, and Memory in El Salvador, 1920–1932*. Durham, NC: Duke University Press, 2008.

Gover, Kevin. "American Indians Serve in the U.S. Military in Greater Numbers Than Any Ethnic Group and Have Since the Revolution." Huffington Post, May 22, 2015. www .huffpost.com/entry/american-indians-serve-in-the-us-military_b_7417854.

Graham, David. "How Much Has Changed since the Birmingham Church Bombing?" *The Atlantic*, June 18, 2015. www.theatlantic.com/politics/archive/2015/06 /historical-background-charleston-shooting/396242/.

Gramsci, Antonio. "The Study of Philosophy: Some Preliminary Points of Reference." In *Selections from the Prison Notebooks of Antonio Gramsci*, edited by Quintin Hoare and Geoffrey Nowell-Smith, 323–30. New York: International Publishers, 1973.

Grandin, Greg. *Empire's Workshop: Latin America, the United States, and the Rise of the New Imperialism*. New York: Metropolitan Books, 2006.

———. *The End of the Myth: From the Frontier to the Border Wall in the Mind of America*. New York: Metropolitan Books, Henry Holt and Company, 2019.

Griffith, James S. *Hecho a Mano: The Traditional Arts of Tucson's Mexican American Community*. Tucson: University of Arizona Press, 2000.

Gruzinski, Serge. *The Mestizo Mind: The Intellectual Dynamics of Colonization and Globalization*. London: Routledge, 2002.

Guidotti-Hernandez, Nicole. *Unspeakable Violence: Remapping U.S. and Mexican National Imaginaries*. Durham, NC: Duke University Press, 2011.

Hackenberg, Robert A., and Beverly H. Hackenberg. "In Memoriam: Ella Gloria Narcho Rumley (1923–2004)." *Human Organization* 63, no. 4 (2004): 513–14.

Haines, Francis. "The Nez Percé Delegation to St. Louis in 1831." *Pacific Historical Review* 6, no. 1 (1937): 71–78.

Haraway, Donna. "Teddy Bear Patriarchy: Taxidermy in the Garden of Eden, New York City, 1908–1936." *Social Text* 11 (1984): 20–64.

Hardaway, Roger D. "Unlawful Love: A History of Arizona's Miscegenation Law." *Journal of Arizona History* 27, no. 4 (1986): 377–90.

Heberling, Lydia. "California Indians Dreamin': Formal and Aesthetic Innovations in Pacific Coast Native Literatures and Arts." PhD diss., University of Washington, Seattle, 2021.

Hirschman, Albert O. *A Propensity to Self-Subversion*. Cambridge, MA: Harvard University Press, 1995.

Holm, Tom. *Strong Hearts, Wounded Souls: Native American Veterans of the Vietnam War.* Austin: University of Texas Press, 1996.

Hondagneu-Sotelo, Pierrette. *God's Heart Has No Borders: How Religious Activists Are Working for Immigrant Rights.* Berkeley: University of California Press, 2008.

Iffland, James. "Roque Dalton: The Magnificent Wound That Never Heals." *ReVista: Harvard Review of Latin America* 15, no. 3 (2016): 36–38.

Johnson, Bailey. "High School Basketball Fans Accused of Racism for 'USA' Chant." CBSnews.com, March 8, 2012. www.cbsnews.com/news/high-school-basketball -fans-accused-of-racism-for-usa-chant/.

Johnston, Basil H. *Indian School Days.* Norman: University of Oklahoma Press, 1998.

Jimmerson, Ellin, dir. *The Second Cooler.* Huntsville, AL: Huntsville Immigration Initiative, LLC, 2012.

Kaganiec-Kamienska, Anna. "Sanctuary Movement." In *Multicultural America: A Multimedia Encyclopedia*, vol. 4, edited by Carlos E. Cortés and Jane E. Sloan, 1865–66. New York: SAGE Reference, 2014.

Kauanui, J. Kēhaulani. *Paradoxes of Hawaiian Sovereignty: Land, Sex, and the Colonial Politics of State Nationalism.* Durham, NC: Duke University Press, 2018.

Kelly, Thomas M., ed. and trans. *Rutilio Grande, S.J.: Homilies and Writings.* Collegeville, MN: Liturgical Press, 2015.

Kirkpatrick, Jeane J. "Dictatorships and Double Standards." *Commentary*, November 1979. www.commentary.org/articles/jeane-kirkpatrick/dictatorships-double-standards/.

———. "The Hobbes Problem: Order, Authority and Legitimacy in Central America." Unpublished paper prepared for the American Enterprise Institute, 1980.

Koening, Sarah. *Providence and the Invention of American History.* New Haven, CT: Yale University Press, 2021.

Kohl, Benjamin, and Linda C. Farthing. "Navigating Narrative: The Antinomies of 'Mediated' *Testimonios.*" *Journal of Latin American and Caribbean Anthropology* 18, no. 1 (2013): 90–107.

Kroeber, Theodora. *Ishi in Two Worlds: A Biography of the Last Wild Indian in North America.* Berkeley: University of California Press, 1976.

Kuhn, Casey. "Untold Arizona: Ajo Artists Colony Brings Century-Old Curley School to Life." *Fronteras*, April 2, 2019. https://fronterasdesk.org/content/847706/untold -arizona-ajo-artists-colony-brings-century-old-curley-school-life.

LaDuke, Winona, and Sean Aaron Cruz. *The Militarization of Indian Country.* 2nd ed. East Lansing: Michigan State University Press, 2013.

LaFeber, Walter. *Inevitable Revolutions: The United States in Central America.* New York: W. W. Norton, 1993.

Landry, Alysa. "Harry S. Truman: Beginning of Termination Era." *Indian Country Today*, August 16, 2016. https://indiancountrytoday.com/archive/harry-s-truman-beginning -of-indian-termination-era.

Lange, Katie. "Why Army Helicopters Have Native American Names." US Department of Defense, November 29, 2019. www.defense.gov/News/Inside-DOD/Blog/article /2052989/why-army-helicopters-have-native-american-names/.

Langston, Donna Hightower. "American Indian Women's Activism in the 1960s and 1970s." *Hypatia* 18, no. 2 (2003): 114–32.

Leal Ugalde, Juan. "La ejecución de Feliciano Ama: Fotografía e historia en la matanza de 1932 en El Salvador." *Istmo. Revista virtual de estudios literarios y culturales centroamericanos* 40 (2020): 82–107. http://istmo.denison.edu/n40/dossier/07.pdf.

Le Guin, Ursula K. "The Art of Fiction No. 221." Interview by John Wray, *The Paris Review*, 206 (Fall 2003). www.theparisreview.org/interviews/6253/the-art-of-fiction-no-221 -ursula-k-le-guin.

Lernoux, Penny. *Cry of the People: The Struggle for Human Rights in Latin America—The Catholic Church in Conflict with U.S. Policy*. New York: Penguin Books, 1980.

Levine, Jeremy, and Landon Van Soest, dirs. *Walking the Line*. New York: Filmakers Library, 2005.

Leza, Christine. *Divided Peoples: Policy, Activism, and Indigenous Identities on the U.S.-Mexico Border*. Tucson: University of Arizona Press, 2019.

Lindo-Fuentes, Hécto, Erik Ching, and Rafael A. Lara-Martínez. *Remembering a Massacre in El Salvador: The Insurrection of 1932, Roque Dalton, and the Politics of Historical Memory*. Albuquerque: University of New Mexico Press, 2007.

Little, John. "Vietnam Akíčita: Lakota and Dakota Military Tradition in the Twentieth Century." PhD diss., University of Minnesota, May 2020.

Lomawaima, K. Tsianina. "Historical Trauma and Healing." Boarding School Healing Webinar Series, June 6, 2019. https://boardingschoolhealing.org/2019-webinar-series/.

———. *They Called It Prairie Light: The Story of Chilocco Indian School*. Lincoln: University of Nebraska Press, 1994.

López Vigil, María. *Monseñor Romero: Piezas para un retrato*. San Salvador: UCA Editores, 1995.

Lorde, Audre. *The Master's Tools Will Never Dismantle the Master's House*. London: Penguin Classics, 2018.

Lucero, José Antonio. "Representing 'Real Indians': The Challenges of Indigenous Authenticity and Strategic Constructivism in Ecuador and Bolivia." *Latin American Research Review* 41, no. 2 (2006): 31–56.

MacMillan, Laurie, dir. *Man in the Maze*. New York: Cinema Guild, 2006. https://vimeo .com/user3591130.

Marak, Andrae M., and Laura Tuennerman. *At the Border of Empires: The Tohono O'odham, Gender, and Assimilation, 1880–1934*. Tucson: University of Arizona Press, 2013.

Mathew, Joseph, dir. *The Long Walk of Carlos Guerrero*. Katha Films, Forthcoming.

Maxwell, David. "Decolonization." In *Missions and Empire*, edited by Norman Etherington, 285–306. Oxford: Oxford University Press, 2005.

Mbembé, Achille. "Necropolitics." *Public Culture* 15, no. 1 (2003): 11–40.

McBride, James. "The Bisbee Deportation in Words and Images." *Mining History Journal* 6 (1990): 63–76.

Melamed, Jodi. "Racial Capitalism." *Critical Ethnic Studies* 1, no. 1 (2015): 76–85.

Menchú, Rigoberta. *I, Rigoberta Menchú: An Indian Woman in Guatemala*. London: Verso Books, 2010.

Merchant, Carolyn. "Shades of Darkness: Race and Environmental History." *Environmental History* 8, no. 3 (2003): 380–94.

Mezzadra, Sandro, and Brett Neilson. *Border as Method, or, the Multiplication of Labor.* Durham, NC: Duke University Press, 2013.

Miller, Todd. *Border Patrol Nation: Dispatches from the Front Lines of Homeland Security.* San Francisco: City Lights Books, 2014.

———. *Empire of Borders: The Expansion of the US Border around the World.* Brooklyn: Verso, 2019.

———. "How Border Patrol Occupied the Tohono O'odham Nation." *In These Times,* June 12, 2019. https://inthesetimes.com/article/us-mexico-border-surveillance -tohono-oodham-nation-border-patrol.

Million, Dian. "Felt Theory: An Indigenous Feminist Approach to Affect and History." *Wicazo Sa Review* 24, no. 2 (2009): 53–76.

Miranda, Deborah A. *Bad Indians: A Tribal Memoir.* Berkeley: Heyday, 2013.

———. "The Bones Speak: Excavation and Reunion." In *Native Voices: Indigenous American Poetry, Craft, and Conversations,* edited by Marie Fuhrman and Dean Rader, 280–97. North Adams, MA: Tupelo Press, 2019.

Montgomery, Tommie Sue. *Revolution in El Salvador: From Civil Strife to Civil Peace.* Boulder, CO: Westview Press, 1992.

Morgan, Mindy J. "'Working' from the Margins: Documenting American Indian Participation in the New Deal Era." In *Why You Can't Teach United States History without American Indians,* edited by Susan Sleeper-Smith, Juliana Barr, Jean M. O'Brien, Nancy Shoemaker, and Scott Manning Stevens, 181–96. Chapel Hill: University of North Carolina Press, 2015.

Morozzo Della Rocca, Roberto. *Oscar Romero: Prophet of Hope.* London: Darton, Longman and Todd, 2015.

Mueller, David, and Lynn Salt, dirs. *A Good Day to Die.* Journeyman Pictures, 2011. www .journeyman.tv.

Nail, Thomas. "The Climate-Migration-Industrial Complex." *Public Seminar,* January 10, 2020. https://publicseminar.org/essays/the-climate-migration-industrial-complex/.

Nash, June. *We Eat the Mines and the Mines Eat Us: Dependency and Exploitation in Bolivian Tin Mines.* New York: Columbia University Press, 1979.

Nevins, Joseph. *Operation Gatekeeper and Beyond: The War on "Illegals" and the Remaking of the U.S.-Mexico Boundary.* New York: Routledge, 2010.

Nguyen, Gia-Quan Thi Anna. "We Became the Cavalry: The Transformation of Native American Warrior Identity during the Vietnam War." University of Washington Undergraduate Research Program, 2014. http://hdl.handle.net/1773/34312.

O'Gara, Nick. "Southside Presbyterian, Birthplace of Sanctuary Movement, Honors Former Pastor." Arizona Public Media, November 17, 2017. https://news.azpm.org/p/news -splash/2017/11/17/120185-southside-presbyterian-birthplace-of-sanctuary -movement-honors-former-pastor/.

Onion, Rebecca. "That Beautiful Barbed Wire." Slate, November 6, 2018. https://slate.com /technology/2018/11/concertina-barbed-wire-border-trump-troops-history.html.

Paniagua, Tony. "Sanctuary Movement: 3 Decades of Activism." Arizona Public Media, March 22, 2012. https://tv.azpm.org/s/8379-sanctuary-movement-3-decades-of -activism.

Parkhurst, Janet H. "Ajo Townsite Historic District, National Register of Historic Places Registration Form." US Department of the Interior, National Park Service, 2001. https://npgallery.nps.gov/GetAsset/11fa9f60-88b3-44a4-b152-a0cbf84fbf26.

PBS NewsHour. "Tribe Divided over Providing Water to Illegal Migrants Crossing Indian Land." PBS NewsHour, September 16, 2008. www.pbs.org/newshour/arts/social _issues-july-dec08-waterstations_09-16.

Perales, Monica. *Smeltertown: Making and Remembering a Southwest Border Community.* Chapel Hill: University of North Carolina Press, 2010.

Pratt, Richard H. "The Advantages of Mingling Indians with Whites." In *Americanizing the American Indians: Writings by the "Friends of the Indian," 1880–1900,* edited by Francis P. Prucha, 260–71. Cambridge, MA: Harvard University Press, 1973.

Rabben, Linda. *Sanctuary and Asylum: A Social and Political History.* Seattle: University of Washington Press, 2016.

The Red Nation. 2020. "Veterans' Day and the Demilitarization of Indian Country with Krystal Two Bulls." *The Red Nation Podcast,* November 10, 2016. https://podcasts.apple .com/in/podcast/veterans-day-demilitarization-indian-country-w-krystal /id1482834485?i=1000498052690.

Regan, Margaret. *The Death of Josseline: Immigration Stories from the Arizona-Mexico Borderlands.* Boston: Beacon Press, 2010.

Riddle, Margaret. "The ASARCO Smokestack—Once the World's Largest—Is Demolished at the Company's Old Copper Smelter in Ruston, North of Tacoma, on Jan. 17, 1993." HistoryLink.org Essay 8744, August 26, 2008. www.historylink.org/File/8744.

Rivas, Ofelia. "Systematic System of Destruction: Sacred Land Destruction Underway on Tohono O'odham Nation for Israeli U.S. Spy Towers." Censored News, April 21, 2020. https://bsnorrell.blogspot.com/2020_04_21_archive.html.

Robinson, Cedric. *Black Marxism: The Making of the Black Radical Tradition.* Chapel Hill: University of North Carolina Press, 2000.

Rosaldo, Renato. "Imperialist Nostalgia." *Representations* 26, no. 26 (1989): 107–22.

Rose, Amanda. 2012. *Showdown in the Sonoran Desert: Religion, Law, and the Immigration Controversy.* Oxford: Oxford University Press, 2012.

Rose, Wendy. *Going to War with All My Relations.* Flagstaff, AZ: Entrada Books, 1993.

Saldaña-Portillo, María Josefina. *Indian Given: Racial Geographies across Mexico and the United States.* Durham, NC: Duke University Press, 2016.

Siegler, Kirk. "Why the U.S. Government Is Dropping Off Migrants in Rural Arizona Towns." National Public Radio, April 15, 2021. www.npr.org/2021/04/15/987618530 /why-the-u-s-government-is-dropping-off-migrants-in-rural-arizona-towns.

Silliman, Stephen W. "The 'Old West' in the Middle East: U.S. Military Metaphors in Real and Imagined Indian Country." *American Anthropologist* 110, no. 2 (2008): 237–47.

Silva, Noenoe K. *Aloha Betrayed: Native Hawaiian Resistance to American Colonialism.* Durham, NC: Duke University Press, 2004.

Simon, Rachel, Leila Borowsky, Siobhan Wescott, and Matthew L. Tobey. "To Advance Well-Being in Indian Country, Limit the Health Harms of Incarceration." *Health Affairs Blog,* July 30, 2019. www.healthaffairs.org/do/10.1377/hblog20190725.492229/full/.

Simpson, Audra. *Mohawk Interruptus: Political Life across the Borders of Settler States*. Durham, NC: Duke University Press, 2014.

Singleton, Sara G. "Not Our Borders: Indigenous People and the Struggle to Maintain Shared Lives and Cultures in Post-9/11 North America." *Border Policy Research Institute Publications*, no. 106 (2009). https://cedar.wwu.edu/bpri_publications/106.

Skidmore, Thomas, and Peter Smith. *Modern Latin America*. New York: Oxford University Press, 2001.

Smith, Andrea, Michelene Pesantubbee, Dianne M. Stewart, Michelle A. Gonzalez, Sylvester Johnson, and Tink Tinker. "Native/First Nation Theology: Roundtable Discussion." *Journal of Feminist Studies in Religion* 22, no. 2 (2006): 85–121.

Smith, Christian. *Disruptive Religion: The Force of Faith in Social-Movement Activism*. New York: Routledge, 1996.

———. *Resisting Reagan: The U.S. Central America Peace Movement*. Chicago: University of Chicago Press, 1996.

Smith, David Ross, dir. *Border Wars*. Season 1, episode 1, "Last Defense." Aired January 2, 2012, on the National Geographic Channel.

Smith, Paul Chaat, and Robert Warrior. *Like a Hurricane: The Indian Movement from Alcatraz to Wounded Knee*. New York: New Press, 1996.

Sonnichsen, C. L. *Tucson: The Life and Times of an American City*. Norman: University of Oklahoma Press, 1982.

Speed, Shannon. *Incarcerated Stories: Indigenous Women Migrants and Violence in the Settler-Capitalist State*. Chapel Hill: University of North Carolina Press, 2019.

Sudermann, Hannelore. "Renamed Campus Road Honors Indigenous History." *University of Washington Magazine*, December 1, 2020. https://magazine.washington.edu/renamed-campus-road-honors-indigenous-history/#.

Sy, Stephanie. "An Arizona Mining Town Reinvents Itself as an Arts Destination." PBS NewsHour, October 21, 2020. www.pbs.org/newshour/show/an-arizona-mining-town-reinvents-itself-as-an-arts-destination.

TallBear, Kim. "Can a DNA Test Make Me Native American?" *All My Relations* podcast, March 12, 2019. www.allmyrelationspodcast.com/podcast/episode/33235119/ep-4-can-a-dna-test-make-me-native-american.

Tate, Cassandra. "Whitman 'Massacre': Are We Past the Whitewashing of History?" Crosscut.com, November 28, 2017. https://crosscut.com/2017/11/whitman-massacre-missionaries-indians-history-colonialism-washington-state.

Tengan, Ty P. Kāwika. "Re-membering Panalā'au: Masculinities, Nation, and Empire in Hawai'i and the Pacific." *Contemporary Pacific* 20, no. 1 (2008): 27–53.

Thrush, Coll. *Native Seattle: Histories from the Crossing-Over Place*. Seattle: University of Washington Press, 2017.

Tinker, George E. *Missionary Conquest: The Gospel and Native American Cultural Genocide*. Minneapolis: Fortress Press, 1993.

Tinker, Tink. "American Indian Traditions." In *Handbook of U.S. Theologies of Liberation*, edited by Miguel A. De la Torre, 330–46. St. Louis: Chalice Press, 2004.

———. "Why I Do Not Believe in a Creator." In *Buffalo Shout, Salmon Cry: Conversations on Creation, Land Justice, and Life Together*, edited by Steven Heinrichs, 167–79. Waterloo, ON: Herald Press, 2013.

Trahant, Mark N. *The Last Great Battle of the Indian Wars: Henry M. Jackson, Forrest J. Gerard and the Campaign for the Self-Determination of America's Indian Tribes*. Fort Hall, ID: Cedars Group, 2010.

Treuer, David. *The Heartbeat of Wounded Knee: Native America from 1890 to the Present*. New York: Penguin, 2019.

Trujillo, Simón. *Land Uprising: Native Story Power and the Insurgent Horizons of Latinx Indigeneity*. Tucson: University of Arizona Press. 2020.

Tuck, Eve. "Suspending Damage: A Letter to Communities." *Harvard Educational Review* 79, no. 3 (2009): 409–27.

Tula, María Teresa, and Lynn Stephen. *Hear My Testimony: María Teresa Tula, Human Rights Activist of El Salvador*. Boston: South End Press, 1994.

Turits, Richard Lee. "A World Destroyed, a Nation Imposed: The 1937 Haitian Massacre in the Dominican Republic." *Hispanic American Historical Review* 82, no. 3 (2002): 589–635.

Turner, Frederick J. *The Significance of the Frontier in American History*. New York: Frederick Ungar Publishing, 1963.

US General Services Administration. "Final Environmental Assessment for the Proposed Construction, Alteration, and Maintenance for US Customs and Border Protection Ajo Housing Development Project, Ajo, Arizona." gsa.gov, April 5, 2011.

Valdes, Marcela. "Their Lawsuit Prevented 400,000 Deportations. Now It's Biden's Call." *New York Times Magazine*, April 7, 2021. www.nytimes.com/2021/04/07/magazine /immigration-el-salvador.html.

Van Leeuw, Philippe, dir. *The Wall*. Brussels: Altitude 100 Production; Luxembourg: Les Films Fauves; Copenhagen: Frau Film, 2023.

Vega, Garcilaso de la. *Comentarios reales de los Incas*. México, DF: Fondo de Cultura Económica, 1995.

Walia, Harsha. *Border and Rule: Global Migration, Capitalism, and the Rise of Racist Nationalism*. Chicago: Haymarket Books, 2021.

Warren, Scott. "Across Papaguería: Copper, Conservation, and Boundary Security in the Arizona-Mexico Borderlands." PhD diss., Arizona State University, 2015.

———. "A New Kind of Company Town." *Journal of Latin American Geography* 18, no. 3 (2019): 188–91.

Warrior, Robert Allen. "A Native American Perspective: Canaanites, Cowboys and Indians." In *Voices from the Margin: Interpreting the Bible in the Third World*, edited by R. S. Sugirtharajah, 277–88. Maryknoll, NY: Orbis Books, 1995.

Weaver, Jace. "From I-Hermeneutics to We-Hermeneutics." In *Native American Religious Identity: Unforgotten Gods*, edited by Jace Weaver, 1–26. Maryknoll, NY: Orbis Books, 1998.

———. "Premodern Ironies: First Nations and Chosen Peoples." In *The Calling of the Nations: Exegesis, Ethnography, and Empire in a Biblical-Historic Present*, edited by Mark Vessey, Sharon V. Betcher, Robert A. Daum, and Harry O. Maier, 291–304. Toronto: University of Toronto Press, 2011.

Whelan, Matthew Philipp. *Blood in the Fields: Óscar Romero, Catholic Social Teaching, and Land Reform*. Washington, DC: Catholic University of America Press, 2020.

White, Cody. "The CCC Indian Division." *Prologue Magazine* 48, no. 2 (Summer 2016). www .archives.gov/publications/prologue/2016/summer/ccc-id.html.

Williams, Robert G. *States and Social Evolution: Coffee and the Rise of National Governments in Central America*. Chapel Hill: University of North Carolina Press, 1994.

Yazzie, Melanie K., Nick Estes, Jennifer Nez Denetdale, and David Correia. "Burning Down the Bordertown." *The Baffler*, February 11, 2021. https://thebaffler.com/latest/burning -down-the-bordertown-yazzie-estes-denetdale-correia.

Ybarra, Megan. "Site Fight! Toward the Abolition of Immigrant Detention on Tacoma's Tar Pits (and Everywhere Else)." *Antipode* 53, no. 1 (2020): 1–20.

Young, Elliott. *Forever Prisoners: How the United States Made the World's Largest Immigrant Detention System*. New York: Oxford University Press, 2021.

Zimmer, Eric Steven. "Building the Red Earth Nation: The Civilian Conservation Corps– Indian Division on the Meskwaki Settlement." *Native American and Indigenous Studies* 2, no. 2 (2015): 106–33.

Index

Page numbers in italics refer to illustrations.

Reserve Officers' Training Corps (ROTC), 91–93

Revelations (band), 33

Robinson, Cedric, 24–25

rock and roll bands, 33, 34

Rodríguez, Paul, 46

Roman Catholic Church, 17–18, 33, 87–90, 108, 115, 119, 130, 144; in El Salvador, 87–90; liberation theology and, 88, 89, 113, 115; schools of, 33, 72

Romero, Óscar, 5

Romero Bosque, Pío, 81

Romero y Galdámez, Óscar Arnulfo, 88, 113, 140

Roosevelt, Franklin Delano, 13, 58

Roosevelt, Theodore, 26

Rosaldo, Renato, 26

Rose, Wendy, 116–19; "Excavation at Santa Barbara Mission," 117

ROTC (Reserve Officers' Training Corps), 91–93

Rounds, David, 42

Ruff, Susan (wife), 126, 127, 138, 149, 167n2

Rumley, Darrell, 33

Rumley, Ella, 10, 33, 51, 162n1

Sacaría Goday, José, 31

Saint Catherine's Mission Church, 12, 17–18

Salvadoran Truth Commission, 85, 89

Samaritans, 147

sanctuary movement, 140–42, 147, 149, 169n3

Sandino, Augusto César, 81

San Francisco Theological Seminary (SFTS), 96–101; Stewart Memorial Chapel at, 96–101, 103–7, 110, 116, 119

segregation, 11, 16–18, 27, 36, 91–93, 159n3

self-determination, 59, 61, 144, 145, 146, 166n29

Si'ahl, Chief, 147

Sinte Gleska (Spotted Tail), 57

Sinte Gleska University, 56–57

Sithole, Ndabaningi, 116

Sixteenth Street Baptist Church, 36, 162n4

smallpox, 108–10

smelting, 21, 22–24

Sonoran Desert, 1, 3, 29, 77, 131, 135, 143, 149

Sonsonate, El Salvador, 66, 72

Southside Presbyterian Church, 101, 140, 141, 169n3, 173n6

sovereignty, tribal, 58, 137–38, 144–47, 153

Soviet Union, 43–44, 64

Spain, 79–80

Spanish-American War, 26

Spotted Tail (Sinte Gleska), 57

Spotted Tail, Charlie, 57

Standing Rock, 166n32

Stevenson, Donny, 148

Stewart Memorial Chapel, 96–101, 103–7, 110, 116, 119

St. Joseph's Hospital, 39–40

"Superfund" geography, 24, 28, 160nn4–5

Suquamish, 147, 149, 175n27

syncretism, 114–16

Tacoma, WA, 23, 28, 160n5

TallBear, Kim, 116

Tandona, La, 71, 73

termination, 58–59, 145, 166n29

testimonio, 5, 158n13

Texas, University of, at El Paso, 21, 22, 160n6

Texas, University of, at San Antonio, 93, 134

Texas National Guard, 154

Thom, Mel, 58, 165n24

Thorpe, Grace, 60

Thorpe, Jim, 55, 60

Tinker, George E., 105, 113, 114, 115

Tohono O'odham: creation story of, 45; in Indian Village, 11, 12, 15, 17, 18, 27, 28; language of, 11, 25, 47, 107, 124; in military, 45–46; Papago as older term for, 25, 38; rock and roll and, 33; traditional homelands of, 9, 25, 157n5, 173n8, 174n11; in Tucson, 32–33

Tohono O'odham Domestic Violence Coalition, 134

Tohono O'odham Hemajkam Rights Network, 157n5

Tohono O'odham Nation: Baboquivari District Council of, 124, 126, 131, 133; Border Patrol on, 3, 4, 7, 8, 29–31, 122, 137, 143, 151–53; on border policy, 8, 135, 174n13; casinos of, 94–95; districts of, 13; Institutional Review Board of, 6, 158n16; jobs on, 15; liberals on, 135–37; map of, 9; migrants on, 3, 7, 10, 24, 101–2, 120–38, 143; schools in, 33; water stations opposed by, 2, 3, 123–25, 131, 135–37, 142, 143–44, 147. *See also* Ajo, AZ

Tohono O'odham Police Department (TOPD), 129, 130, 151–52

Topawa, AZ, 15–16

totalitarianism, authoritarianism vs., 85

Trahant, Mark, 166n29

Trail of Tears, 114

tribal sovereignty, 58, 137–38, 144–47, 153

Trujillo, Rafael Leónidas, 44, 168n10

Truman, Harry S., 58–59

Trump, Donald, 30

Tucson, AZ, 18–21, 32–41

Tucson Indian Center, 32, 33, 38

Tucson Indian Training School, 48

Turner, Frederick Jackson, 26

Ukraine, 141

Union Theological Seminary, 112

Unitarian Universalist Church, 94

United Fruit Company, 168n10

United Indians of All Tribes, 58, 166n25

United Nations Declaration on the Rights of Indigenous Peoples, 135

US Army. *See* Army, US

US Army War College, 164n9

US Capitol, 110

US Commission on Civil Rights, 18, 38, 159n3

US Congress, 121, 137, 165n18, 166n1

US Department of Homeland Security, 28

Vatican II, 88, 89

Vavages, Juan (Harry Wilson; paternal grandfather), 10, 47, 48, 49, 52, 164n1

Vietnam War, 41, 49–50, 57, 60, 86

Walking the Line (documentary), 2, 5, 139

War on Poverty, 40

Warren, Scott, 29–30

Warrior, Robert, 112, 114–15

Washington, University of, 108, 171n18, 171n23; Wilson at, 5, 22, 78–79

Washington Post, 31

Washington State, 110

water stations, 2, 3, 30–31, 101–2, 121–38, 131, 149; as human right, 134–37; named for Gospels, 124, 130; opposed by Papago United Presbyterian Church, 123, 132–34, 142, 143–44; opposed by Tohono O'odham Nation, 2, 3, 123–25, 131, 135–37, 142, 143–44, 147

Weaver, Jace, 113–14

Westmoreland, William, 86

Whelan, Matthew, 89

white privilege, 28, 92–93, 137

white supremacy, whiteness, 28, 162n4

Whitman, Marcus, 107–10, *109*, *111*

Whitman, Narcissa, 107–8, *109*

Whitman College, 107

Wilderness Act (1964), 170n7

Williams, Raymond, 87

Wilson, Art (cousin), 47

Wilson, Bertha (mother), 13, 15, 17, 20, 35

Wilson, Cecilia Maria "Ceci" (daughter), 41

Wilson, Dick, 61

Wilson, Harry (Juan Vavages) (paternal grandfather), 10, 47, 48, 49, 52, 164n1

Wilson, Joe, Jr. (brother), 35

Wilson, Joseph Anthony (son), 36, 40, 41, 128

Wilson, José Vavages (father), 15–16, 20, 33, 35; military service of, 45, 47

Wilson, Laura C. Cruz (ex-wife), 36, 40, 41, 42, 91

Wilson, María Eliza "Lisa" (daughter), 41

Wilson, Michael (uncle), 46

Wilson, Michael Steven "Mike": in Ajo, 11–18; on Aztlán, 137, 173n8; birth of, 13; civil rights testimony of, 18, 38, 159n3; on Cold War, 10, 43–44, 62, 64, 84–85, 90; at college, 39–40, 41; in documentaries, 2, 2, 5, 122, 138, 139–40, 144; in El Salvador, 2, 50, 62–77, 78–79, 84–85, 86–87, 90; as farmworker, 35–36; Fife's relationship with, 95, 101, 139–40, 147; Lucero's collaboration with, 5–7; marriage and fatherhood of, 36; military service of, 2, 41–44, 49–50, 62–77, 78–79, 84–85, 90, 91–93, 126; multigenerational story of, 10; O'odham identity of, 11, 18; Presbyterian church joined by, 93–95; as Presbyterian lay pastor, 1, 3, 101–2, 120–38, 143, 173n6; on Raymond Mattia's death, 152–53; road to Damascus of, 74–77; as ROTC instructor, 91–93; at seminary, 96–102, 103–4, 107, 116, 119; sheet metal accident of, 41–42; as teenager, 32–41; University of Washington talks of, 5, 22, 78–79; "voice and exit" options of, 149–50; water stations maintained by, 2, 3, 30–31, 101–2, 121–38, 142, 143–44, 147, 149

Wilson, Stanley "Tykie" (brother), 13, 20–21, 27, 28

Wobblies, 26–27

World War I, 25, 27

World War II, 45, 46, 163n11

Wounded Knee confrontation, 60, 61

Yahi, 100

Yale Summer School, 34–35

Yazzie, Melanie, 164n13

Ybarra, Megan, 28

Yellow Thunder, Raymond, 61

Young, S. Hall, 97, 98, 103–5, 110, 113–14, 170n7; *Alaska Days with John Muir*, 104

Zimmer, Eric, 159n1

9 781469 675589